Dear Everybody
Letters From the Heart

Dear Everybody

Letters From the Heart

Stephanie Smith

Silver Pennies Press
Camden, Maine

Cover Image: Linen tablecloth that belonged to Hannah
Book Design: Jonna Bragg

This book is dedicated to Hannah, Margaret, and Ann who provided lessons on life's intangibles, and to my father, Richmond, who gave me directions to find my way home.

"How can we know who we are or where we are headed if we don't know anything about where we have come from and what we have been through, the courage shown, the costs paid, to be where we are?"

Robert McCullough

Table of Contents

Dear Everybody

Chapter One

Instructions

The man who was not one to give advice was doing just that. He stood in the living room entry of his 18th-century Cape Cod house, slight hunch in his shoulders, watching me rummage through the old sea chest filled with family photos. The man was my father, a shell of the physically fit man he once was, now stooped over, ninety-year old muscles giving way, unspoken grief for my mother taking its toll. Images rose up of when he was in his prime wearing his white physician's coat with "RWS" monogrammed on the upper left pocket, his posture strong and confident. He had a presence that commanded your attention. Even at ninety, I came to attention when he stood in front of me, my hands holding the manila envelope full of letters from my grandmother, his mother-in-law, Hannah Stevenson Trimble. Over the years I had glanced at them with little interest. My grandmother had always felt distant to me, a formal and formidable woman we called Grandmother, a more than fitting term. She was grand with a capital G and an emphasis on grand. I stopped my rummaging in the chest, put the envelope down beside me and took heed when my father stated with no hesitation, "You should do something with those letters."

I had come to Maine from California that July to check on my father, and to also check on myself. Maine is a good place for that, far away from California. Too many "D" words were floating in my life: death, divorce, decline and my kids dangling by threads with all these "Ds". My mother's death was a year before, my father's health was in rapid decline, I was in the middle of a long, difficult divorce, my daughter was wishing her struggles to get through college were over, and my son was flirting with the dangers of adolescence. I needed Maine to anchor myself.

On that day when my father stood in the doorway delivering his instructions, I was delving into the past, sitting on the living room floor, the old sea chest in front of me, my back against the couch, and my legs folded underneath me. My mother's glass-fronted secretary desk across the room caught my attention now and again; it housed her most valued handcrafted items, nothing showy, each understated in its beauty, much like my mother. Two Curry Bohm paintings of rural Indiana, once Hannah's, hung on opposing walls. The humidity that day, soft and comforting, not oppressive, was coupled with a fresh breeze off the river as it wended down to the ocean. A welcome contrast to the dry, parched summer days of California. I appreciated giving no thought to my hair, which transformed into gentle waves with the slightest humidity. I welcomed the plain pea-green skort I was wearing and the sleeveless seersucker shirt, both from the recesses of my closet, both items I always packed for my trips to Maine as they looked too "back east" for Marin County, California.

More than once, my Marin friends heard me pronounce, no doubt with pride, that it didn't matter what you wore in Maine, and it didn't matter how your hair looked. Clothes and hair, however, mattered to my mother. Even after moving to Maine, she never fully let go of her sense of style. She warned me not to become like my father's five New England sisters who, as she put it, "let themselves go." New England women can do that, she cautioned. My mother was also concerned about how much leg showed above the knee. She was discrete, her skirts mid-knee or slightly above at most. Despite the attractiveness of her legs, her mantra was, "Women's knees aren't attractive." When I was a teenager, she disapproved of my short skirts, made sure to let me know, and I quote her exactly: "One needs to leave something to the imagination." The "one" she referred to was me. She was one to use the word "one" to depersonalize a situation, even though one knew which one she was talking about. When I was older, she kept quiet about my clothes. Her mother mantras still float through my head as they did on that day in July. Sometimes I pretend that my hair and my clothes aren't important, but on most days they are. I missed my mother, her style, beauty and grace. The Camden house was different without her. The living room was full of my mother and her mother, the house exemplified my father, and both wrapped me in comfort. Looking up at my father in the doorway, I pushed back thoughts that soon he would no longer be alive. Our family was good at pushing back feelings, even thoughts about feelings.

I sighed to myself as I looked at my father. After his proclamation about the letters and not being one to linger, he left the room and left me floating in thoughts about the one parent I still had in my life and the one who was no more. I was awash with memories. My love for both ran deep. I did not have a traumatic childhood. Both provided a secure home.

My father, an unaffected, solid, self-reliant man full of integrity was dedicated to the greater good. His New England tendencies or maybe eccentricities stood out during my Michigan childhood in Grosse Pointe. He climbed up two-story ladders to clean out our gutters or put up wooden storm windows. He worked long hours during the week and a half-day on Saturday caring for his patients, chairing the Department of Medicine at Ford Hospital in Detroit, and leading research into endocrine diseases. He made house calls and took a shift to provide medical care to the indigent who came into the Emergency Room. He was never idle, never extravagant and had a renegade streak. When my mother was hospitalized, he snuck me in to visit her on the days when children were not allowed. A creator and inventor, he designed an early version of the game Battleship and created a headless man Halloween costume for me using coat hangers attached to an old orange life preserver for the frame of the body. In winter, he jumped rope in our garage to stay fit, and wearing paint spattered clothes, puttered in his workshop.

Every summer our family left Detroit, and to use my father's words, left "the armpit of the nation to head to God's country," aka New England. My mother grew up in the southern Indiana city of Evansville. She fit easily into Grosse Pointe society, served on non-profit boards, was an avid reader, played bridge, tended to her garden, and made sure my sister and I were on task. She had her hair done weekly and dressed each day as if she was going to a social event even if she wasn't.

Sitting on the living room floor, surrounded by the beauty my mother created, much of which was due to *her* mother, I acknowledged the sacrifice she made moving to Maine to allow my father to have the retirement life he wanted. Long before my parents met, when my father sailed off the coast of Maine as a young man in medical school, he dreamed of owning a stone house overlooking the ocean. In the 1960s, he drew up plans for his house and spent summers helping with its building. In the late 1970s he retired from his medical career, and he and my mother moved to Maine to live year round on a hilltop, down a long dirt road on a remote peninsula overlooking Penobscot Bay, ten miles from a fishing village. My mother's reaction after forty plus years living in Grosse Pointe was in line with her "make the best of it" and "grin and bear it" comments.

Once age caught up with them, and my mother grew increasingly weary of coping with the rural life she never wanted, she prevailed and they moved to Camden, a town with activity and social doings. True to her words, my mother made the best of it. She blew dry her own hair, served on non-profit boards, tended her garden, joined a book club and broke part of her vow that upon moving to Maine she would never quilt and jam. She made quilts, many of them.

The dichotomy between my mother's and father's worlds was striking. She liked a social life and what Midwest cities offered, he preferred isolation and the ruggedness of rural New England. I straddled each of their worlds and valued both, a Midwest/New England hybrid who had been dragged by a husband to live in California, a place where I had never wanted to live. I shook off thoughts along with emotions of how I ended up marrying someone whose values and worlds were different from mine. With my divorce pending, I knew I no longer needed to have a life I didn't want.

~

With my grandmother's letters beside me, I had not a clue what my father's request to "do something with the letters," meant. I pushed back that thought and let in my sadness of how hard it was seeing my father alone and on his own. No more Richmond and Margaret, no more Dr. and Mrs. Smith. During the year after my mother's death, he called several times and announced ". . . it was time," meaning he thought he was about to die. I hopped on the red-eye and flew out to Maine. I had mastered the travel routine: board a nine p.m. red-eye flight from San Francisco to Boston, put on eye shades and ear plugs and settle into my window seat, talk to no-one. The hum of the plane numbed me, and with a few hours of light sleep, I would exit the plane with bleary eyes, rent a car, and navigate out of Boston, stopping at the first place along my route that had a decent cappuccino. Living in Marin County for almost twenty years, the ultimate, made-to-perfection cappuccino, wet or dry, with milks of every sort was the norm. I had fallen under the spell of California coffee while bristling at people who announced their list of qualifiers on how they wanted their coffee. With a cappuccino at my side, small not tall, regular milk please, I would head north on I-95 and take a deep rejuvenating breath as I crossed into the state whose slogan resonated: "Maine, the way life should be." My next marker would be the coastal Route 1 exit sign, which started my mental checklist of each upcoming town: Brunswick, Bath, Wiscasset, Damariscotta, Nobleboro, Waldoboro, Warren. When the Route 90 by-pass sign appeared, I would savor the remaining foam from my now cold coffee, knowing I was almost to Camden.

I found Maine reassuring and comforting with its mixture of ocean, lakes, rivers, pines, and the solid feeling of the rocky coast, the granite foundations and doorsteps of the old houses, and the lines and lines of stone walls in forests and fields. On each of these trips, I needed comforting as I traveled with thoughts that this may be what my father called "the time." I would arrive, and he would perk up. He was lonely. Keeping loneliness at bay was no easy task. My grandmother, a widow for forty-three years, had to have spent many years at that task. With my pending divorce, I wondered how I would fare. I was lonely in my marriage. Now I faced being lonely alone. Words my mother wrote long ago surfaced from the recesses of my memory, words that we basically all live alone. Uncomfortable words to which she added, "though, thank heaven"—a qualifier often used—"we hope that we are able to get close to someone." And then another qualifier, that "those are transient moments to treasure." I never forgot her message. The "L" words haunted me: love, loss and loneliness. I hungered for real love with a partner and feared the loneliness that was to come once both parents were gone. I wanted treasured moments that would not disappear.

My father said nothing more about the letters. He didn't tell me what to do with them or why and I didn't ask. Before I closed up the sea chest and placed my mother's coffee table books back on top, I took the letters out of the envelope, all on fragile onion skin papers, many were carbon copies, all typed single space. I glanced at the first one in the pile, a letter written to my father during WWII in November 1943 when he was on a destroyer. It began:

Saturday the 13th

Dear Rich,

Here goes the calliope on the Island Queen again, which is nosed in against the plaza. It always makes me think of Sunday School picnics and round cakes with icing that sticks just a little to the wax paper that wraps it around. I can remember how the wind felt on our faces and how our hair blew back when we sat on whatever it is that you call the part of the boat that sticks out in front.

And just around the bend of the shore more ships are being made under brilliant light that reflects on the water. They are ships of less kindly intent. The sound of their riveting follows me to my bed and I think of you and hope they will hurry with the ships.

Further down the page I read with astonishment the advice she was giving to her new son-in-law:

Personally, from my aged point in living, I would not think of it as disloyalty at all if you stabilized your nerves as other men do. We are machines that cannot pull the load when the strain is too great on any one part of us. Margaret need not know – what is better for you is also better for her.

Many a night I have gotten up and walked about, taken a cold bath in the middle of the night – and by the way, a cold bath clears a lot of warmer emotions. Try it. Or don't Destroyers have showers? Even so results are imperfect. The root of the trouble is that we do not want to clear ourselves -- we do not want to become shells of human desire – it is usually only when all other avenues are closed that we accept that eventuality. I am fifty-six years old now and still I do not embrace the idea. Subconsciously I still hope for escape that I know will not come. But yours will.

I flipped to another war era letter to my father and this sentence caught my eye:

Now she is washing her panties and stockings against the week that has already begun to cast its shadow.

7

The "she" in that sentence was my mother, Margaret. Hannah wrote to her son-in-law about her daughter washing her panties. I turned to the last letter at the bottom of the stack, one of her travel letters written to family and friends. It started with "Dear Everybody" and included this comment about loneliness:

> When I went to bed, I felt lonesome without my hat tree with the fingernails but I have a recessed, marble lavatory, and an upper light that has a cartwheel of ruffled, cherry colored glass below it.

And ended with:

> P.S. I have just found an unnoticed item in my bathroom. No, I don't mean that one. It is a round mirror on an arm that juts out from the wall. It is attached to a cord with a switch. When you press a button a circle in the mirror at the bottom flashes on a light and you can look at any area you wish to scrutinize. I switched the light off quickly. I would rather live behind my face in semi darkness.

My eye landed on another nugget:

> His smile was as sweet as the honey of Lebanon - - tender as first love, and meant exactly nothing.

Then another:

> Our bench was underneath a linden tree. There were purple beeches, and weeping birch and rhododendron and azaleas. English dai-sies sprinkled on the grass. (What makes them English? They're in Paris and Vienna and in front of a motel in New York). This spring I picked some as I entered a motel in Carolina. Girls pushed baby buggies among the aging men and women who sat alone on benches. It is a triumphant thing to push a baby carriage. I notice some feel grave importance. Others flaunt their triumph. For babies

are a proof that mothers have been singled out and loved and needed. Babies are good advertising.

With Hannah's letters in my hands, the few portions I read intrigued, and I needed intrigue that wasn't about my life. I held letters which had been saved for more than seventy years, letters about love, beauty and loneliness sprinkled with a sense of humor which I never imagined my grandmother had. Delving into the letters meant I would learn more about my grandmother, a woman widowed at age forty-one who never re-married, a woman who remained single.

I had mixed feelings about becoming single. While fear was pervasive about what my life would be like as a divorcee, I was relieved to be free. For most of my marriage, my husband didn't really understand me and what I held dear, which wasn't money. I retreated and the marriage bonds unraveled. I recoiled from the life my husband grew to value. A Grand Canyon gap formed. For our first Christmas in California, he gave me a substantial diamond ring. I burst into tears. I didn't want an expensive ring. I wanted a marriage with reciprocity, compassion and a shared sense of what mattered—things of the spirit to hold gently. A friend reminded me that jewelry stores don't have warm bread. I needed to understand how I got myself into the situation I was in, hanging out where I didn't belong. Classic to my mother, when I told her during a Fall trip to Maine that a divorce was inevitable, she replied, simply, "We wondered what took you so long." I was stunned. Yet, not. My parents never meddled in my affairs. I was left on my own to sort things out, and now I was about to march out into the world on my own with fear on one side and hope on the other.

I was longing to feel rooted, to belong somewhere, to feel connected with those who valued what I valued. I had no idea that July day when my father told me "to do something with those letters," how much Hannah would guide and nudge me along in the years ahead and how patterns in previous generations were rooted deep within me.

Dear Everybody

Chapter Two

Feeling All Tucked in With Family

Returning from my July trip to Maine with photocopies of Hannah's letters and a stack of old photos, I was sapped of energy. The flight from Boston to San Francisco was longer than usual with the headwinds resisting westward movement, too much time for divorce worries to invade my thoughts, and not enough emotional energy to push those aside. I opened the door of the house I had purchased during the divorce and the stale air hit me. I left my bag by the door and walked around the room, surveying all the photographs I had already put on display. With my divorce and father's death pending, I needed family where I could see them. I counted six photographs in a cluster on the antique tilt-top table. The ceiling-to-floor bookshelves on either side of the fireplace had photographs of previous generations sprinkled throughout including a portrait of Hannah and one of her mother, Fanny Rose, both in the same wedding dress. Handsome George Arthur, Hannah's husband, was on a nearby shelf. The photograph that stood out was another portrait of Hannah, her eyes full of warmth, flowing with love and kindness, a tender closed-lip smile was framed by soft curls of her white hair close to her head. I walked up closer, looked straight into her eyes and smiled at her. She smiled back at me. Tears welled up. She was telling me all would be okay.

I had to turn away, the emotions were too much. I focused on the low table behind the couch where I had three eight-by-ten photographs taken by Hannah, each of my mother and her sister, Ann, as little children. In one, they are about three and four years old wearing white, lacy dresses, smiling, holding hands walking down a garden path. Margaret had a daisy in one outstretched hand as though to give the flower to the photographer, who was Hannah. In the other photo Ann and Margaret were in a farm field, my mother sitting in a wooden box wagon with the words "Use Berry Brother's celebrated varnishes and architectural finishes" on the side. She was wearing a knitted hat on her head and was looking back toward something, sad and unsure. Ann was sitting on the dirt next to the wagon, legs out straight, dark leather shoes with side buttons up to the ankles, the back of her straw hat facing the photographer. It was hard to believe that Hannah didn't stage this photo. In the third photograph, my mother and her sister were wearing white dresses, patent leather buckle shoes, white socks almost up to their knees, and matching large-brimmed black hats with ribbons. My mother was reaching for Ann's hand with a look on her face, wondering if everything was alright. Ann looked endearingly up at their mother. For the first time, it dawned on me that Hannah was a talented photographer. Her keen eye captured the essence of childhood, the insecurities, the innocence, the joy. These were not amateurish photographs. The woman behind the lens created photographs that told a story. I couldn't imagine she took such dreamy romantic images of her children to have them stored in a sea chest as my mother had done.

My parents' Maine house had no photographs on display, and my childhood home had only two that I recall. Family images were not scattered about for those coming to the house to see, for us to absorb unconsciously as we walked by throughout a day. The volume of photographs tucked away in that sea chest in Maine was a reminder of how private my parents were, not ones to draw attention to themselves, or put themselves "out there." On the day I walked into my house with Hannah's letters and was greeted by family photos, I remembered a sentence of hers that jumped out when I was photocopying the letters: "I feel all tucked in with these people…" That captured my feeling. I felt all tucked in with these photographs of my people. I was part of them. I belonged.

~

I never felt I belonged in the house my husband and I bought when we moved to California. The 1950s ranch with a cathedral ceiling living room and a silo-like addition at the end wasn't me. We couldn't afford anything in the area north of San Francisco with the back-east look I needed. Deciduous trees were my must-haves, and the town we picked had those. I did the best I could for ten years living in a house that wasn't me.

When I was dealing with the death of my mother and with my divorce underway, my husband insisted upon selling the house. At the top of my divorce fears was where I would live. To fend off that fear, my best friend and I went to open houses to survey the market. I couldn't imagine living in any of the houses we saw, and my fear wasn't being squelched until one Sunday, the two of us found a 1920 grey shingled cottage in the town where she and I lived on a street we never knew existed. We walked through the front gate, past four apple trees, entered through the front door, and my friend pronounced, "This is your house." I looked at her and said, "Yes, this is my house." Old by Marin standards, the house looked like New England. Nothing was gussied up inside, and the original horse barn was in the backyard with ivy growing up between the wide floor boards. I did a double take when the realtor told me the owners were selling to move to the wife's family farm in Maine.

Buying a house in 2007 in Marin was a highly competitive activity, and my realtor advised I write a letter to the owners to increase my chances. She sleuthed out that the wife went to the same college in Maine as my sister. I had a way in. Maine had come to me in Marin. I wrote the letter explaining all the connections with assurances that I would honor the New England integrity of their house. With some negotiations on price, the house became mine on June 30, 2007. I was ecstatic. Navigating divorce and the fallout with our children, an air-raid shelter had been needed on too many days. I was out of the house that had been covered with a dark divorce cloud. I realized that I had carted around the wrong life for too long, married to the wrong person. I breathed a sigh of contentment with my Marin house that felt like Maine.

~

Once I returned home after the July visit with my father, my life left little time to focus on Hannah's letters. I managed to sort them into two categories, those to her new son-in-law during WWII when he was on a destroyer and those to her "Dear Everybody" group written during her travels. After sorting, I put all pages in a binder with an enlarged copy of Hannah's portrait photo on the cover. Her photo was a comfort. I also dug around for and found my grandmother's scrapbook which my mother turned over to me years ago and I'd since shoved in a closet. At the time my mother passed along the scrapbook, its importance was lost on me. I made a mental note of the white Mystic Tape holding the cover together and the haphazard way Hannah had glued and taped in the many letters from publishers, editors, and admirers of her writing. There were stray essays stashed in the back. The scrapbook looked like it was created by someone who cared little about organization. I photocopied the essays and added a third tab in my binder for them.

With hopes for family input, I mailed a hard copy of the letters, all 123 pages to my sister and maternal cousins knowing full well reading the copies would be a challenge as they had been for me. The ink was blurry and page numbers were few. Photocopying added to the blur. The response I received told me that I was the only one who had read each and every page. They were interested yet not as immersed as I had become. Their response included the question, "What are you going to do with these?" without any help with the answer.

Summer in Marin with the never-ending string of sunny days made being indoors hard for me, and Hannah's letters sat, unattended. Hiking, weeding my garden and trimming my hedges fended off worry about my father's health and the impact of the divorce on my children. I was working full-time and had traveled to various states to find a school for my son that would settle him. He, my daughter, and I were all unsettled. The complicated issues in my divorce were in the hands of experts who would proclaim in a few months what should be done. I had married a man of industry, a man dedicated to money, a man who lived with his guard up. The untangling of our lives, dividing our assets was not simple. Co-parenting was never simple and was now more complicated. Despite this backdrop, when I was alone on weekend nights, I skimmed through a few essays, and began transcribing passages into a document I titled "Nuggets from Hannah." Randomly I started with her essay "This Changing World," and found messages about character and men.

> Before trees gave way to parking lots and handkerchiefs to Kleenex, my grandmother bought a book, designed for and addressed to ladies and gentlemen of that period. It was a thick book in a red binding and was titled *Manners, Culture and Dress*. In its preface which was signed by the author he makes clear his objectives. "My aim," he wrote, "is to cultivate the heart as well as the mind, and to produce a well-rounded symmetrical character." That phrase alone would keep him off the best seller list today. There are those who would prefer to have no character at all than to be well-rounded.

Three generations of women holding onto a book about manners and character. Hannah Trimble had character in spades, that I had known. I wondered if in passing this book along to Hannah, her mother saw a little too much "character" in her daughter for her liking. The quality of one's character was held in high regard as I grew up, including cultivation of the heart, being kind-spirited and compassionate while simultaneously developing an inquisitive mind. Not a small order. As my married years added up, there was no avoiding the truth—my marriage lacked what is cultivated by the heart, and we didn't have a well-rounded life together. Hannah's commentary continued:

His approach to ladies is far less demanding. It makes me think of a valentine which I once received from a gentleman - - well, maybe a synthetic gentleman. He had chosen it because of a picture of an old fashioned dress form - - the kind women used when we made our own clothes. Beneath this, enclosed in a lovely red heart were printed these words, "Darling I am adjustable."

My husband never called me darling and would never be described as adjustable. I wondered who the synthetic gentleman was that my grandmother knew. Interesting word choice for a man, "synthetic." One thing I knew about my grandmother, she wasn't typical and wasn't shy letting others know:

Talking upon subjects of which I know nothing is my favorite indoor sport. I have a friend who simply cannot stand me when I do this. She says, "And WHAT is your authority for that statement?" Such a frontal attack sharpens the wits and develops a creative faculty. A good time is had by all.

Hannah's passage provided a much-needed smile. I needed Hannah, her letters and her essays. I needed a woman with character. A woman who reflected on her life as I reflected on mine.

Fall arrived as it does, and with my son and daughter at school, and daylight shorter and shorter, my time alone inside grew. I was alone a lot in my marriage and lonely without a soulmate, but alone on my own was different. I was content leaving behind all the drama of the marriage. My after-dinner companions became Hannah's binder, post-it-notes, and a yellow highlighter. Her warm smile on the cover was full of love that radiated to me. I worked my way through her letters at a slow pace, reading and highlighting paragraphs or phrases that stood out. Without someone next to me to turn to and say, "Listen to this," I emailed select passages to girlfriends. What I received back was, "You need to do something with these." My father's words echoed. Friends who knew nothing about my grandmother were telling me she was a person whose life was worth exploring. Hannah was taking up residence with me. With my "Nuggets from Hannah" document now more than a few pages, I was stunned by the beauty of her writing, stunned by her astute observations of people, and stunned by her humor and the intimate thoughts she shared. What I was reading didn't match the woman I knew. That seemed fitting, as the life I had been in for the last twenty-four years, didn't match who I was.

Dear Everybody

Chapter Three

Saying Goodbye

On the day before Thanksgiving, a little more than eighteen months after my mother died, and almost one year to the day since my divorce, the phone rang. My father's favorite caregiver, Lisa Pendleton, had called and put him on the phone. He always dialed himself. I knew something had changed. His words seared into me: "I will hold on until you get here."

During my July trip, my father had announced that he didn't want to live through another winter alone. He had made it through one without my mother and had no intention of living through another. Winters in Maine are long, cold, and dark. My sister and I believed him. I had flown to Maine at least three times since my mother's death when my father called to say, "This is it. You need to come now." During the last two trips, with the good-bye at the mud-room door, he gave me a hug, had tears in his eyes, and said, "I love you." I had never seen him with tears. He had never said those words as best I could remember, though I always knew his love was there. Talking openly about love or feelings wasn't done. When the word love was spoken, I took notice.

During the year of his "come now" requests my stress was piling up along with divorce papers from the Superior Court of the State of California, County of Marin. I had filed for divorce, beat my husband to it. After he said he wanted a divorce, I found an attorney, and she advised: "You need to file fast and freeze the assets." I heeded her advice. Our settlement conference, the official "now you are divorced" event, took place one year later, and things were still not settled. Stipulations, domestic relations orders, copies, and filings had to be managed. Hannah's letters had become a diversion. Diving into her letters took me away, floated me to another time, off to another world. The letters she wrote during WWII to my father were letters on behalf of love, and I submerged myself, as she did, in my parent's romance. Both Hannah and I were without a love of our own. With my mother's death, my father's memories of these letters must have held extra meaning for him.

[Letter dated "Saturday the 13th"]

Whether you think of her or not, she will be here, thinking of you. There will be an end to your waiting. When you come back to her, her love and her loyalty is not going to be measured or increased by the hours on deck you have held her close in your thoughts.

[Letter dated "Tuesday the 11th of January"]

Life seldom allows two people to love and have one another in so perfect a way as you have. I'm scared. I hope it will not be months, after all, that you cannot reach to her. You are very right to tell her bare facts, as nearly as you may, tho. It is always easier to face any eventuality than to drag thru days of uncertainty. In the meantime keep on and on saying the loving things that lie in your heart.

My mother and father met eight times before they married on June 19, 1943. My mother called it "a war wedding." She wore a suit, hem just below the knee, a garland of flowers on her head, one toe peeking out of each shoe with heels making her just about the same height as my father. He wore his white, Navy officer's uniform. They wed in the Grosse Pointe Episcopal church though neither were religious, let alone Episcopal. My father reported for duty in Seattle a month later, and Hannah, his new mother-in-law, if she hesitated at all, pushed any hesitation aside, and in the following twenty-two months wrote twenty letters to her daughter's new husband, keeping her daughter Margaret fresh in his mind and fear at bay.

I thought of my father alone without her, alone after sixty-three years of marriage. While the inner workings of their marriage were private, it was clear their years together forged a strong bond. It was common for him to tease her with a twinkle and a smile. She responded batting him away, looking annoyed. I don't remember any out and out fights, or on the other side of the ledger any outpouring of physical affection other than a quick kiss when my father walked in the door after work. My mother longed for more attention, acknowledgment and affection. I do remember two comments directed at my father. Two lines, each on different occasions. My mother's voice floated out, calm and firm, "If you didn't want someone to challenge you, you should have married someone else." My father had five accomplished sisters who no doubt challenged him. The other line of my mother's stunned me the most, first because of what she said, and second because she said it within earshot of me when I was sitting at the kitchen counter doing my high school homework: "I am not your maid and concubine."

After my mother's first stroke, my father put his wedding ring on for the first time since they married. According to my mother, his claim was that wearing a ring on a destroyer was a hazard. Then, post war, he claimed rings bothered him. Signs of my father's love came out in the open as my mother's life faded. Through her stroke fog, I hope she noticed that he put on the ring. I noticed when my mother told me Hannah made known to both my mother and her sister, Ann, that marrying a doctor wasn't all it was "cracked up to be." Maybe Hannah felt no marriage was all it was cracked up to be. Mine certainly wasn't. Maybe that's why she never remarried. Maybe that's why I am searching for clues on how to push back both the fear of being unpartnered and the fear of being swallowed up in partnership again.

When the phone rang that November, I was setting the Thanksgiving table, smoothing out an unironed linen napkin. Looking at caller ID, I took a deep breath and turned to the misty view out the window. Early in the week there were calls full of stress from my kids about going to their father's house for another holiday with the new girlfriend in residence. There was stress about how to navigate splitting a holiday now that our marriage had split. I was like a beaker full of water. One more drop and I would spill over, and that is what happened when my father's caregiver handed the phone to my father, and he said, "I will hold on until you get here."

After I hung up, I pulled myself together and pulled the dining room bamboo shades down all the way attempting to keep out the dreary chill. A gentle rain was starting to fall. My focus had been on setting the traditional Thanksgiving dining room table to send a message of family togetherness and warmth, my family consisting of my two children and me and our two Golden Retrievers. I continued to put out family items and pushed back tears remembering that several months before, I needed a notarized statement from my father listing all the items he and my mother had gifted to me to fend off my soon-to-be ex who was trying to claim these cherished items in the divorce process. I would have been unmoored without those connections to my family.

Family items filled my dining room and many were from Hannah. On my table were silver candlesticks with two outstretched arms, a gift to my mother from Hannah's trip to South America. The lace dining room tablecloth, once Hannah's, spread halfway down to the floor as I didn't need extra table leaves for just the three of us. The Audubon bird plates on the table were from the stack of twelve Hannah gave to my mother. Hidden in the sideboard were Royal Daulton flower plates and serving pieces, also from Hannah. The Russian Samovar on the butler's tray was passed along from Hannah's cousin, Gertrude Hubbs Hornbrook. The two hand-hammered brass wall sconces from Sweden, courtesy of Hannah, sported hearts at the top. As a wedding present, my mother's sister, Ann, gave me antique telescoping candlesticks with the copper showing where the silver had worn off. One candlestick no longer telescoped, the flaws part of their appeal. I was in my dining room facing my father's pending death with my grandmother, mother, and aunt around me.

Before Lisa put my father on the phone, she told me I should fly out soon. My kids were flying in that afternoon for the Thanksgiving weekend and flying out on Sunday. My father knew this. I hear his words now as if he had just said them, "Have Thanksgiving with the kids, come after they leave. I will hold on until you get here." My sister and I often heard our parents say, "We don't want to trouble you." My father didn't want to trouble me and ruin Thanksgiving with my kids. The anxiety in my chest told me this would be the real red-eye trip, and tears welled up. I shoved them down. Anxiety stayed. "See you Monday late morning." I told him and then, the words, "Love you." They just came out. I couldn't keep them in. I hung up and booked the red-eye flight for Sunday night.

My father held on. Lisa and my sister gave me the update when I arrived. He hadn't eaten in days, hadn't gotten out of bed. Until a few months ago, he still crawled up the narrow, twisty steep stairs to his bedroom on the second floor. He had put white Mystic Tape on the top stair tread, a warning, watch out, steep going ahead. The treads, wooden and uncarpeted, accommodate a size seven woman's shoe. I measured it once with my foot. Anything larger, the toe hits the riser and the heel hangs over. Half way up, the stairway curves sharply to the left. The treads become triangles at that point. How he navigated up and down those stairs in the last few years of his life I never knew. What he did near the end of his driving days was a clue. He taped a V on the steering wheel of his car as a reminder for him to be vigilant. He was determined and vigilant. When the time came for a hospital bed, my father resisted. We convinced him, explaining it was easier for Lisa to care for him. He cared about Lisa, and acquiesced to the bed, but refused to have it in the living room.

Lisa wasn't just his favorite caregiver. Lisa was a Pendleton related to the Pendleton who built the house and the Pendleton who married into my father's side of the family back in the early 1800s. The house was meant to come back to our family, and Lisa was meant to come care for our father. The coincidence was hard to shake off.

The hospital bed was put in upstairs, and out went the two twin beds my parents had throughout their sixty-four-year marriage. I time-dated the sagging mattresses to about 1950 given the manufacturer's satin hand-sewn on labels. I carefully cut the threads and saved one of the labels before the beds were taken away. Like T.V.'s Ozzie and Harriet, Lucy and Ricky, Richmond and Margaret slept in single beds.

As a physician, my father knew how to hurry death on: stop eating, stop drinking. My sister came up from her place in Portland as she had done many times. We both had an inkling that I might need to cancel my return flight to San Francisco which was only a few days away. I stood silently by his bed holding his hand. The window shades were down. The room, dimly lit by the hallway light, had a softness to it. Only the hospital bed, one chair and a drop-leaf table, all leaves in the down position, were in the room, which was cramped when the two single beds were there. We had removed the braided throw rugs from the wide plank wooden floor to prevent slipping. The air was still. The only sound was my father's uneven breathing, long pauses between breaths. Pauses that made me pause. Checking to be sure he was still alive, I put my head close to his chest to hear his heart. He said very little that day, only a few words about my mother. He said that she had packed her bags. These were unusual words given she died almost two years before. Probing further might bring up emotions, and I knew better than to do that. The morning my sister and I told him that our mother had died at the hospital in the night, he stared straight ahead and said, "Something is wrong with my emotional thermostat." My emotional thermostat was out of whack as I sat by his bedside listening to breathing that I knew could fade away at any time.

I held my father's hand. He seemed unaware of his surroundings. With hesitation from the years when emotions and physical expression of love were kept in check, I leaned over and stroked his head, slowly, tenderly, gently, over and over. Memories welled up of times when love was on full display, moments as a little girl when he tickled me, put me up on his shoulders on walks, played "airplane" lying on his back with the soles of his feet on my stomach, holding both of my arms, extending his legs with me atop his feet so I would fly in the air above him. When saying my goodnights, I jumped on his lap as he read the *New York Times*, flung my arms around his neck and gave him butterfly kisses. One night when I was about nine or ten, my mother told me I was too old to do that, "Time to get off his lap," she said. I did. I don't remember kisses and hugs after that, except at my wedding.

I stroked his head again and again, put my arms around him and told him I loved him. I pulled the chair closer and sat by his bedside for a few more moments. I rested my head on his chest, on the man who was true to himself. His old station wagon flashed through my mind, with "V" for vigilant on the steering wheel. I felt anchored. A pervasive calmness came over me. I felt the integrity of my father as he was dying. I knew at that moment I wasn't losing the essence of my father. What transferred from him to me was a security in knowing what our family stood for, how I was meant to go through life. He spoke of my mother, and her essence was there also. When I was single and just out of college, struggling to find my way, she wrote to reassure me that I knew who I was. I uncovered her letter in the process of sorting through Hannah's letters and only then did it fully resonate.

> At least you know who you are and who your family is, and what we stand for, and the fact that you are part of all of us . . . Really, the only security any of us can have, in the end, is security within ourselves - - -I do think you have that - - - the process of achieving it is painful at times, but you have done well in developing it - - you have decided on certain values that are important and help guide your decisions, you have discovered some of your skills and have developed them. You know who you are and where you came from.

Somewhere during my marriage, I lost track of what had become of me. Maybe what I felt sitting next to my father as he died was that what I stood for was a feeling of being integrated, a term I would come to discover that Hannah used many times in her writing, exploring whether someone, including herself, was "integrated," a unity of all parts of oneself and one's life as a whole. Maybe my father knew Hannah's writing would help me rediscover what I had lost.

After I said goodbye to my father, I took a deep breath to keep it together and headed down the stairway, minding the white mystic tape at the top. He died that night, December 1. Someone once told me that people die as they lived, and given who my father was, the odds were that he would die in private. That was what he did. He said he would hold on until I got there, and that was what he did. He was true to himself to the end.

Chapter 4

Christmas Memories

I wasn't sure how Christmas would feel now that I was what one cousin called "an adult orphan." One thing was certain, I looked forward to setting up Christmas on my own, no fuming as in the past when I struggled to put up the generously sized Christmas tree by myself while my husband sequestered himself in his office. Each year when the time came, he was too busy. "I'll help later" was his comment, which meant, never. In a letter I had skimmed, a line jumped out about what Hannah would do to husbands who didn't help their wives: "I'd knock their blocks off." I was never brave enough to do that, and I wonder if she ever did that to my grandfather. It had been two weeks since my father's death, my second Christmas without a spouse and my first without parents. No packages would arrive from Maine. No card from my mother with a check inside and her traditional message, "Treat yourself. This is JUST for you." I would carry on Christmas traditions, many carry-overs from my childhood, many to do with Hannah. Her several Christmas visits made their mark. One of the letters in my Hannah binder was a thank-you to my father. Unlike other letters, it was short. When I first read it while sorting out the stack of letters from the Maine sea chest, I pushed back tears. I pushed back tears again when I photocopied it, when I put it in the binder, and when, remembering its message, I sat in my living room with boxes of ornaments in front of me.

Wednesday, January 7/59

Dear Rich - -

This is a thank you note, for your generously offered Christmas. I am glad that you have thank yous, too, for a life that contains honor, love and lovely children in a home that reflects good taste, high ideals and the only kind of security there is - - - the security sustained by a unity of purpose.

It is cold as everything here. I kinda like it. Good year ahead of you!

Lovingly,
Hannah Trimble

Her insight was spot on, "security sustained by a unity of purpose." My husband and I, often at odds about core values, could not claim to have that.

Following tradition, I put my right-sized tree up ten days before Christmas, all by myself, accompanied by tears. The California sun was shining and temperatures were in the low seventies, not a Christmas spirit day in my mind. Even after ten years in California, I couldn't acclimate to Christmas weather that felt like the tropics. With the warmth and humidity, I learned I had to do away with the childhood tradition of hanging candy canes on the tree as the canes elongated and sticky syrupy goo dripped on branches and the floor. The tradition Hannah introduced of hanging ribbon candy would be hopeless. Chocolate mice strung up by their tails, another Hannah tradition, did work. Hannah's Santa Lucia Wreath on the coffee table was a must. As I unpacked each Christmas item my mother had passed along, I heard her words, "This is from your grandmother." Her words did as she intended; they anchored me to family, and made sure I didn't forget my heritage and our traditions.

As the sun went down, I lit the candles on the wreath, turned off the lights, glass of wine at my side, and sank into peace and harmony while listening to Dylan Thomas read *A Child's Christmas in Wales*.

~

Grandmother with a capital "G" and an emphasis on grand, made a grand entrance when traveling up for Christmas from Evansville. Her arrival at the Detroit airport almost needed trumpets. When she exited the jet runway, I stood up straight and snapped into a polite, don't-be-a Goop mode. I would never have wanted to be a Goop in her presence. The Goops were characters in a book, *More Goops and How Not to Be Them: A Manual of Manners for Polite Infants*, publication date 1900, which Hannah bought for my mother and her sister when they were children and later became part of my childhood. The tattered book, pages falling out, the cover barely hanging on, has a valued place on my bookshelf. Hannah reinforced the book's messages as did my mother: "Whenever you are eating soup, remember not to be a Goop," and "The Goops they lick their fingers, Goops they lick their knives . . . Goops lead disgusting lives." Goops were part of the upbringing of three generations. I bought a re-issued edition for my children and tried to instill a few poems in them, though none seemed to stick.

Hannah arrived dressed for a Michigan December; her oversized wool coat with saucer-like buttons was draped over both shoulders; her arms within the coat, but not in the sleeves, created a rectangular outline for her solid frame. Her sweaters were also worn in that way, top button buttoned, arms out of the sleeves. Hannah was a woman whose chest deserved the word bosom, and the chunky artistic silver necklaces she wore accentuated that bosom. Necklaces, her junk jewelry as she called them, were a staple in her wardrobe. Her legs were solid, no delicate ankles like my mother's. Hannah's fur-topped galoshes, unzipped half way, revealed underneath the only shoes I ever saw her wear—black Archlock orthopedics laced up below her ankles, the chunky solid heels anchoring her to the ground. During my early meanderings through her letters, certain words leapt off the page.

Archlocks was one. On a trip to Austria after WWII, she referenced her shoes: "This is sure the place for me. In comparison, my Archlock shoes are positively dainty."

In the midst of a day of transcribing Hannah's letters, I took a break and searched for a pair of Archlocks on eBay. Success. In her memory I placed the order. When they arrived, I shoved in my feet, laced up the laces, looked in the mirror and gave thanks for my mother's ankles. My feet are happy in graceful flats or shoes with thin 1 ½" heels. Archlocks don't even come close to being dainty. My search for these shoes told me the depth of my search to find myself.

When Hannah was before me in the Detroit airport, hair as white as white, gentle curls held close to her head with white bobby bins, I would walk toward her with trepidation and a polite, "Hi Grandmother" greeting. Her standard reply, "Hello darling." I don't remember hugs, but if there were any, they were not the long deep hugs you melted into. Unlike the effusive warmth I discovered in her writing, my memory of her was someone with distanced, deliberate restraint. Quite a contrast to the effort I required to slow down and stop moving. When skimming through her essay, "A Daughter's a Daughter the Rest of Your Life," I nodded as I took note of her opinion:

> . . . my daughter, in conference with her husband, decided to name
> my grandchild Stephanie - - why, I have never exactly understood. I
> like a short, sturdy name, with a pioneer flavor.

> Stephanie turned out to be a hilarious extrovert - - the only one in
> our blood stream. Her name was shortened to Bubs.

"Hilarious extrovert" may be a stretch. I do think she liked what my father referred to as my "spunk" and didn't want to suppress it, that is, as long as I was polite, manners intact, and not behaving like a Goop. I lost my spunk somewhere in my twenty-four years of marriage, and maybe my father wanted me to read these words. He was the one who dubbed me Bubs.

After arriving back at the house from the airport, I followed Grandmother upstairs to the guestroom. I was around nine years old that year, time-stamping this by the year we moved into the house with a guest room. A three-quarter bed once belonging to Hannah's mother Fanny Rose took up most of the room, its head and footboard boasting holes for ropes that once held the mattress. This odd-sized bed was perfect for the room, as the only other items that fit were a dresser and a Detroit factory chair. I stood politely by her side as she put her suitcase on the bed, pushed opened the latches, snap left, snap right, and the lid of her leather suitcase opened revealing the satin pocket on the inside of the lid, puckered by elastic, sagging with its soft contents. Soft somethings inside that pocket protected what was on top of her clothes. I knew what was inside, strands and strands of popcorn for our Christmas tree, strands Hannah strung with her knobby, arthritic hands. She took the strands out, one by one, and draped each over my outstretched arm while providing instructions on the proper way for me to carry them so they wouldn't tangle on the way downstairs to the tree. Her labor of love needed proper handling.

Further down in her suitcase, deep in between her clothes was something else I was after. She lifted a layer of well-folded clothes and put them on the bed, and there was the box of dark chocolate mice. Each mouse lay on its stomach, twine as tails, white nonpareil candy eyes. Just by looking, I could taste their white cool-mint innards. The popcorn strands were placed first on the tree and the mice were next. We hung them by their tails and were allowed, on three occasions, to take a mouse off the tree: to offer one to a friend which also meant having one ourselves, then one on Christmas eve, and one on Christmas day. If any remained, they would be parceled out. Our tree sported mice, popcorn strands, candy canes, ribbon candy, popcorn balls, honey locust-seed pods, pine cones, and ornaments Hannah collected from her trips to Europe. The tree's position in the room was next to the Victrola which housed my father's seventy-five rpm opera records, and the onyx and pearl inlaid writing desk of Hannah's grandfather, her publications within. After Christmas, our tree was propped up in the backyard so the birds could feast on the popcorn. These Christmas ceremonies created magical moments for me, one of many ways Hannah noodled her way into my life despite her rare visits.

When I had children, I wanted them to have the same Christmas-mice pleasure Hannah provided. Evansville no longer made the mice so I searched to find another source. Success in New Hampshire, chocolate mice, hand crafted. These mice have one problem, they don't show their best side when hanging on the tree. The arrival of the mice delighted my children, in part because they arrived in a wooden box with a hinged lid, a wide satin ribbon tied around the box, and a gold-colored wax stamp securing the ribbon. When the box opened, mouse faces peeked out. These are not the sturdy Midwest Indiana mice of Hannah's day but sophisticated, velvety, whipped ganache with toasted-almond ears and a "hint of port."

Besides mice and popcorn strands, Christmas with Hannah included many games of Canasta played in the living room on a card table next to the window with the steam radiator underneath. I was toasty warm during those games, and when I didn't know what card to play, staring at the stack of books and hand-hammered brass dish on the radiator top was a good distraction. The radiator hissed now and then, a good backdrop to winning and losing at cards. Hannah always beat me at canasta, her skills honed on her freighter trips across the Atlantic. I beat Hannah at my favorite game, Slapjack. Arthritis made it hard for her to top my speed when the Jack turned up. She never complained. There was an unspoken understanding that we both needed to win at our own favorie games. Her thoughtful intellectual play of her hand in canasta, and my quick-as-a-flash, barely-think-about-it slap or hold-back in Slapjack suited each of us.

Memories of Hannah and Christmas aren't complete without horehound. Winter made worse what she called a "tickle" in her throat. I am mindful of a tickle whenever I clear my throat. Hers meant she pulled a horehound candy out from her pocket or purse. She offered me one once. I never accepted another, never even saw them in stores, until a few years ago when, to my shock, at the checkout stand at a trendy grocery store in Marin were Horehound candy bags designed to mimic those of a century ago. With the spirit of Hannah on my shoulder, I bought a bag thinking I might like them with a mature palate. Not true. Even at age fifty-four, I had the same reaction as when I was eight. Never again will I put one in my mouth. The taste is described as bittersweet. I would say bitter is ninety percent of it. I never understood how she could like horehound, and I doubt it will have a resurgence even with clever packaging, even in Marin where the expression, "It's all good," wins over anything bitter without a balanced dose of sweet. While Hannah carried horehound candies in her purse, I carry dark chocolate squares, bittersweet in proper proportions. They melt in my mouth, a soft creamy sensation, a delight on my tongue. Horehound and chocolate, both Hannah and I had what soothed us close at hand.

Having decorated my right-sized Christmas tree and the Santa Lucia wreath aglow on my coffee table, I had no qualms treating myself to a chocolate mouse as the weight I had lost during the divorce stayed off during the period my parents were dying. I opened my box of ganache mice, popped one in my mouth, put the red satin mouse tail on the table and admired the ornaments on my tree. Gone was the guilt I once had when I put my mother-in-law's factory-made ornaments on the back of the tree. When I went through the ornaments to give a fair share to my ex-husband, those from his mother were the first to go. They never matched the handcrafted ornaments Hannah collected on her travels. For several years I tried stringing popcorn, following Hannah's rule to let the popcorn get stale to prevent splitting during the threading. Stringing popcorn is laborious work. Too many split kernels, and I lacked the required patience. With memories of my parents, I've held onto the few remaining pinecones and locust pod ornaments they used when they had limited resources, ornaments I associated with their young love. I can't avoid what is becoming clear, I am a sucker for nostalgia, for romance, for what soothes.

Only a few months before, when browsing through Hannah's World War II letters, I tabbed down the corner of one written near Christmas, infused with sweet, warm and romantic words. I put aside my sit-up-straight, be polite, all-should-be-proper impression of my grandmother, and smiled at her creative method of dating her letters, never noting the year. By my calculation, this letter was Tuesday, December 19, 1944. Hannah was fifty-six, two years older than I was when I read her letter. My father was twenty-seven and had been at sea, away from his new bride, Margaret, for a second Christmas.

Tuesday the 19th of Christmas

Here, so near to Christmas, and where you are - - what? When you say March, I'm simply scared to death – don't say it! Sneak up on it - - barefoot, with shoes in hand, on tip toe - - we want it to be true so - - that it scares us. I didn't get flowers for Margaret with your Christmas check - - instead I got a beeyootiful night gown, because I knew she wanted it - - she says she is going to start to gather a hope chest again. She has a wreath of holly on her curtain and has filled a small brass bowl with silver bells and red and green. They reflect in our little breakfast coffee pot - - made in Russia of shining brass. On the dressing table she has a silver vase with English holly, which with luck, I found a week ago. I knew it was that kind you broke from trees in Seattle, so, quick, I brought it to her. This is the evening for her hours at the canteen. In another hour she will be back, hang her uniform neatly on its hanger, stick her feet into those enormous red wooly mules, thrust her arms into the sleeves of the quilted dressing gown with rosebuds over it, and I'll bet, sit down and write to you before she goes to bed.

I have just finished a letter or two myself - - I found a delicious picture of a kitchen for your father - - he was always muttering last summer that a modern kitchen had no soul - - that it needed a big black stove with red fire in it and a pump on the sink - - the picture had it all - - the seven children, - - even the dog, exactly like the one who comes to bedroom doors to say good morning at your house.

And I sent a note to your Aunt Agnes - - did Margaret tell you of a green calico rooster that had suffered the indignity of becoming a pot holder, which Aunt Agnes sent her? It hangs over our breakfast coffee pot - - I like Aunt Agnes.

You are the only doctor I have ever known who actually - - what is it you call it in Basic English - - sticks out his neck? I mean actually asks about an aging lady's ailments We like it far too much. I'm really fine - - no ache or pain - - too bad, with such a chance to have an audience. But thank you anyway.

Did you ever go into the Women's City Club in Detroit? Of course not. Why would you. Except that your wedding cake came out of its kitchen. I stayed there again last summer and every morning loved watching the sweet old ladies - - just one short jump ahead of me - - if you listen as they talk you will find that their doctors are their heroes - - the only men left in their lives - - "He said to me" - - "I said to him." I was accepted into their group at once because I limped - - if I had lent myself to their little game, just think what wonderful material the Ford Hospital had given me. What's the one who works under Dr. Mc Coll? "Why in the hell don't you get off that foot?" he said. "Damned quick" he added. I didn't dare to quote unquote further to my old ladies who WERE ladies.

Jean (renter in the building) is below my stairway making Christmas cookies - - can you smell them? I'm going down and help her - - goodnight. I'll save you at least one. Don't let a black cat cross your path. Come home in March.

Lovingly, Mother

Christmases laden rich with memories. One Christmas, chocolate mice and popcorn strings aside, there were fireworks. Hannah would have been in her mid-seventies, and I in my teenage years was old enough to remember the fireworks and old enough for my parents to explain why my father said what he said, his voice raised and angry. It was early afternoon on Christmas, and I was by the phone in the breakfast room. My father was in the living room on the other side of the house, the dining room, front hall and stairs were in between us. I could hear his words, clear and firm, directed at Hannah: "If you don't behave yourself, I am going to put you on a plane and send you back home." I was stunned not just hearing him raise his voice but that he was talking to my grandmother with a tone sounding like he was talking to a child. Realizing I had overheard the conversation, my mother came to explain. What triggered my father's outburst was that Hannah had pouted and complained she hadn't gotten enough Christmas presents.

Christmas can hang heavy with emotion. December 2005 marked the year my husband and I had announced to our children that we were getting a divorce. Two years later, my children still were struggling, and I was plagued with memories about the day we told the kids our "news." I credit him for taking the initiative to end a marriage that had died. I couldn't do that. I wasn't brave enough to break up the family. I was raised to buck up under stress and duress. I thought a divorce would be particularly hard on our kids who we adopted at birth. Another loss, I thought. Another rejection. That Christmas season of the telling was as horrid as I imagined. I dreaded the thought. If I had been my mother, she would have said, "Perish the thought." She perished many thoughts. I couldn't. I begged my husband to wait until after Christmas to break the news, and to my surprise he agreed. How many days after Christmas before we dropped the bombshell, I analyzed and over-analyzed, one of those analysis conversations I have with myself that can go on and on. I wanted enough time for the children to settle in with what they heard before they headed back to their schools, though I knew this news never settles comfortably.

I was also surprised that I was still surprised when my husband came up with an idea that was the opposite of what I was thinking. That was typical. If I thought X, he thought Y. In this situation, he wanted to tell the kids the news in the living room. I refused. The Christmas tree was still up, the wooden box of chocolate mice was still on the table next to the couch with a few mice waiting to be eaten. The living room was not a good backdrop for the announcement that was to come. The supporting props for Christmas cheer were all around, and I couldn't agree to give the news that the family was splitting apart in a room that was supposed to be full of warm holiday feelings. Divorce announcements are seared in for life. A Christmas tree does not belong in the picture. I convinced my husband that the kitchen was the right location. I stood with my children on either side of me. He was across from us. That was not how family therapy experts advised. The mother and father were to be side by side, facing the children. I couldn't bring myself to do that, any more than I could agree to make the announcement in the living room.

With the Christmas of the divorce announcement in the past, a holiday never to be lived again, I breathed a deep sigh as I created a Christmas without a husband in my post-divorce house, in a house that was meant to be mine, in a California house sold to me by a couple moving to Maine, a house with apple trees in front and kitchen and bathrooms that were as they were meant to be, rooms aged with character. It was a Christmas without conflict, disappointments and tears. During quiet moments as the holiday approached, the tree in front of me, my feet up on the coffee table, family photos around me, I finished reading all of Hannah's letters and the essays in her scrapbook. I had Post-it notes on pages and pages. I felt hope rising in my chest, again. I had thoughts of buying a "beeyoutiful" nightgown for myself. A gift to me from me. I felt connected to family with chocolate mice, the Silent Night music box, the fragile German advent calendar whose twenty-five doors still opened and closed, the Santa Lucia wreath, and the Opal Wheeler Christmas song book on the coffee table. The piano left with the marriage. I had hopes that maybe my kids would play Slapjack with me after they arrived. Thoughts that if they did, I would probably lose. Arthritis was creeping into my hands, hands that were starting to look like Hannah's.

Chapter 5

Settling in with Hannah

With Christmas behind me and my children back in school, the house was empty and the alone-on-my-own feeling welled up. One Saturday morning, early in January, I dove back into Hannah's letters. Why not enter my grandmother's life and escape mine? Maybe an idea would form on what to do with them. I made a cup of coffee, grabbed my laptop and the binder of her letters and settled in at the dining room table. Outside the January rains had begun, and the forecast showed heavy rain and wind all throughout the weekend. I turned to one of the pages I had marked with a Post-it to remind me of sections in her letters that had resonated. The letter was written to my mother and her sister from the Cali, Colombia airport in 1953:

> It is knowing about people from the inside out like that which helps me with that awful feeling of fear, whatever it is. Don't know why, but it does. I have always thought that this idea about a power that followed each person doesn't make sense, but I am beginning to wonder. So many times this week when I needed it most, someone has reached out a hand and straightened me up.

A murder of crows had gathered outside my dining room window on the soggy grass, and as I watched them, I wondered how long the fear that had welled up during my divorce would have a hold on me. Turning away from the crows, I typed a few more sentences into my laptop and could picture Hannah opening the case of her Smith Corona typewriter, poised to type one of her many letters.

> I am writing with my typewriter on my knees in the airport at Cali,
> on the way to Lima. When I left Bogota, it was still dark. Those
> low-lying gray clouds that cover the savannah and hide the peaks
> were still shot with silver from sunrise, and circled with vultures.

The power that followed her was taking ahold of me, I felt as if she was reaching out a hand with her letters to straighten me up. As I read on, Hannah created scenes for me, escape hatches.

I was cloistered inside, heavy rain outside, and typing up the various chunks I had tabbed was a welcome relief. A full day went by without contact with another person. Going out risked flooded roads, falling trees. As a transplanted eastcoast person, California floods, mudslides, fires, and earthquakes still triggered fear even knowing my neighbors, if needed, would be at my house in a flash. Thinking of the tax papers I had pushed aside, more fear arose, even knowing the grandfatherly man who managed my finances would help. I wouldn't be alone. A finance man with a warm heart had arrived in my grandmother's world of letters too. Hannah let on that a man from the Ex Printer bank came to her aid in Cali.

> While "the nice man" weighed my bags all of a sudden here I was
> going to pieces again. The lean Dutch man from Ex Printer turned
> into a human being and took me over to a table in the crowd, where
> we were brought coffee and orange juice. Then he talked about him-
> self. In halting English. "I know what being alone is," he told me. "I
> go home to my desk and my bed and sometimes, tho I am a man, I
> weep." This is some of what he told me.

My grandmother going to pieces. I couldn't imagine that. Finance men giving comfort. I wasn't used to that. My ex was a finance man, and not one to give comfort. All the years of our marriage, I kept hoping for comfort from him. I was the one who had wept.

On that rainy January day as I looked out my dining room window over my backyard grass pooling with water, I paused after transcribing those words, fingering the smooth front and angled back of my citrine necklace, a habit I have formed, sensory input to soothe. The necklace once belonged to my mother, a purchase I assume Hannah made during her trip to South America. When my mother announced that her neck was too wrinkled to draw attention to with necklaces, she gave it to me. I wear it every day unless an occasion calls for something more dramatic. Typically, what replaces it is a necklace that once was Hannah's. Her necklaces bring compliments, the citrine one in particular with its dime-sized gem in an arts-and-crafts silver setting with an abstract leaf swirl at the top, and a tulip like opening underneath into which the chain is threaded. With each compliment, I give credit to Hannah and feel her smile, a bit smug, full of delight. In my aloneness, Hannah's artifacts were there for me. Her jewelry had become a talisman of sorts for me, helping dispel that unpleasant free floating feeling of having no anchor now that my parents had died.

Over the past few months during my first full reading of the letters, I had put Post-it notes wherever she mentioned her jewelry. There were lots of Post-it notes. I couldn't resist. My association with Hannah and jewelry is powerful, stemming back to my childhood. Memories of her bosom always sporting a necklace to intrigue are vivid. My mother reinforced the jewelry bond between us. Most of her necklaces were once Hannah's. I admired them, and as a child was allowed to explore her jewelry drawer, something I did over and over, my mother giving explanations about the provenance of an item as warranted. Accessories on behalf of beauty, connections to people and places.

Nuggets from Hannah's letters on jewelry:

Aboard the freighter, the SS *American Planter*, she wrote about a fellow passenger:

> Around her throat was clasped a rhinestone necklace, from which a cluster of rhinestones hung as a pendant. (a dead ringer for me.)

When in Vienna:

> While we waited in a line she lighted up about my necklace (the way they all do here when they are pleased with something). The necklace was that black and silver Siamese one. So, I yanked off my earrings and gave them to her.

Hannah yanked off and gave away her earrings? I paused in amazement that she did that and wondered if I could do that. My answer: doubtful. I am not so impulsive around strangers. Hannah's behavior unsettled me. Not what I expected.

In Badgastein, Austria:

> When I reached the Weismayr it was time for dinner . . . I changed my necklace and started in on dinner.

Another from Badgastein:

> I change my necklace to conform each night.

My attachment to Hannah's citrine necklace overpowers notions of changing out the necklace to conform. I am also attached to the black opal ring which my mother gave me in my early twenties, a ring I never take off. I have a habit of twirling it on my finger, gazing down at the gem, transfixed by the rich multi-colored stone when I need to think or be transported from thought. If I admitted that items have become a part of me, I would be telling the truth, a truth possibly for psychiatric probing. With the rain beating on the window adding to my grey mood, reveling in another of Hannah's jewelry nuggets suited me. This one written aboard the freighter SS *American Planter*:

> As we approached Beirut the sun set gloriously. Above it, a silver thread of moon, with lifted horns. It floated in its misted radiance, which, reflecting on the water, left a softly glowing wish from it to me. From the forward deck we watched night absorb the twilight. We saw the skyline of the merchant city emerge from shadows in a glittering razzle dazzle of electric lights. Rows of storage sheds along the shoreline became scarfs of light, adorned with swimming neon. A jeweled necklace of hot bulbs outlined the docks....

The word jewels in that passage, and the dreamy romantic images she painted, conjured up fantastical wanderings which squashed the ever invasive memories of my chilly life with a mathematically minded husband. Hannah held on to the sublime. Time for me to immerse in the sublime, jewelry and all.

∽

When I needed a mooring to shake off any unpleasant feelings, I fell back on my skill at organizing and buck up to work, an inheritance from my father, a skill well-honed over the years. I pulled myself out of rainy day jewelry thoughts and decided on my next step with Hannah. To know her "from the inside out," to use her words, meant typing up her letters, every word, every page, all one hundred and twenty-three of them. It also meant revisiting her essays, unpublished and published, including the two lengthy ones from the *New York Times Magazine*. It meant looking at her scrapbook with letters related to those publications. I started my search for anything related to Hannah Trimble. What I would do with the transcription of her work remained a mystery. What I was doing was the next right thing, word by word, to understand what lay underneath her "awful feeling of fear," her immersion in magnificence, her delight in junk jewelry, and her urge to travel. I was puzzled why she wrote as she did to my father during the war, why she collected and gave away what she did, and most of all, how she handled living alone for over forty-five years. Hannah's power pulled me in, away from the dark clouds that were in my life.

The first task was to start where her letters started which meant attempting to put them in chronological order, a challenge given her unique method of dating her letters which never included the year. Sometimes she offered up the month, the date, and a tidbit: "September the 5th after two days of school." Other times she let on about the day of the week and date: "Tuesday the 7th." When feeling clever she added a clue about the time of year: "Monday morning the 16th and still dark." To not be outdone, one time she felt the day of the week alone would suffice, "Thursday." Having recently put to practice my skill with details to "settle up" funds in that unsettled period in a divorce from "date of separation" to "date accounts were disentangled," proving my ex-husband incorrect, proving he owed me money, proving I did not owe him, I started in on Hannah's dates. With monthly calendars spanning the years my father was out at sea, I sleuthed out the day of the week, the month, and the year of each letter.

With her letters in order, I transcribed her first correspondence to my father, sent from Evansville, Indiana, November 1943, and then researched what was going on in Evansville at that time. To my surprise, Evansville played more than a minor role in the war effort. Several of the city's industries had converted to manufacturing war materiel: bullets, ships, fighter planes. On Evansville's banks of the Ohio River was a forty-five acre shipyard which made the city the largest producer of landing tank ships in the nation. Another factory turned out bullets by the billions. All this in Hannah's backyard. Her mother, Fanny Rose, lived around the corner in Hannah's childhood home on SE 1st Street, two blocks up from the Ohio River. Hannah's father, Thomas Burke Stevenson Jr., had died four years earlier several months apart from her sister, Lulie, who died of heart and kidney disease. Her two brothers, Basnett and Frank, lived in the area. Hannah was a seasoned third grade teacher at the

Fulton School, and had published seven articles about teaching in national journals. Her daughter Ann, married to a surgeon, had one child, Thomas Trimble, not yet two. Thomas's twin, George Arthur, died as an infant the year before, a piece of family history not talked about. As the namesake of Hannah's husband, the death of Ann's infant had to have hit Hannah and Ann to the core. Her other daughter, my mother, newly married to my father, left Detroit to live in Evansville with Hannah "in this more than synthetic way of living," as Hannah wrote to her Navy officer son-in-law. It was wartime, and life seemed surreal with ration stamps and the sounds of riveting from the factory on the Ohio river. I sensed fear was in the air.

Lieutenant Richmond Smith Jr., Navy Assistant Surgeon, shipped out to sea October 13, 1943, on the destroyer USS *Hailey*, a mere six months after he married my mother. Hannah's letter was one month later to the date. I digress to point out an item I found in my father's war scrapbook when I went in search of the date he shipped out to sea. A three-by-five card, written in his measured handwriting, noted key points of irony about his ship, linking him, a true blooded Yankee, to his new bride, Margaret:

> Named for Capt. Hailey, hero of the 1812 war, who commanded
> the American privateer "True Blooded Yankee," a fast 16 gun brig
> of French construction, fitted out as an American Privateer. Sailed
> 3/1/1813 under Capt. Hailey. Her first prize was the coastal craft, the
> "O Margaret."

In times of war and love, coincidences and serendipity were not ignored. Good omens were needed. Not much could make one feel more vulnerable than life on the *Hailey*, a 376-foot destroyer stocked with guns, torpedoes, and 320 men in close quarters, on dangerous missions away from land and safety for weeks and weeks.

Hannah's first letter was sent when my father had been out to sea for two months away from Margaret, his new bride. This letter is the one that I mention most often to others, and the one that makes them ask, "She is your father's mother-in-law, correct?' This letter made its mark on me with her vivid descriptions, humor, and most of all, her intimate revelations and advice to my father. I was shocked with how freely she revealed her inner self given the short time she had known my father and how much my family kept hidden within. Hannah's letter implied that he wrote to her worrying that he was "cracking up." Her reply stunned me, made me have both sympathy and respect for her, made me start to absorb the fact that my grandmother was no ordinary woman, was a woman who danced over the edge of protocol to comment on what I would never imagine could be brought to the surface. On top of it all, her depths of loneliness resonated as I wrestled with being on my own at about the same age she was when she wrote this letter. My grandmother, a fifty-six year old widow, shared with her son-in-law her feelings about being alone without the intimacy of her beloved husband, George Arthur.

Saturday, the 13th [November, 1943]

Dear Rich,

Here goes the calliope on the Island Queen again, which is nosed in against the plaza. It always makes me think of Sunday School picnics and round cakes with icing that sticks just a little to the wax paper that wraps it around. I can remember how the wind felt on our faces and how our hair blew back when we sat on whatever it is that you call the part of the boat that sticks out in front.

And just around the bend of the shore more ships are being made under brilliant light that reflects on the water. They are ships of less kindly intent. The sound of their riveting follows me to my bed and I think of you and hope they will hurry with the ships.

We wonder if you are near Formosa. We fear so. We leave our radios on, in a whisper, into the night, to verify the report --- there are no surface ships injured. You are coming nearer and nearer to a nephew of Arthur's, who looked so like him. He was and may be now in

Spanish College in Manila – a Japanese prisoner. Who knows – you may see him – the impossible seems to be the actual now.

Rich, I didn't give Margaret the letter you sent to me. Didn't tell her I had it. No, you are not cracking up. And you won't. It is amazing what human beings can stand. It is a good idea to write what you think. Many's the time I have propped a similar envelope under a lamp until morning when I found it has served its purpose and could be torn into bits and thrown into the scrap basket. I am a very good person to talk to when clouds cover the moon. My moon has been covered so long that I can understand when you speak.

I wish I knew the answers that are a cure. I doubt anyone does – when we accept as a civilized pattern a way of living that suppresses forces that can't be rubbed out any more than can freckles from our noses, we are in for trouble. People like you who cannot release strain with whiskey or women as such, have a terrific price to pay.

I learned a few things by myself a long time ago. I learned that I could not deliberately take time when work was finished and I could be alone, to close my eyes and recall the many things that I was refusing to allow to become dim in my thoughts. Mostly those were things that had been made beautiful by the senses. I suspect that on nights when you are alone you do the same thing. And that you find, as I did, that the price in pain is more than you can pay.

When I found that I was destroying my usefulness I denied myself that indulgence – that is what it really was, Rich. That is what it is for you too. I think you must for your own sanity, living the abnormal life you must, do that too. I think you must put Margaret out of your thoughts more and more. It can be done tho you do not think it can. Fix your mind on common place things – you can think of only one thing at a time. Remember there is no finality in your separation.

Whether you think of her or not, she will be here, thinking of you. There will be an end to your waiting. When you come back to her, her love and her loyalty is not going to be measured or increased by the hours on deck you have held her close in your thoughts. You will be more useful to her and to yourself if by an act of will you put her aside for parts of the present. Personally, from my aged point in living, I would not think of it as disloyalty at all if you stabilized your nerves as other men do. We are machines that cannot pull the load when the strain is too great on any one part of us. Margaret need not know — what is better for you is also better for her.

None of this makes sense, I am afraid to you. It would have seemed strange advice when I was your age. If you are what Margaret calls herself – a practical idealist – that is good. These times are certainly the acid test.

I don't underestimate the job. Many a night I have gotten up and walked about, taken a cold bath in the middle of the night – and by the way, a cold bath clears a lot of warmer emotions. Try it. Or don't Destroyers have showers? Even so results are imperfect. The root of the trouble is that we do not want to clear ourselves -- we do not want to become shells of human desire – it is usually only when all other avenues are closed that we accept that eventuality. I am fifty-six years old now and still I do not embrace the idea. Subconsciously I still hope for escape that I know will not come. But yours will. Pretty soon you will be making plans for a house on Penobscot Bay.

The calliope has stopped. Good night. Do you have Grimes Golden apples in New England? They are ripe now. And so are those little tough burnished chrysanthemums that come first of all and last until frost. We have bowls of both.

Goodnight again. Lovingly, Mother.

Thanks a lot for asking about my insides. I noticed at the City Club
this summer that their doctors were heroes in the lives of all the
sweet little old ladies who gathered round to ask me why I limped.

Hannah's words, "we do not want to become shells of human desire,"
are hard to shake off. I envision an empty shell, the contents long gone, the
succulent luscious oyster once within, now only a memory. I had been an
empty shell for more years than I wanted to acknowledge. Any desire for
intimacy had slithered out of me year by year during my marriage. Never
had I considered my grandmother having physical desire. Once more
I adjusted my image of her, making room for a woman full of passion,
a woman who longed for the days when she had romance under a full
moon, a moon now covered by clouds, blocking out the magical light
that shines in the night. "The calliope has stopped." The playful fanciful
tunes that dance carefree in the air were over even while her memories
were fresh of Sunday school picnics with wind on her face. Hannah still
hoped for an escape that she knew would not come. A fifty-six year old
widow was trying to push back thoughts that romance, passion and desire
had ended. How could anyone read her letter and not grieve for her loss,
a woman full of passion, who believed "that things made beautiful by the
senses . . ." may not be in her future? Her calliope had stopped, yet she
turned toward the joy of Grimes apples and chrysanthemums.

When I first read this letter, I was fifty-six, a new divorcee. I felt a
whole new life of romance might be ahead of me. I had no intentions
of becoming a shell, empty of desire. With many readings of this letter
and after its full transcription, I remained puzzled how she stepped over
a protocol line and wrote this advice to her son-in-law:

Personally, from my aged point in living, I would not think of it
as disloyalty at all if you stabilized your nerves as other men do . . .
Margaret need not know.

My mother, discrete as she was, never shared with me what she thought
of any of her mother's letters. She had to have known her mother was

ahead of her time, would never be one of those "sweet little old ladies" Hannah described at the Woman's City Club. When my father told me to do something with the letters, he opened the door to the inner workings of their private lives. The letters held intimate information about him as well as my mother and grandmother. I knew he meant doing something was more than my reading them. I had to let go of hesitations that I was opening up their lives for others to read. As private as he was, my father wanted the letters known. I fingered the citrine necklace, opened a Word doc and went on with my transcribing, Hannah on my shoulder.

Chapter 6

Love and War

As I transcribed the second of nineteen wartime letters to my father, I was swept into the lives of my parents as newlyweds, an odd place to be at the end of my marriage. Odd also was how Hannah swept herself into a more than typical mother-in-law relationship. When one has been alone without romance for years, it's hard to know what one might do.

Thursday the 6th of January [1943]

Rich darling,

THANK YOU FOR THE PICTURE! I have brought it down to Margaret's room where we both see it most often. It stands, arms folded, on a green painted shelf over her bed couch, guarding its own down below. The one that is just you, she wants across the room on a small chest. It is under a light and a mirror and beside a green bubbly glass jar of pink snapdragons and white chrysanthemums. The horrible tin things Margaret puts her hair up on at night, push against you, in a wee lemon wood box, lacquered in Mexico, by an unfaithful Matador, whose Indian wife taught him his craft before he deserted her. (Good Heavens, what a sentence, if you can call it that.) But now you can see yourself, close to us.

Speaking of achievements . . . Margaret attacks her hair fiercely each night with a hair brush and emerges shining as never before. I have even contributed another brush, since the life of this one cannot be long. She is so firm in her determinations born of love. She will, she says, wear her hair exactly one way until you come home, because you like it that way - - like swearing you will have none of haircuts until the Republicans are in again. She is really quite well again and has been sleeping mornings, which is wonderful for her. After having waked her with my alarm and my lavatory which gurgles, and with my own squeaky board... on which I tiptoe, I leave her with a kiss on the top of her head . . . Then we have supper from Pink Minton china on a rosebuddy cloth and she reads me such scraps from your letters as are seemly. Each day, I, like Peg, like you more. We are allowed only conversation at dinner, because your mother orders it that way, so my bad.*

Radio News of the World habits are breaking away. And she makes me take my shoes off before I lie on her pretty day bed. Has she made you see her room in this more than synthetic way of living? Her room faces south which means sunshine - - the whole south wall is windows, to the ceiling, since it once was part of a sun parlor - - a brown rug - - a brown arm chair and a dusty rose corduroy cover on the bed. Pushed into a corner of it is a bed rest - - a fat pillow with arms out to you. Besides there are chintz pillows . . . soft gray with hand blocked pansies - - a huge soft one, a fat long one and a thin short one to stuff under her neck. Your big metal tray we put on a green baggage rack - - behold! It becomes a coffee table. I found lamps out of the past with new shades out of Kentucky where there is still a gift shop. I'll bet she has told you of the wonderful map of your sea which

---

* Note to reader: analysis to follow!

we have under glass on the green wicker desk. We pour over it daily and I become more confused. And I pray more desperately that nothing in it can harm you and Peg.

You have opened doors for her that reticence had kept closed. She can look into my eyes and speak my language now as well as her father's . . . she can let me comfort her in tiny bits. At night when she thinks I can no longer hear, and cries into her pillow, she lets me come to her. She could never have done that before.

Last night she came in, sodden with rain and after ringing door bells for a job – The Republic - - the Thunderbolt place* offers her some endless suggestions, at time and overtime for fifty eight hours a week. They wanted a snap "YES" or "No." I pestered her into "No." My swan song was "Rich does not want that." It worked. There is a nursery school beckoning - - I hope she does that…. it will be easy and pleasant - - so few children that it is wicked to spend the thousands that the govern-ment has been throwing that way. It is needed but whether or not, parents mistrust it - - the sort that should use it. Instead, they let their children get up in empty houses and eat hamburgers on corners. But I swear - - I am hushed - - However, my fingers are crossed.

In two shakes, we are going to Town Hall, to hear a war correspon-dent. In between then and now, I have to wash a small clean circle around my nose, and change what Marg calls my hair do. So good-night, darling. I will talk to you again soon if I may.

Lovingly,
Mother

Using all CAPS, Hannah emphasized her appreciation for his photo. A few sentences later, starting with: "The horrible tin things Margaret

---

* Republic Aviation manufactured the Thunderbolt fighter plane. The factory built over 6,000 P-47s and employed thousands of workers.

puts her hair up on at night, push against you . . ." I can't help reading between the lines. Pushing against Rich, intriguing word choice. Enter the Matador. Was she sending a warning about the Matador who deserted his wife or was it she couldn't resist thoughts of an escapade with a Matador, or am I the one traveling to thoughts of a Matador on the loose? A single woman on the loose can escape into fantasies. I may be in good company with my grandmother.

Hannah doesn't hesitate pulling her new son-in-law close, sharing intimate thoughts. She credited him with adding the language of the heart to her daughter's repertoire, the romantic, warm expressions of desire Hannah knew and used so well. She implied that Margaret had only used her father's language, a language that matched how I view him in his photos, starched like his collars and tied up like his ties. Arthur's reticence was passed down to his daughter, a hard-wired Trimble trait. Alta Trimble Griffith, Arthur's niece wrote: "It was never easy for her (Arthur's mother) to show emotion.....her desire to give out fondness and warmth she felt was thwarted by a reserve she found so difficult to break through." That sentence could describe my mother. She wasn't cold and distant. There was warmth and love within, yet speaking it aloud was rare, no enveloping hugs, no affectionate nothings whispered. Unlike Hannah who had an outlet through writing, my mother kept feelings within. I bow to inheritance and my hesitation to speak the language of my heart. If it affected my marriage, maybe I also didn't know that language.

Hannah, a middle-aged single woman, was more than a footnote in her daughter's marriage; and I, her granddaughter, a single middle-aged woman, was reading between the lines in her letters, trying to imagine how my grandmother inserted herself so easily into that relationship. Even though raised at the end of the romantic Victorian era, she pushed the edge of social boundaries with the images she created for her son-in-law. A letter from Hannah's daughter, Ann, provided clues:

> Your grandmother was an incurable romantic, as I am, but have learned the hard way, the only approach is that of the pragmatic realist . . .

She was, whether due to her early widowhood, terribly possessive of her children which I always retreated from and your mother, finally did. I always felt my mother would resent anyone I decided I was mature enough to marry for better or worse.

If I were Margaret and had read even a few of her mother's letters, I would have protested, begged her to stop. I would have said, "How could you have written that, mother??!!" Multiple exclamation points needed.

Among photos in the sea chest is one from Ann's wedding, a photo spilling over with romantic notions. Ann's wedding train extended in front of all seven in the wedding party. Lavish flower bouquets so large they overflowed in my mother's arms. A maid of honor used her hat to carry the flowers. Romantic dreams prevailed. Somewhere along the years, Ann became a self-proclaimed "pragmatic realist" and left behind the notions she once nurtured. Bravo to Hannah for keeping her notions of romance alive, even if hopeless. I take note of my aunt's and grandmother's positions as I navigate life as a singleton, this time with lessons learned about red flags that were flying when I said, "Yes, I will marry you." Like my aunt, I learned too late that the career my ex wanted precluded family life. There was a chasm. For now, my thoughts are how sad it is to live without dreams and hopes for romance.

Hannah hinted she didn't follow the order by my father's mother to stick with light conversation at dinner. As a romantic, how could she? She jumped right in even knowing her daughter might be uncomfortable with talk of emotions. Hannah pegged her daughter as a "forthright practical person" and couldn't resist muting that trait, loosening Margaret up, trying to pull out feelings held in reserve. What a contrast. Hannah and Margaret. In telling me to do something with these letters, my father may have wanted to make known matters of the heart. His family didn't speak of them. My mother didn't speak of them. Not too late for me, he might have thought.

Five days later, Hannah wrote her third letter with an opening which gave pause, ". . . the twenty-fourth, which is also our anniversary." I noted the word "our." It had been fifteen years since her husband's death. The roses she bought on behalf of Rich for "Margaret's table" carried thoughts of her own wedding anniversary. I rarely celebrated thoughts of my wedding anniversary even when married. Once a marriage dies, remembrances belong in the graveyard. Hannah carried anniversary thoughts years after Arthur's death as she joined in her daughter's marriage, a romance she was determined to nurture, even if it meant stepping over a line. Her declaration "my bad," and her proclamation in the next letter, "Maybe if I'm good I may be allowed . . ." reinforced she knew she was off the mark.

Tuesday the 11th of January [1944]

Rich darling,

I have your letter and will have the loveliest roses in Evansville in a crystal jar on Margaret's table on the twenty fourth, which is also our anniversary. Three of your letters were waiting for your lady - - she sat on her feet in the brown chair and read them over and over and then shared bits with me. So that you may see her better - - she was wearing a blue green sweater, Silver Mexican beads . . . around her neck. I have beaten her down on the question of the car and we are using it in turn, week in - - week out. Our busses move only on impulse which does not often check with your needs. Any way that arrangement allows me to beat her home and have baked potatoes in the oven, the table set and music in her little brown radio. After dinner we went to a concert . . . in between every tenor Metropolitan Aria, she told me what a wonderful voice you have and how in High School you sang the lead in the operas.

She REALLY is going to like the nursery. I held my thumbs at first. I felt that to have human beings in her care would absorb her more than office work, and I also thought that the class of children she would have would give back to her obedience and affection which sons of Ford overlords did not have to offer. She has already felt that difference - - "They are sweet!" "They mind what I say!" . . . she says with a bewildered delight . . . Tonight she is going to make you fudge which is coming in a tin chalk box off of the Third Grade, Fulton. Maybe if I'm good I may be allowed to beat it. Or wrap.

Rich, I'm scared. I hope it will never show in my eyes when I look at Margaret. Life seldom allows two people to love and have one another in so perfect a way as you have. I'm scared. I hope it will not be months . . . that you cannot reach her. You are very right to tell her bare facts . . . It is always easier to face any eventuality than to drag thru days of uncertainty. In the meantime keep on and on saying the loving things that lie in your heart. Those are things for which women scrub floors on their knees with a smile. We will stand what looks hard to onlookers and not feel its presence, because of a tender word that belongs only to us. Women are always like that. So few men know it - - not many have the magic gift you have. Please dodge behind coils of rope when torpedoes or bombs or anything harmful heads toward you.

And by the way, I have learned some nautical terms - - - me, I live top side, from which I will in one minute climb down the hatch, rush out the bow of my house, and take off for school.

By the way again - - Margaret has this week been wearing her loveliest soft wool dress, cherry red, and not once has she slipped it on that she has not said, "I WISH I had had this in Seattle. Rich would have liked it."

Lovingly, Mother.

Hannah either remembered tender words spoken to her or she longed for them as I do. What she knew was fear. Fear surrounded her as a young mother when her husband died at her side. Fear had to have been a close companion for years thereafter as a single mother during the Great Depression with money in short supply. Death lurked. Hannah's father and sister died in 1939, then in 1944 her daughter Ann gave birth to twins, and the one named for George Arthur died one month after birth. Now the husband of her daughter was on a destroyer with the possibility of death all around. Fear had to have been triggered in my mother also. She was twelve when her father died, and now her new husband was in the line of fire. Fear hovers and shows up on its own terms. Triple fear had to have been with Hannah's mother, Fanny Rose, who lived around the corner and was witness to the losses of her daughter, granddaughters, and the losses in her childhood family. Three generations living within blocks of each other, living with the fear that Margaret's new husband might not return.

Hannah had lessons on how to deal with fear when facing the world alone.

Saturday the 15th of January [1944]

Dear Rich,

Such funny hours I steal to talk to you! Dark outside, punctured by yellow squares of light that mark early risers in the hotel across back yards. Smoke from furnace chimneys - - not clean and drifting, like your Maine wood smoke - - Marg is doing what is known as "putting on her face" - - she has sleepily swallowed another farm hand breakfast - - While she washed her undies last night I went armed with a list, and bought you presents - - , coming back I gathered up two chocolate Sundays, dripping with goo . . . we ate them and talked of the news from your mother, and were glad she had the picture which she could not help but love.

Your wife loves almond toast - - I keep it on her table where she reaches without knowing - - tell me when to stop fattening her up. When I was a little girl I had a book about a cat. "his mistress said to her husband every morning, "Oh, Solomon, see him grow fat! Our erstwhile skinny, diaphanous Pat!" That's what is happening at our (and your) house . . . your wife is going to sleep now . . . instead of tossing for hours, wide eyed. She is learning to hide the thoughts that she lives with - - if I did not know so well how that defense is built up and how costly to yourself the victory is, I could look with more peace to myself. But beyond standing by, and loving you both, I cannot do much. PLEASE DODGE!

Lovingly, Mother.

P.S. The weekend is nicely taken care of. We have two dinner invitations - - without ration stamps.

Humor and images to delight, both can scrub out fear, for a moment or two. If my mother knew her undies were highlighted, she may not have been humored. I have a suspicion Hannah played into my father's hand, providing a regular dose of humor, knowing his skill with the same.

When my father stood before me, Hannah's letters in my hand, he knew I had lost my playful side and may have hoped Hannah might revive me, remind me of the price that might be paid when hiding feelings, and he was a man who knew about hiding feelings.

Monday the 24th [January, 1944]

Rich darling,

And now you're gone where we can't see your background - - nothing familiar - - only fears in Margaret's eyes. I am glad you sent her home to me - - to have been alone in any other place with that frozen look that breaks into tears would be worse than this. And nothing I can say - - nothing I can do, but stand by. As I remember, that helps some.

Your red roses have opened wide and fill the room with fragrance. We had a birthday cake - - very beautiful, dripping with thick icing, for my mother's birthday and since it is also the shadow of the day on which I was married as well as your day, I lifted my glass and said, "This is to you, and to you, and to Rich, who is here with us" - - Marg said, "to you too mother" and there we all were - - but I shouldn'tuv - - should have skirted the edges - - Supper was good - -

lamb chops and asparagus and an ice - - sounds like spring, doesn't it? And it looks like it out of doors - - yesterday we went to the "shacks" and scrambled down the river bank, walked in the muddy rocks and climbed up again. Lilac bushes have green tipped buds and forsythia too. The poor silly things - - and this be only January. We came home nice and muddy - - at one point the hunting dog and I slid, causing an avalanche and landing bottom side up with care. Josephine Leich had just come back from Mexico where she had been living the life of the embassy in Tampico . . .

I operate on the feeling that the tireder Peg becomes from other things than thoughts - - the more sleep at night - - there are no contemporaries, so off we go together - - ever see "Holy Matrimony" with Gracie Fields? That wrung laughter from her - - I have learned that tears are good when they are in sympathy for the sadness of someone else - - movies offer that - - when we came out we walked home in the cold and dollars to doughnuts she went right to sleep.

I wish for the moment I could live on your ship - - or even there would I wake up with soot on my pillow - - Marg goes about bewildered - - headlights/pale wet glow in the smoky fog each morning - - our best way follows the river and the lights from the shipyards mark the shoreline on the curve - - cars nose to tail hurry to the morning shift. We are taking turns with the car - - - have a little extra gasoline because the nursery school is for defense workers' children. The feller who has the car has to do the marketing too, so - - goody! Goody! This week I shall wander in like a princess and ask, "And WHAT will we have for supper?"

Into bed I go - - in only a minute I shall be rolling out at six in the morning. We have another thing in common, I hear - - we both are wearing certain of our garments rough - - very rough dried? Your hair sounds awful!!

Lovingly, Mother

Hannah was in standby mode for her daughter, remembering that others stood by her when she faced life without her husband. Memories had to have surfaced on January 24, the date of this letter, the date of her wedding anniversary. Pushing away anything which might drag her down, she transitioned to roses, a birthday cake, and a frolic down the river bank, her descriptions so vivid I can almost see her "bottom side up" by the Ohio River. She moved with ease from the outer world to her inner world of emotions which she couldn't resist sharing. Her words about what movies offer resonated with how I was raised: keep your emotions within, yet acknowledge emotions of others. How I wish I could read my father's response to her letter. Did he stay on safe ground writing about routine life on the ship? How could he or any son-in-law respond to:

> "I wish for the moment I could live on your ship - - or even there
> would I wake up with soot on my pillow . . ."

There is no way to think about that comment as anything but "way out there." The question keeps rising up: what possessed my grandmother to insert herself as she did? Was her loneliness that deep?

For several months after my father shipped out, Hannah sent one letter every week. She was quick to size up people, and recognized what humor might do for her son-in-law, a man with a wry sense of humor. He had to have smiled reading her letters.

> I looked - - hard - - at the Kodak picture of you. The one in a sweat
> shirt. I can't find you. You had a very boyish and alluring grin, I
> mean when I last saw you . . . this didn't look as if you would wink
> in passing as you did in the apartment in Grosse Pointe. But body
> and bones, you looked sturdy. Am I right?

If my father shared sections of her letters with others on the destroyer, it would have been with Captain Brady who entertained the ship's crew with antics and wrote tongue-in-cheek letters to my mother, though

I note there can be a kernel of truth in any joke. "Why don't you be a pal and write the good Doctor a ten-page letter for a change? The poor guy looks terribly disappointed when he reads those two pagers of yours." Reticent Margaret. A fear of exposure. A fear of vulnerability. Hannah warned there is a costly risk in reticence. Time to turn the mirror on myself.

Humor was an obvious antidote to life on the destroyer, and Hannah sent envelope after envelope of letter joy. My father endured twenty-two months of uninterrupted operational and combat assignments, the longest WWII Navy cruise. The *Hailey* was part of the Leyte Gulf battle, considered to be the largest Navy battle in history, and experienced the first use of kamikaze attacks. The *Hailey* was also involved in the Okinawa Assault in which twelve U.S. destroyers were sunk. Aside from harrowing naval battles, Margaret's new husband performed an appendectomy out at sea, and in December 1944, the *Hailey* barely survived the historic typhoon Cobra. There was terror from the skies and terror on the sea, and Hannah and Margaret tracked all this as best as the news and letters reported. Fear could be smudged out for a moment with humor. Hannah knew it, my father knew it. Hold on to humor is my takeaway.

Hannah babbled on, letter after letter. She mentioned watching Margaret write letters to my father. I found none. Quite odd. Also odd was not finding any letters from my father to my mother. Only Hannah's letters were saved along with items he carefully preserved in his war scrapbook, one of which was a single communication from my mother, a telegram. Fortuitous as it may be, during a visit to Maine with his scrapbook in my lap, when removing his navy portrait from its protective cover, a paper, folded in half, fell out from behind. I unfolded the paper, read the header, the date and "Dear Trim" and knew immediately. My father had hidden a love letter, written the day he sailed off from Seattle, away from his new bride. Tears welled up. I read the letter he identified as "Letter #1."

U.S.S. Hailey
October 28, 1943
9:15 PM

Dear Trim:

The moment came quickly. We left silently, cutting through the thick fog. The buildings of the city lay hidden somewhere behind the gray curtain. I tried hard to spot the Harborview Hospital, hoping perhaps its height might allow me to see it. Tho, Trim darling, there was nothing but fog. But I saw you. I felt you, sweetheart, and on my dry lips I tasted the sweetest tears that have flowed from your eyes. And your fingers pressed lightly against my cheeks, as if the kiss might break away too soon. I ran to the bow and the light wind of our headway dried my face.

The fog is still here. We are moving ahead with increasing speed to redeem yesterday's loss. Something moist hits my cheek but perhaps it the fog. There's no more to say now. Tomorrow I will write with a healed spirit, as you would have me now. But I can't darling, for the most beautiful thing in this world has been left behind. God be with you, precious and good night. Ours is the perfect love.

Rich

Tears turned to sobs. Love was out in the open, daylighted. Such warm, open expression of tender caring overwhelmed my heart. Tears for the man whose words were before me, tears for the woman who read them long ago, words which would melt a beloved. Over the years my father's expressions of love went underground, and my mother longed for more affection and attentiveness. Tears for both of them. Tears for me, which I've yet to understand. Tears for the elusive perfect love. Once I calmed the emotional flood, I checked all pages for other hidden letters. Underneath a photograph of the USS *Hailey*, a love letter from my mother fell out, a letter written near the end of his tour of duty, two years after they had parted.

My darling Rich,

Nowhere is there anyone more wonderful, more thoughtful nor more loved than you. Two years – two years of the most happiness and the most completeness of my whole life. Out of the blue there you were – all I'd wanted for and longed for and even tho you're on the other side of the world now, we have more than most in our love that holds us close in our hearts and grows stronger and deeper with each passing day. Thank you, darling for it all – for being as you are and giving me you to love and to live for – Thank you for the two roses that mean so much and are so beautiful as they remind me of the two of the happiest years of my life – tho much of the time have brought us a loneliness deeper than any that seemed possible, they have brought us so close together that nothing will ever separate us.

Tis after midnight now – I'll write a nice long letter tomorrow but I had to send special love and prayers to you tonight – for all day I've been with you as I am every day that passes.

Goodnight sweetheart – till tomorrow

Trim

Hiding the letters, keeping them private was a classic move by my father. My mother might have been in cahoots (as she might say). Both private people, ever so fitting that neither wanted their love letters made known, and now, a voyeur in their romance, I was doing that. Did my parents read all the letters, decide which two to save, then discard the rest? Or did my father do that on his own? Two letters saved, hidden, tucked away. If he were alive now, I would ask, "Why did you save and hide only two when you saved all of Hannah's letters?"

Letters provide glimpses into the past with opportunities for deeper understanding of the lives within. The demise of letter writing is a loss for generations to come. Emails are rarely printed out and tucked away for future insight. At one point in typing up Hannah's letters, I searched for all the letters I had saved. Letters in my desk, in boxes, in file folders. One letter I found from my mother written sometime after college, I read anew, gaining a new perspective on her.

October 3

His feelings deeper than mine (I think) but he's unable to open them to others. I'm bad enough – he is worse. Only thru letters (written during the 2 years in the Pacific) did he ever express intimate feelings. Also, I really don't think he knows how to play (neither does Aunt Ann). I would guess (hope) you aren't cursed with that! Too intense.

Believe it or not, until - when I can't figure out, tho heaven knows, I'm too serious about too many things, there were years when I really had FUN - - plain unadulterated fun - - - one could say I wasn't really an adult, but who wants to be one all the time - - - I used to love to dance - - - it was marvelous - - and when I last had a really good laugh, I can't remember, tho I used to - - - actually, Mrs. Stearns and I used to laugh at things - - sometimes when what was actually going on was awful - - So, try not to lose the side of you that likes a good laugh and cuddle.

I wondered if her marriage or having children took away her fun. My mother became jaded over the years. Maybe there wasn't enough emotional feedback from my father, or maybe she didn't recognize it when it came her way. If I could send a message to her, I would tell her not to worry about my being cursed. I am learning to play again, laugh and dance. In the arena of expressing emotions, with two parents reluctant to do that, it will take time for me to change. As I typed up my mother's words, I vowed to not lose what she had lost. I vowed to let go of the fear emotions could engender when sharing the truth in my heart. Love, loss, longing and belonging. Words I carry, wondering how well I will do with my vow.

Dear Everybody

Chapter 7

Moons, Dreams, and War

To keep Hannah front and center as my Marin winter marched on, I put a photo of her on my desk in the passageway connecting my kitchen and utility room. Of the many photos I had gathered, one called out, maybe because of the curly Persian Lamb jacket she was wearing, and the slight smug smile on her face, and the scrunched red hat smack dab center on her head. The photo's appeal could also have been how she folded her arms within her jacket, or the irony, which she no doubt knew, that she was posing in a marina with a boat named "Deb" behind her as she was hardly a "deb" (term for debutante in that era). I digressed to the *Urban Dictionary* definition and found more irony: "Deb: Independent, Intelligent, Beautiful, Strong Minded, Easily Adapts in Different Situations, Is the Focus of Attention, Great Sense of Humor, Sassy, Loving Caregiver, Well Rounded Interests, The Girl Every Guy wants to be With, Super Sexy. Delightful Exotic Beauty."

Hannah was looking directly at the photographer, and as a result, she looks right at me. With the jacket draped over her shoulders she would be warm yet not confined, arms crossed in confidence as teachers do when demonstrating who is in charge. Her lips were together, slightly upturned, and her prominent cheeks and eyes confirmed the smile challenging the photographer to take her picture. The background looked as though she was in Detroit. My guess is she was in her early seventies. All bets are off on who took the photograph.

With Hannah in front of me, her citrine necklace around my neck and my mother's opal ring on my finger, adult orphan feelings were pushed back and a sense of belonging comforted. I am doubtful about the power of gems, but I felt the power of the opal and citrine. My rational brain succumbed to the mysterious as I transcribed the next letter, and I felt Hannah had invited me, along with my father, into her day. A birthday that was full of magics and moons. I needed magics. My days had none. Friends had suggested online dating, "You never know," they would say. "Yes, I know," was my reply, followed by "Ugh and Yuck." Like magic near the end of her letter, a man appeared who I associated with romance.

Tuesday the 7th [March, 1944]

Good Evening, Dr. Smith,

I am sitting on the edge of Mrs. Smith's bed with an African violet staring me in the face. Margaret is sitting on her feet in a brown chair, reading Glamour, doubtless against your return, since there is a limited field for practice of same.

This evening we nosed our car into the wooden horses which barred the way to the river, and watched the sun go down over the muddy waves, full of tossing brush. A tidy little tug which pushes oil barges up and down from Shreveport, was tied up below us. A yellow flag with a black circle whipped over its little pilot house. I took it for a weather flag, but a fat policeman assured me that it was a Coast Guard way of saying that the crew was complete. How time changes us. I knew the fat policeman when he was a slim guard at the Country Club pool in the good old days when we idled. He looked so muffled up in brass buttons instead of a bathing suit.

We have eaten the last of the last birthday cake - - Mine it was with trimmings to match the Minton china. We took it to Josephine's and lighted a conservative number of candles - - I blew hard on my wish because it was for you and Margaret. Part of that household is going to Mexico so the evening was made of good-byes. I wonder what she will find for herself in Mexico - - it will not be in the wonderful, filthy markets which I loved to frequent - - She is a dainty creature who moves about in compartments.

We went to see a movie the other night - - called Lost Angel - - whose star was a wonderful little girl who had been an experiment - - shut away from the world . . . living with kindly professors. A reporter sent to interview her, tells her that magic is true - - I have been seeing our own magics ever since – even the tug which had come out of Chicago, had one – its pilot house moved up and down like gas in a station tank . . . We become so used to magics that we fail to find them. I wish I could conjure one for you and Margaret. She tried hard to be brave, but she's scared and lonely without you. Tomorrow she is going to play bridge with friends – I hope that will keep her too busy to watch the moon, which is pretty big and round at the moment. Moons are bad for morale. I still hate 'em myself and I have looked at a lot of them by myself.

John York has not come yet – we had hoped he would, as he hoped to get a leave. And we had hoped that he might have much to say that would make us seem nearer to you. Did Marg tell you that he is going to be married? He wrote me that he wanted to have breakfast with me again, and to lie on the floor, so I had the rugs cleaned and my pillows all plumped up and pushed into clean covers. But no luck.

Margaret is pretending to be asleep. Her pink slippers – the ones with wee flowers are sitting pigeon toed on the floor where she kicked them…. the quilted blue dressing gown is across her feet. We have gone into reverse – now it's me in the brown chair. The radio is shouting that CBS World News will report the landings on Los Negros and on New Britain…... What we want really to know, is that you are safe. Goodnight, Rich – the time that is gone will not have to be lived again. Cross it off of your calendar.

Mother.

Enter John York along with moons and "magics" to bolster everyone up. I stopped transcribing and launched an internet search to unravel the family connection to the man I had heard about from my mother. He popped up in the 1940 census as a lodger in the home of Hannah's friend Josephine Leich. More research netted that John was an officer on the USS *Wyoming*, matching the photo my mother had given me. Befuddling was fifty-six-year old Hannah writing that she was propping up pillows on the floor in anticipation of his visit, a man the age of her daughter. While it would be understandable to be lonely as a widow, I struggled to make sense of John lying on her floor. Did she dream of him gazing up at her while she sat in a chair, almost as if she was holding court? Did she make up that scene for effect? Whichever it was, she was disappointed that the man she prepared for didn't show. Sometimes, I too, have said, "No luck," regarding the world of men. At least the men I have had on my mind are my age plus or minus a few years.

John York wasn't just any friend of my mother's. John was the man my mother revealed more than once she wished she had married. The photo of him with her writing at the top—"John York"—and an arrow pointing to a handsome navy officer accompanied the black opal ring she gave me, a ring she said he acquired for her in Australia, presumably during the war. The oval gem, beautiful beyond beautiful, substantial and rare, sits in a simple gold beveled setting. Hannah had to have known John was a "special" friend. Maybe letting my father know that John was to be married dismissed concerns he might have had about a former boyfriend. I was complicit with my family's practice not to pry, which meant I never asked my mother the full story. I assume John asked her to marry him and she declined. That is the story I created. Online digging exposed that John married Genevieve "Kitty" Flickner from an early Evansville family. My mother married a New England man and fantasized about life with the opal ring man.

John's hold on my mother was deep. She believed he would have been doting and a good travel partner. My father, content on his own, wasn't interested in traveling and he didn't dote. More sleuthing. John grew up in New Jersey. His Morristown High School Yearbook hinted he was a hit with the girls:

> We've often wondered if Johnnie is really as wise as he looks. Anyone who takes math for a personal hobby must be. Johnnie has won for himself many friends and has been popular with everyone. The girls especially are bound to miss him.

My mother missed him or better to say, she missed her fantasy about him. Whatever happened to Johnnie? His life didn't turn out as my mother imagined. No abroad travel records were found for him. He stayed in Evansville and had a series of jobs as a salesman and supervisor. He died of cancer at age thirty-nine. After my divorce, I tracked down two men about whom I wondered: what if I had married them? Neither ventured farther than where they grew up. That answered my question about the life I might have led with them—limited.

What was my mother's intent in telling me about John? She could have given me the opal with the simple explanation that it was a gift when she was young from a man she once knew. Instead, she tagged on a message about marriage. If that was a warning for me to watch out whom I married, I didn't get the message. My internal overseer was off duty when I said, "Yes I will," to the man who asked, "Will you marry me?" Just like my Aunt Ann, I was lost in romantic dreams of weddings and men destined for success. My mother told me more than once, "You are just like Ann." That was a warning. It was only during my divorce, while standing in line for Southwest Airlines did I learn what I never knew about whom not to marry. While in a converswation about our lives, the woman in front of me looked straight at me and said, "Didn't your mother tell you never to marry someone who doesn't love his mother?" "No," I said, "She never told me that." If she had, that would have been a clear message I might have absorbed. My family's habit of not talking with candor about matters of the heart is a liability.

I have worn the opal every day since my early twenties. The ring, my birthstone, serves as a talisman. While not superstitious, I feel it holds "magics." I have it in my head that something bad will happen if I am not wearing it. An irrational fear rises up. I tell myself it is simply a ring, yet, in the let's-be-honest-with-ourselves-department (to borrow a Hannah phrase), it connects me to deep feelings not yet sorted out. With a cautionary note about mystical magical information on the internet, I couldn't ignore my impulse to look up the meaning of opals. Jewelsforme.com revealed:

> An opal amplifies traits, whether good or bad . . . brings characteristics to the surface for transformation . . . helps stimulate originality and dynamic creativity, encourages an interest in the arts . . . aids in accessing one's true self . . . encourages putting out positive emotions and teaches that what you put out comes back to you. The opal is a protective stone in dangerous places.

> Opal has always been associated with love and passion, as well as desire and eroticism. It is a seductive stone that intensifies emotional states and releases inhibitions. It can also act as an emotional stabilizer.

Love, passion, desire and eroticism, an appealing package accompanies my ring.

After several years of getting my single-life bearings, I moved past my protests and joined the online dating world, listing Maine as my location. I was in no rush, and going back and forth from Marin to Maine as I was, Maine felt safe if I met someone, which I did. The me that showed up when offered emotional warmth surprised both of us. His message: my school-board-trustee, foreman-of-the-jury exterior hid the passion within. His other message: "You have been in an emotional desert for too long."

Hannah, can you channel in from the grave and comment? Love and desire, the pull John York had on my mother and the pull I feel through his ring is inexplicable. For now, I am content to associate that ring with another Hannah phrase, each mention of which I highlighted when first scanning her letters, a message for my heart: "Who lives with beauty hath no need of fear."

~

Leaving John behind, moons are the next subject, another topic related to love, loneliness and longing. Hannah's "Tuesday the 7th" letter wasn't the only time she wrote about moons that touch deep within:

Essay, "The Inner Me"
Those privileged hours when the moon walks from left to right on the old colonial windows, awakens that someone who lives down deep within me. That 'within me.' I do not know what it is, but I know it is there . . . The thoughts of night are whisked away by silver brooms on a full moon.

Letter, Saturday the 13th, 1944
I am a very good person to talk to when clouds cover the moon. My moon has been covered so long that I can understand when you speak.

In Maine the moon shines in the windows on either side of my bed and brings futures to imagine, not luscious memories never to be lived again. To write about moons as Hannah did, she had to have had romantic moments with Arthur, handsome husband that he was, moments she longed for under moonlight. I think about her loss, "le morte d'Arthur," and how fear could well up as she witnessed the fear and loneliness in her daughter's eyes with a new husband out at sea with guns and torpedoes. Hannah didn't hide her fears. She brought them to the fore and called up distractions, painting alluring scenes of my mother, images to enchant, while ending many a letter with zingers. I remind myself to not forget the small "magics" in life, and I will be sure to have slippers that bring me joy. They won't be pink like my mother's.

Uplift with beauty, laugh with honesty. Vivid mentions of my mother's beauty and descriptions of her clothes were one of many threads Hannah wove to fend off fear, while nurturing love and longing. Excerpts:

Sunday – the one they call Palm Sunday

Another thing – don't give me away – I am going to get flowers for Marg on Easter and tell her that you told me to do it . . .

You like to have me tell you the things Margaret does not tell – so here goes – She is still thinner – and more beautiful than ever. We went the other night to church for supper to hear a friend who had been driving ambulances for Britain. I felt almost chic enough for the cover of Vogue – in a new hat with a huge white rose, also in a new gray suit. Acquaintances kept turning toward me and shaping words with their lips, from long distance. I took my bows with smug acceptance until I discovered that they were all saying "M-a-r-g-a-r-e-t Beautiful!" So, I applied myself to creamed chicken on biscuit and choked down my disappointment.

Last Sunday she got out the dress she had bought to wear when she met you at the coast, and put it on. I knew she had accepted postponement. Neither of us said anything.

It is really spring / we drove yesterday to a hilltop and came away with great yellow pansies which now blow in the wind from Margaret's window sill, from a green metal box. Jonquils are giving way to japonica and the woods are clouded with a promise of green. And in the oven is an honest to goodness rib roast bought with saved up stamps. The eating of it will be a real test of our selflessness. If we are selfish pigs and I'll bet it turns out that we are, we will ask no one to supper, nor will we put it under an arm and set out for the home of a friend. We do not yet know the answer, but we will report, (honestly or dishonestly) to you.

P.S. Later
One-thirty – we have eaten the roast beef behind closed doors. More shame on us.

Hannah was over the top, making bare her desire to have life be other than it was. This letter must have created smiles for my father, a relief arriving as it did after performing his first ever appendectomy, a man's life in his hands while Hannah had a roast beef in hers. Ten days later Hannah followed her letter of Palm Sunday with another "let me help you escape from the destroyer," letter, a "will you smile with mention again of your wife's panties?" letter. The letter found me once again scouring the internet to learn about Hannah's friends, to learn more about my grandmother. Friends are invaluable, and I wanted to know who Hannah valued. Enter Janie Veatch.

Thursday, [April 13, 1944]

Hello, there, Rich,

The jonquils have given way to lilacs on Margaret's desk. That should bring us one jump nearer to summer but no - - there is lethargy between me and my electric pad. Dog wood winter, the farmers call it - - then there will be a blackberry winter before I can put my fur coat in the basement.

I all but invited you to supper tonight - - we had a real party - - butter instead of oleomargarine....fresh asparagus on slices of chicken breast on toast with curly bits of bacon, and scrambled eggs on the side - - hen eggs, new born - - not powdered - - and for dessert, frozen pears with a swoosh of fresh strawberry preserves..... To say nothing of hot cross buns - - do you like hot cross buns? The one a penny, two a penny kind - - the if your daughters don't like 'em give 'em to your sons variety. They came out of Mother Goose and were to be eaten only on Easter.

I went to Bloomington for Easter- - and Janie Veatch's three year old daughter waited for us under the big wild cherry tree where the violets had long stems. I slept, because I am a stubborn woman, in the tower of the Union Building on the campus and when I wakened, looked down over the roofs of the college town, and listened to the carillon bells at the early church service.

We came home after dark, in rain that beat upon the road and bounced up. The next morning the piston in my car broke. Two blocks from a garage, it broke. Who says I have not lived a good life? Fifteen bucks it cost me - - So I wrote him a check and went away feeling as Ann must have felt when she wrote me from camp in Carolina and said "Come down here mother. It will pay you whether you can afford it or not." I have always used that idea to justify my most erratic behavior patterns since then. You'd be surprised to know how well it works.

Margaret is a very forthright practical person, isn't she? I dragged her to Audubon Park to look at "dogwood ivory trays" when she wanted to wash her panties. I said humbly, guilty that "there was only one such moment and that you waited a whole year for it." She answered that there was always something else to look at. Which is too too true. And I wish you would come home. Good gracious how I wish it. Can't you develop a contagious disease like leprosy that would keep you in quarantine in San Francisco until they found that after all it was nothing but an allergy for Chocolate bars???

You'd better let your hair grow my dear - - Margaret feels nostalgia for the days of yesteryear. Besides, she has told trusting friends that it is beautiful - - with waves and such.

Goodnight, dear - - it is a strange game that makes it impossible for me as for you, to talk of more than inconsequentials - - I hope that to you as to us, even those empty-ish words bring people who love one another, closer.

Easter Sunday and Hannah was in Bloomington, Indiana visiting Janie. An online "In Memoriam" indicated she was the "beloved wife" of Evansville's Henry Veatch, a professor at Indiana University and one of the leading twentieth-century neo-Aristotelian philosophers, and added, "Those who ever had the good fortune of spending an evening of conversation with them knew of their wit, wisdom, and devotion to each other." One of Hannah's good fortunes was sharing wit and wisdom with female friends of depth and substance. Hannah needed more than beauty and humor to march through life alone. My fortune has been the same. My female friends have pulled me into a lifeboat, provided deep conversation, and offered up healthy doses of honesty and humor about what life has dished out and how I have grappled with it all.

In another letter, Hannah displayed self-awareness, which she did now and again, "just a smidge," as Margaret might say. She confessed to erratic behavior such as: ". . . unless I talk too much I say too little." I began a list of Hannah's self-professed traits, remembering a quote I found somewhere: "Current patterns may be rooted in previous generations." If any of her traits landed in me, time to decide which were keepers or which were discards. A trait that she never called out, that jumped off the pages and made her charming and her writing irresistible, was her sense of humor. She may not have needed to mention it as it spoke for itself. Until I launched into her writing, humor would have been the last trait I would assign to Hannah. Would her friends say she was humorous in person? Her outside self may not have matched her self within, a self which emerged in her writing. Humor aside, Hannah also had tremendous insight, messages for everybody.

- - it is a strange game that makes it impossible for me as for you, to talk of more than inconsequentials - - I hope that to you as to us, even those empty-ish words bring people who love one another, closer.

If I were the umpire of that strange game, I would say she won. Hannah was bringing the people I loved close.

Her next letter contained another proclamation by Hannah, one more trait to add to the list of Hannah's reflections on herself: "And besides, I am such a transparent person . . ." Her letter also waxed on in a charming way with philosophic musings about life, "scraping off a lot of barnacles.....polishing up on the verities of our lives" which she mixed in with imaginings, flower blooms and once again, her daughter's panties. I think the count of panty mentions is up to three or four. Hannah was unfettered. My mother would have been mortified.

Sunday, April 23 [1944]

Dear Rich,

If I hadn't seen so many letters rolling off the assembly line and sent to your South Seas, I would have been typing away with one finger to tell you our news.....besides, I am such a transparent person that to say that everything was simply wonderful, while Margaret had the flu and went to school the bravado of youth and determination, then to bed too sick to pretend - -. Now she has pink cheeks again and can laugh - - today we went to the cliffs on the river - - the ones she has told you of - - and planted the rose bush you sent her for Easter - - It will climb on a fence that looks down on the river and out across a hill to a wood. The wild crabs are in bud – the lilacs, wild phlox and larkspur - - and the slopes are covered with blooming Virginia cowslips. Winter wheat spreads to the edge of the dogwood, and alfalfa is green under grey wind full clouds that blow apart to let sunshine thru.

Margaret wore wool socks and a sweater which you haven't seen - - a greyed blue green one that matches her eyes - - she caught tadpoles....and wanted you with her. Then we came home, starving, and ate cold fried chicken and ice cream with fresh peaches and angel food cake. Now she is washing her panties and stockings against the week that has already begun to cast its shadow.

It is so much easier to imagine you here, at the river, with us, than as part of the war - - Sometimes the war seems only a sick feeling in the pit of my stomach and a twist of a radio dial - - and the look in Margaret's eyes.

When you can be casual about an emergency appendix, I will help you dig an asparagus bed for the house on the cliff . . . And you will laugh because you are happy . . . I suspect that by then you won't even need a house - - just to see each other will be enough - - our demands upon life are pretty basic just now - - we are scraping off a lot of barnacles - - yesterday I came upon a friend. She had gone to buy one of the swings you call a glider-- - there were none - - she decided new cushions would do - - no cushions. Nonsense - - she would get more canvas and cover the old ones - - no canvas for the duration. I found her scrubbing the old pillows and was completely satisfied . . . That all must sound very inconsequential to you, on a Destroyer. It isn't. It marks progress and progress once made allows more polishing up of the verities of our lives.

Take care, please Rich - - lovingly - -
Mother

The inconsequentials which Hannah wrote about are significant clues into who she was. I'll hold on to her wisdom while keeping an eye out for "magics" and moons that bewitch. Typing up her letters, losing myself in her life, I was scraping off barnacles from my married life and making progress, and progress once made allowed more understanding of the verities of my life. I gazed over at the photo of Hannah in her fur jacket and nodded with appreciation for the woman who instilled in me a sense of beauty long before I knew that was what she was up to. Her "I told you so smile" revealed she knew what I discovered during a trip to the Florida Keys.

Every other year for over a decade, eight childhood girlfriends, now living all throughout the country, have gotten together to bask in our shared bond.

Women of depth and substance committed to each other. Our year to gather was 2007. My mother had been dead for eight months, and I needed lifetime girlfriends who shored me up. We met in Miami, and as we caravanned in two cars down Highway One to the Keys, friends in the car in front of mine spotted a consignment shop. They turned in. We followed. Once inside, it was clear this was worth the stop. The 1920s bungalow was packed full of hats, shoes, dresses, coats. With my mother's interest in consignment shops well ingrained, I was game to explore, though with my divorce in full throttle and watching my funds, I knew this would be a spectator sport. I wandered around feigning interest, thumbing through a few racks, and soon headed to wait by the door.

The rack at the door had fur coats. Coats of no use for anyone living in Florida, coats such as a Persian curly lamb jacket which looked directly at me from the middle of the rack. It said, touch me, or was Hannah calling me? My best friend whose husband had taken business risks with their money was also feigning interest, looked over at me, looked at the coat, and her eyes reinforced the words floating in my head, "Try it on." I lifted it off the rack. She then said the words out loud, as I was putting the jacket back on the rack, "Try it on." Then "Come on, try it on," floated across the shop, now a chorus from my other close friend, and then everyone was watching. "It's gorgeous." said another. I lifted it off the rack again. What's the harm, I thought. I ran my hand up and down the sleeve. This time, touching turned into trying it on. I raised the collar around my neck and burrowed in. A strange voice chimed in over the racks of clothes, "It looks great with your hair." Now the sales clerk was involved. Indeed, she was right. My salt-and-pepper hair, mostly grey-silver, matched the fur. The coat's silver satin lining had the previous owner's initials above the name of the St Louis furrier. I didn't know at the time that St. Louis was where Hannah's Uncle John, who had provided Hannah's mother with the best of fabric and lace for her wedding dress, owned a merchandise shop. It felt surreal. I was in Florida, wearing a Persian curly lamb jacket like my grandmother's, a luscious silver sensuous jacket. I put it back on the rack.

"Buy it," my friends insisted. The price tag, $300. "I have no place to wear it," I told them. Secretly I wished I had some place to wear it. One friend who gave fashion advice had the answer, "Wear it with jeans." I took the jacket off the rack, off the hanger, put it on again, looked at myself in the mirror, and pulled the collar up, to feel once again the softness on my neck and cheeks. "It doesn't make sense. I can't spend the money. I won't wear it," I told my friends. The jacket went back on the hanger, back on the rack. The practical me just couldn't do it, and it was getting close to the time to check into our rental. Time to get back in our cars.

All throughout our gathering, the jacket that reminded me of Hannah, that felt and looked like home, took up too much real estate in my brain. The conversation I had with myself kept repeating, "Gorgeous jacket, go ahead and splurge," and was countered with, "What are you thinking? $300 for something you'll never wear?" Then a new voice appeared in my head, "Why not keep it in the closet as an item that pulls up dreams and desires?" Hannah had no trouble wearing a fur jacket in a marina. She had an eye for clothes that captured attention. She had a knack for clothes that created alluring images intended to keep desire alive.

Days later the gathering of friends ended. The time was arriving to face my life of estate and divorce papers coupled with stressful emails from my ex-husband about money. His underlying theme, "You took all my money. You pay for what the kids need." My underlying theme, "I could be a bag lady." Fears and tears welled up weekly, sometimes daily. I was driving back to Miami alone to catch a plane for a short trip to Maine to see my father, alone without his wife of so many years. The jacket, its softness, beauty and comfort, was still in my head. Words Hannah wrote to my father haunted and captured what swirled within, words she wrote when she was fifty-six years old, cautionary words:

> The root of the trouble is that we do not want to clear ourselves - -
> we do not want to become shells of human desire.

There I was, in Florida, age fifty-four, worrying about being a bag lady, pushing away desire and fears that I could be that empty shell. The consignment shop was on my route to the airport. On impulse, or maybe on underlying, premeditated desire, with Hannah whispering in my ear, I put on my blinker, pulled over, parked and walked into the shop. The Persian lamb jacket with the collar that enveloped was still on the rack. I bought it. I have worn it to holiday parties in California accompanied by "Wow" comments. With each glance at Hannah's photo, I nod, smile, and think of the coat that hangs in my closet, a coat of beauty surrounded by memories and dreams for future magics.

Chapter Eight

Navigating Winter and War

Two years had gone by since I started transcribing Hannah's letters, a slow process, or perhaps a process I made slow to fill empty wet winter moments. California is either in drought or deluge. This was the year of deluge. Days of rain; I had no desire to venture out. Alone inside. Time to escape my aloneness with Hannah. The next eight war letters continued a theme that offset the dreary feeling I carried within—beauty. Hannah wasn't shy about painting evocative images of my mother:

> she looks lovely beyond words. She is as slim as even you want her
> to be - - every one speaks of her beauty as tho they had not seen it
> before.

Not to be ignored were references to "being integrated," reinforcing that external beauty alone wasn't enough. Hannah kept blowing on the embers of desire, hers snuffed out long ago.

In her practice identifying days in a clever way, she "dated" her twelfth letter, "Your Birthday," which meant she was typing away on my father's birthday in mid-June 1944. I ignored a chunky paragraph filled with news about comings and goings until my interest was captured when Hannah stated she was going "native" and putting on "the minimum of garments" for a summer job at *Life Magazine*. I struggled to conjure up an image of her in whatever attire that was. Images of her buxom bosom interfered. My father may have not wanted to try.

Your Birthday

Dear Rich,

Happy Birthday! This is one time when I can hope you'll have a lot more just like it. Maybe next time it will be the Atlantic, and you and Margaret will be making fat sandwiches to take out in your sailboat. I hope so.

Our summer is in full blast - - in no time at all I shall have gone native - - - Margaret remains amazingly dainty, - - I am glad to be free to see that she has food that will tempt her.

Now I must put on at least the minimum of garments and start out to help do a survey which Life Magazine wants done - - to establish in their minds exactly the things women like. I think I could tell them without asking questions. Women have changed less than their world. That is one of the things that make them - - what is it psychiatrists call it - - "not integrated'? We're like the mice that the textbooks talk of - - the ones that are bewildered beyond their power to shift gears.

Bye, Rich - - each week brings you nearer to return - - we are trying hard to remember that.

Lovingly,
Mother

Previous clues hinted at what Hannah thought women would like. Beautiful clothes would be one, compliments from men another, women friends a third. Hannah patched in a summer job during school break, and her life expanded before my eyes: here was a woman from southern Indiana working for *Life Magazine*. The evidence for how she did that once again pointed to Josephine Leich, whose son's future wife and Swarthmore girlfriend, Jean, was on the staff of the magazine. It would be no surprise that Hannah met Jean at the Leichs', and Jean realized in short time that Hannah, a woman with opinions, would be perfect for the job. Some of Hannah's opinions befuddle me, such as including herself in her statement about women being like mice, bewildered beyond their power to shift gears. That seemed far from reality. If anything, Hannah had the power to bewilder others. With her comment about psychiatric thinking, she may have put herself in the category of women who were not integrated. Hannah wrote about "being integrated" several times, which made me suspect that she was on a mission to sort that out about herself, making me suspect I have a mission in that area. How to align my "serious-get-the-job-done, be-of-service-to-others self," with my yen to wallow in delight? How to reconcile the woods and dirty garden knees with Jimmy Choo shoes and a Persian curly lamb jacket?

Another letter, and again, "being integrated" was on her mind, this time in reference to Margaret. Hannah also looked inward and during a trip to my father's childhood homes, she took in feedback, that she, Hannah Trimble, was a "social parasite" when it came to certain foodstuffs. I could insist she also hooked onto social connections, though the negative connotation of the word parasite is troubling.

August the 20th [1944]

Dear Rich,

I have been to Walpole! Now all of the people you love most and all of the places you like to remember are more than names to me. It is quite easy to see why you are proud to belong to them. Your mother and father represent the finest of what we mean when we speak of American traditions. In a day and the scrap of another day I learned to love and admire them.

I am, your father insists, a social parasite because I drink powdered coffee and eat Cross and Blackwell's marmalade produced with blue stamps and not with hours of honest labor. I left him hunting for a cabbage knife with which he was going to make sour (how on earth should it be spelled?) kraut.

You will be glad to know how completely and happily Margaret has become one of them….I have not seen her look so wonderfully well - - isn't the word "integrated"? She had gained weight, was a gorgeous sunburned brown . . . the hunted look was gone. I think she is definitely happier there than in Evansville - - she feels nearer to you . . .

We went to Princeton and ran upstairs and down. If you ever miss those wonderful wrought iron candlesticks that fold their hands and pray and make a shadow on the wall, search me first. If there had been any possible way to spirit them off I should have done so.

Please hurry home. There is them that misses you.

Lovingly,
Hannah Trimble

Clever is as clever does. Hannah fiddled with how she signed her letters. The mood must have hit her to sign her full name.

Hannah full of style and pizazz, and my mother slim as could be, meeting my father's unadorned New England family, solid stock with no flourishes, must have been quite an event. Glamourous clothes were not high on the list for my father's five sisters and mother. Walpole would have been a time for my mother to make note of the home in which her new husband grew up. Hannah made note. My father's family made their own food and Hannah bought hers. Where she was wrong, my mother was not becoming one of them. She never felt fully accepted by his family. If my mother was anything like me, we both ignored what we saw in our spouse's parents that were clues about how our married life might roll out. I am reminded of two of my mother's many sayings: "A good marriage is mostly about luck," and "When you are ready to get married, you turn around and look who is beside you and get married." I am not sure I would repeat those to my daughter. Instead, I'll say, "Look carefully at his family. There are clues there about what he may or may not value."

Hannah's words resonated: the fading of an actual presence . . . with conscious effort you can bring it close. I was doing precisely that, bringing my mother, father, and grandmother close as I transcribed, grabbing onto their essence, keeping them alive. After four years since my divorce and my father's death, I needed family. I heard it took one year of healing for every five of marriage. With my twenty-six years, I had a way to go, and was glad for Hannah's companionship. I was up to letter #14, emmeshed in her practice of infusing doses of my mother's beauty in her son-in-law. I zeroed in on the paragraph about beauty and what Hannah thought wives should do.

September the 5th, after two days of school [1944]

Dear Rich,

I am forwarding another letter for Margaret - - she has written that she is going to get reservations for home and will let me know - - that she has enjoyed the weeks in Boston - - has laughed as of old.

I understand just how it must be - - this fading of an actual presence - - for awhile with conscious effort you can bring it close - - then it no longer has substance. Margaret is very real, with a summer freckle on the nose and brown where she was pink and white. I will slice off any extra pounds that destroy glamour. Boxes that look like an overflow of summer clothes have begun to come so I think she too will soon be here.

I drove to Lexington to help Ann, who was to arrive with a baby under each arm. They have a darling little doll house - - standing in the doorway you can almost turn on water in the kitchen - - - has a wee back yard with a peach tree and lilac bush to say nothing of a white painted gate . . . A call came from Boston, some sort of answer to a surgeon's prayer. All of us but Kenneth fell silent and scared for the little house . . . Ann spoke up as wives should and said she'd go wherever best - - it was a temporary offer, so the feminine side of the household smiled. He has rented an office and bought instruments for chopping people . . . I feel that the ghost of ambition and Boston is not laid - - if they write again I will poison them. Lexington is the sweetest town - - except of course, Camden Maine . . .

It is getting dark and I can't reach the lamp, so I shall fall over and let it get dark - - me asleep on all of the couch pillows - - when the first week of school has toughened me, I'll write again. There are fifty children in my room, Heaven help them and me.

Love - - Mother - - the second one

"Mother - - the second one" let on that when visiting my father's family, my mother had boxes of summer clothes which may explain why she didn't feel welcome, that her "long legs" were commented on in a way that she felt criticized by those whose attire and legs were not so attractive.

Longing to belong. Husbands striving for success. Complaisant wives going along with husbands. Not hard to picture Hannah behind the scenes trying to influence said husbands. If women were as bewildered as she wrote, was that a ploy Hannah used to feign and accomplish what she wanted? Hannah was emerging as savvy beyond imagination. She wanted her daughter Ann nearby, hoping Boston would not lure her husband, taking Ann and grandchildren far from Evansville. "Mother

- - the second one" also mentioned Camden, Maine, a response to a possible letter from my father with his vision of living there, a vision he accomplished. He knew what he wanted. Hannah knew she didn't have what she longed for. She was well acquainted with the fading presence of Arthur who by 1944 had been deceased for fifteen years. Not able to bring back Arthur, she was determined to keep visions of my mother's presence alive for my father. Longing, a yearning desire, a word within the word belonging.

Next letter and my mother's appearance again took top billing. My ex-husband was not attuned to my looks, distracted by his striving for success. His only comment about my clothes was, "Is that new?" implying he was worried money was spent. I long for someone who would notice that which isn't about money. Excerpt from a letter dated, Sunday the 24th of September [1944]:

> She weighs no more than a sugar plum and we shall not allow so much as an almond toast lest your ideal be shattered. She complains such treatment is unnecessary - - that if she hears you are on the way home she will be too excited to eat anyway and will be wasted away before you see her.

> She is rested and lovely looking . . . We went to church this morn-ing - - last winter we couldn't - - she cried through the service…. and so we went no more. This time she sang the hymns… Would you like to see her - - she wore a soft blue tweed suit off of Mr. Peck and Peck from a New York sale - - with a wee brown felt hat and bag and shoes with her last shoe stamp. Her blouse had a little frou frou under her chin, which bobbed when she walked.

> After dinner she changed into a pale yellow sweater and we went to the cliffs which you hear of- - John Leich is back from Tampico before he goes overseas - - and another John, having finished fifty missions in the air over Europe, walked with us too. The third John, whom you barely missed seeing has reported in the Brooklyn Navy yards . . .

Now there is nothing left of the day but bed - - I wish yours were as comfortable as mine - - even so, I'll bet it is as tempting.

Lovingly,
Mother.

For whatever reason, Hannah felt compelled to report on the three Johns in her daughter's life, one of which was John York. My father had to have known my mother attracted young men.

Why the reminder? Hannah couldn't resist, as she couldn't resist mention of clothes. Sacrifices must have been made when funds were scarce for my mother to acquire a Mr. Peck and Peck of New York. Never had I imagined my mother's emphasis on being attractive went back to my grandmother. What crept into my mind, was if Hannah's mother seeded that in her? Understanding generations further back will be needed to understand the me of today.

Throughout my mother's life, she sought out sales, shopped and volunteered at thrift shops searching for the best at a bargain. As a child I tagged along, and as the keeper of memories, my closet holds three of her Peck and Peck cabled sweaters with round, crocheted buttons, each a different color. The sweaters look as good today as when she bought them. Frequenting sales and thrift shops, even when nothing is needed, is part of my inheritance, along with dressing with care and not "letting myself go." Three generations strong and maybe more. To quote Emerson, "Every man is a quotation from all his ancestors." Replace man with woman, the message is the same.

Another letter, no surprise, provided more sensory input about Margaret with the smell of fudge and a message on the "what ifs" of life tagged on. More than once my mother declared, "If it hadn't been for the war, I might have made another decision." She meant a decision about marrying. She said this once in front of my sister's children. There are always wonderings about the "what ifs." Pushing mine back for now, I'll let in another image of my mother, excerpts of "what ifs" included:

Monday morning - - the 16th and still dark [October, 1944]

Good morning!

Margaret is asleep - - I THINK. She sleeps down stairs now - - I threw her out. She rests longer that way . . . she looks like a lovely thing - - so that you can see her, she wore a blue green soft colored sweater with a rose brown skirt which is another one that she wishes you had seen. Around her neck the little brown clay pots bobbed on a wool cord that Indians braid into their hair. Her hair is still done your way and is brushed dutifully every night. Our hall way was smelly with fudge last night which I will take to the Vulcan to have wrapped scientifically, on the way to school - - watch for it - -

I am so sorry to hear that Don's baby will not live to be what they hoped. Marg said to tell you what I thought of your decision to have none just now - - - I did answer that in the letter - - there is no answer - - no one knows what is best today - - we just make decisions and hope . . .

Must run - - Lovingly, Mother

Hannah's words lingered, a message for all time: "No one knows what is best today - - we just make decisions and hope." Blot out fear with beauty and hope.

With the war dragging into 1944, my father had been out to sea for one year. Hannah's next letter included poems, one about fear and the other moons, both subjects which kept rising up. She also added another slice of self-reflection, a line to add to the list I started of what Hannah knew about herself: "I wish my imagination were less sensitive." She may have wished that, though I don't. The consequences might negate the astuteness of her observations, the richness of her writing, the nuances of her photographs, and her sense of humor. No surprise, she offered up beauty as an offset to fear and "torn hearts." While no war is waging

around me, I embrace her words to offset fear. My heart doesn't want
to embrace loneliness.

Sunday the 29th of October, [1944]

(at church bell time)

Dear Rich - -

And no one is going because there are not enough hours in the day
for jobs that follow you to bed. It is still the golden moment of Fall.
You can almost manage to

"Walk where the rock hangs red
with the sumac's cheer
-- - Breathe deep and forget your fear."

There's another that lies in my thoughts when the days are like this - -

"We walk thru fallen leaves while lingering light
Mellows against the outline of blue hills.
The alley smokes with golden haze
The warm moon rises. We walk through crumbling leaves."

And with you - - I wish my imagination were less sensitive. Two
destroyers report sunk. Out of - - how many? The chances surely are
good. Nevertheless, climb over the edge of your ship and swim to a
post office when no one is looking and report to us.

And Rich, in spite of the cross section which magazines give....we
are a nation of anxious serious people.... waiting, working hard,
sleeping restlessly and praying more. There have always been and
will be diamond necklaces and nightclubs - - even those may be
nothing but a moment of effort to make thoughts we live with, more
bearable. There are so few of us now who do not take to bed the
thought of someone we love, who is in danger. Knowing that, does
it seem reasonable that many of us can feel really profligate and gay

and devil may care in our hearts? We have to go thru the motions – living tho something has died inside of us - - we have to use familiar words when we speak and try to make them casual because no one can live and show open wounds to friends.

And sometimes we still can't make the grade and reach for anesthetics - - if a night club is within reach and measures our resources, it maybe in that form. Maybe a new hat which we cannot afford - - maybe any inconsequential thing which would in spotlight, be misinterpreted. And photographed by whatever publicity channel, open to contempt.

Last night I met a friend whose nineteen year old is with the army in Europe. He had been trained for the big guns, but is being used for replacement duty, reconnaissance behind the German lines. They have not heard since the 23rd of September. She said "When I get into a soft bed, it seems so cruelly unfair." . . . We have a hard end too, Rich, altho it is not made up of the pain of torn bodies. It is only a torn heart that we carry about.

. . . this is a halting answer to a letter Margaret gave me, because she said she could not answer you - - her way of clearing ideas is to settle them behind her closed doors, and not muddle around with words, which I do, and which I am noticing you also try to do. Words clear ideas to me whether or not they are badly chosen. The trouble with them is that to each person a different image rises in reply to a word….what I say may mean one thing to me and another to you. I'll bet you have a shadow of an idea of what I am driving toward.

Now I will wash my stockings, clean my rooms and dress to go out to dinner with Margaret. We are going to Mrs. Igleheart and her niece, who is almost blind and has never to my memory, mentioned it. There are so many kinds of courage.

Lovingly, Mother

Hannah cleared herself of ideas. No hiding them, and she did far more than "muddle around with words." I would insist that she was a premier word muddler, word juggler extraordinaire. Her description of her daughter settling ideas behind closed doors needs a qualifier. In her mid-fifties, my mother opened up her closed doors a crack, writing letters about our family and her life. Mention of her feelings was noticeably absent, which brought to mind Hannah's sentence in "They Call it Creative Writing," *Progressive Education*, 1943. "The point is: to release emotions, you must be honest." Hannah, honest, released her emotions with her own qualifier . . . "no one can live and show open wounds to friends." Her boundary bore a striking resemblance to my mother's . . . "To a certain extent, tho I do think we have to 'keep it together.'" The need to present as intact, no wounds, no falling apart, not letting oneself go are family badges. Which leads me back to the first-aid bandages of clothes and beauty.

Hannah had a cure for open wounds: hats. Hats were the same cure my mother once used to "keep it together." Her words during a difficult spot in my life mirror that of her mother:

> Have a good cry now and then (I've done it many a time) then rush
> yourself off – get yourself something you don't need (we used to go
> buy a new hat!)

I never ran out and bought a hat. I never felt I looked good in hats, but throughout my divorce, each Friday I walked into What Poppy Wants, a vintage consignment shop, and walked out with clothes. Three generations reaching for anesthetics of the clothes variety. Poppy was the owner's dog who lay on the floor of the shop, and what Poppy wanted, Poppy got. Valerie's shop was full of classic European and vintage clothes. Dresses and gowns hung from the ceiling. A mannequin greeted you at the door often wearing a dress for an F. Scott Fitzgerald party. Chanel shoes with grosgrain ribbons stood in the window along with Jimmy Choos and other designer shoes unknown to me. Valerie was one of a kind. Her wild, dark hair was pulled back off her face, volumes of uncontrolled curls spread out behind. She wore clothes only Valerie could dare wear, clothes with a flair, a twist that surprised or shocked. One memorable outfit was a black laced-up camisole with a 1950s maroon swing skirt and a slice of a hat, bobby pinned on to hold the lace veil off her face. She always looked great. I looked worn out from work, teenage kids, and divorce documents. My wardrobe was as weary as I was.

Valerie and I hit it off, opposites attracted. She retooled my wardrobe, listened to my tales of woe and encouraged me on. Classic with a twist, she advised. She knew my qualifiers. Nothing shiny or brash. No sequins or bobbles. When she showed me clothes with flash and gaud and even the slightest bit of "wow," I scrunched up my face and said two words, "No way." Slowly over time I bought form-fitting dresses, skirts, and shirts with fronts that could reveal depending on buttons or zippers done or undone. The process was slow. Many Fridays went like this: I stepped out of the dressing room for her advice and stated, "I just don't know." She replied, "You look great!" Next comment from me, "I have no place to wear it." Next comment from Valerie, "You'll find a place. You look stupendous." Next comment from me, "The wildlife biologist in Maine who I told you about doesn't care about clothes." Comment from Valerie, "Don't be too sure. Men are visual." Valerie knew. Hannah knew.

My mother and Hannah always looked "put together." Not so my mother's sister. Ann had a style of throwing on whatever struck her. During a summer visit to my aunt's, my mother was appalled that Ann had forgotten to zip up her slacks, and what was showing should not have been showing. She had forgotten to wear what goes underneath. My mother told her sister, "Go take care of yourself and fix your slacks." Childhood memories made their mark. My mother's style, understated elegance, accentuated her beauty and grace. Hannah's clothes reflected that she was a woman of substance. I was sorting out where I fit. Looking back, Valerie was a version of Hannah. A woman with Hannah's "If this don't beat all" attitude. Both women pushed the edges of etiquette. Valerie's "Stuuupendous!" proclamation was a variation on Hannah's "beeyootiful." Both knew clothes can fend off tough times and boost morale. My mother's words revealed she knew also, words written when my first young adult romance went south:

Right now, I do think it perfectly O.K. to get some pretty clothes that make you feel good, for we do have to present a fairly intact, cheerful front or the gloom will only backfire and scare people off.

~

Clothes aside, in a Tuesday the 19th of Christmas letter, Hannah wrote, "Come home in March." Wishful thinking. At that time, the *Hailey* had barely survived Typhoon Cobra's 100-mile-an-hour winds. Three destroyers had sunk, 790 sailors drowned, and nine ships sustained heavy damage, and Hannah was again painting pictures of beauty, making jokes, pushing back fear. "Don't let a black cat cross your path," she pleaded.

Excerpts from another letter dated Tuesday the 20th of February [1945] in which Hannah expressed wishful thinking:

Rich, darling, who but you would send the sweet birthday note! (Margaret's birthday was February 19) Can't you possibly come home to say "happy birthday again?"

I haven't been good about writing - -- - I am very poor at producing a cheery atmosphere when I am scared to death - - thru that month when it was impossible for you to get letters thru, when I looked at the circles under Margaret's eyes, I simply could do nothing but tear up letters designed to give you the kind of news you wanted. When the package of letters came we began to live again - - now we point out pin pricks of islands on the blue map under her desk glass and hope you are not there.

I found a gift for the ten dollars you sent. The stores are so empty of beautiful things - - but in a little shop there was a copper coffee pot made in Russia a long time ago. It is put together and pounded into shape by hand. The coffee pours from the mouth of an outward curving snake - - you can put it into a traveling bag without break- ing it – breakfast coffee on any little window ledge. I put it on her tray yesterday morning.

Margaret has packed all of the dresses she thinks you will like - - carefully away - - the undies have fresh ribbons and the pink dressing gown new slippers - - her little wedding hat has been revamped - - the flowers sit rakishly over one ear now - - she looks lovely beyond words. She is as slim as even you want her to be - - every one speaks of her beauty as tho they had not seen it before. But me, I would really be happy not to have her here - - because I know that when she is gone, she will be with you, and the look in her eyes will be gone, too. You seemed so sure of coming - - is the whole picture changed or just postponed. Can't you stop being ethical for one letter - - just for once - - and tell what delays the plans?

Believe it or not, son-in-law, I have a pot of forsythia branches with tiny green leaves. A little nature faking, and patient sitting on a shelf, but at last, green leaves! And purty soon, betchu, yellow flowers. The Graveyard shift at the shipyards is folding up - - Aladdin's city of lights around the river bend no longer pricks the smoky fog when I leave for school in the mornings. Children whose fathers have been dismissed are leaving for Tennessee and Kentucky - - everybody is shifting about like checker men - - I want to believe yours will be one of the empty squares that will be filled again, quick-like.

If you will just keep out of headlines until then, the first of May will be even prettier than the first of April. We will accept no longer delay - - you will miss the dogwood.

Lovingly, Mother

Hannah was pleading for the impossible when she asked my father to stop being ethical. His standards were exceeding high, his ethics beyond reproach. Hannah might risk crossing over a small ethics line if a greater good would be served or some beauty would be had. In a previous letter, she emphasized that while the ladies at the Detroit Women's City club "WERE" ladies, she hinted that she herself might

NOT be such a lady. Letter nineteen was case in point, her last letter in which Hannah mentioned her daughter's undies. I doubt the City Club ladies would have done that. Was her intent to engender sexual thoughts? What else could be the reason? I picture my father with a twinkle in his eye, standing next to Captain Brady, reading the letter and commenting, "Well, here she goes again, my mother-in-law wanting me to know about Margaret's undies." Undies aside, I admire my grandmother's renegade spirit and gumption. She never hesitated to zero in on what may lurk within and to share those thoughts, either about herself or what she observed in others, a trait that could be enlightening or off-putting. Note to self: rediscover your gumption and spunk and tap down judgmental opinions.

The last war letter was seven days after the start of the Okinawa assault, one of the most lethal American battles, during which numerous ships went down. News of this battle had to have reached my mother and Hannah. So far my father had made it through almost two years of duty unscathed. The previous letter and this last one implied he was to return soon. To be so close to a safe return only to be in the middle of the largest battle had to be terrifying on the sea and in Evansville.

Sunday, April 8 (1945)

Rich, dear,

Please hurry to a port where you can send us the quickest message to tell us you are all right! We are living with the knowledge that three Destroyers have sunk.

Until we know, our life is suspended. Margaret is going to Detroit for the week that she chose thinking you might spend it together. At least it will occupy her and she will be among friends. Contemporaries are easier to talk to about the war - - perhaps because we who are older catch our breath even more sharply, remembering what life can do even without the horrors of today. They can manage to be more casual.

I was right about leaving Margaret at Easter - - she went to church
- - she would not have gone with me - - and proudly reported that
the music did not make her cry - - then she went to Newburgh with
Tante and raked leaves from the wild flower beds - - our little window box does not give her scope for gardening. If she makes public
her wish to take a hoe and a shovel and dig till she gently perspires
I suspect she will be surrounded with a hopeful crowd like the ones
that gather about market stalls before the farmer appears - - Yesterday I emerged from such a gathering triumphant. I had managed a
bunch of asparagus, and Marg loves asparagus - -

My mother, who made sure I knew women don't sweat, was gently
perspiring, a possible glowing beauty for the hopeful crowd. The letter
ended with asparagus. The next page was missing. May 24, 1945, a month
and a half after this letter, my father detached from the *Hailey*. Rich and
Margaret were reunited and lived on Parris Island, South Carolina during
his temporary duty. After release, he completed his residency at New
York Hospital. With her daughter and son-in-law together, life changed
for fifty-seven-year old Hannah. She was once again on her own, living
alone. If there is an arc to every story, this one peaks with beauty and
fear and keeps returning to the place of alone.

Dear Everybody

Chapter Nine

Family Foundations

D uring that El Nino winter of endless rain, the winter after my father's
death and four years after I heard the words, "I want a divorce," I
was in the last phases of transcribing Hannah's travel letters, wondering
whether California or Maine would be home. Thumbing through her
papers, I found a gem, words confirming her sense of place, leading to
a watershed moment for me. I may need to look back to look forward,
to understand who I am and where I feel rooted. Transcribing, reading
and re-reading Hannah's words confirmed that where I belonged, my
sense of place, mattered. Without that, I felt unmoored.

> News item, I'm learning. I can tell the girls who're looking forward
> from those who're looking back. It's quite easy to distinguish the
> married ones. They don't entwine and take each step except the last
> and final one, on the sidewalk. Girls play up to their men in Paris.
> I'd rather live in Indiana, thank you. 1955 from Paris

I have not been rooted in one place as Hannah had been. When people
ask where I am from, I don't know how to reply. Do they want to know

where I was born, where I lived last, where I lived longest? My father declared there were three places you never would want to live: Texas, Florida, and California. He never explained his biases. I didn't want to move to California but went when my husband took a job there. If I had stayed married, I would have lived in two out of the three.

Hannah preferred to live in Indiana, and that is exactly what she did all her life. Hannah's roots to her place ran deep. Two of her unpublished essays created images of her childhood, slow dreamy days, simple days, days sitting on her front porch or on a bank by a bayou, days with the love from her mother and her Aunt Hannah Hubbs all around her.

Unpublished essay, "Anyone with Half an Eye Can See."

When I was a very little girl I spent at least a part of every summer with Aunt Hannah, who had no children of her own. She wore purple pansies on her bonnets and lived in a cool, dim upstanding house where life moved rhythmically forward. At night I lay small and quiet, and very happy, in a great four-poster, under a canopy of mosquito netting. When morning came, I worked. Responsibilities were dusted on me as lightly as pollen on a bumblebee. With an apron tied about my neck, I cut out thimble biscuits for our breakfast. I gathered potatoes from the cinnamon vines and onions from among the morning glory seeds. These I sold in open market to Aunt Hannah, who paid in full with dry tasteless crackers, shaped into rosettes which powdered as I bit them.

When my work was finished, I spent long hours in the front entry between guarding tubs of oleanders, where I played jacks and watched for mule cars. I marked off solitary games of hopscotch on the sidewalk, with sticks of carbon dropped from arc lights at the corner. I fed the chickens and hollered down Aunt Hannah's well. I strung elderberry blossoms and made them into finger rings and bracelets. At four I "dressed" and sat beside Aunt Hannah in a smaller chair. She often read aloud to me.....I was not a psychopathic lonely child. I had Aunt Hannah. She, like my mother, was for me that "feeling."

Unpublished essay, "Whatever Miss T Eats Turns into Miss T."
My mother offered me the stuff dreams are made of. It lay
all about me, in quiet places where time is never measured by
the hours; where chipmunks lived in acorn trees and toadstools
were knee deep in moss. Out of bounds, behind our stables, was
a marshy bayou into which, each spring, a river overflowed . . .
I liked to sit on these, my feet drawn up beneath me. It was my
favorite pretending throne. A hermit thrush provided orchestra-
tion. My dreams were highly improbable, wildly exhilarating . . .
Maybe I was just lucky.

Hannah's connections to the land, to the joy she found in nature,
lasted throughout her adulthood. Her imagination was fueled by her
highly tuned ability to take in the sensory world, recalling William
Blake's words: "The tree which moves some to tears of joy is in the eyes
of others only a green thing which stands in the way, for as man is, so he
sees." Young Hannah saw beyond what most others see. What she took
in as a child became touchpoints as an adult. Her Indiana childhood
full of pretendings and dreams sustained her, shaped her career, shaped
my mother, and shaped me. The saying that "the child is father to the
man" I alter on behalf of Hannah: "the child is mother to the woman."
Hollyhocks, chipmunks, granite steppingstones, soft moss, and pine
needle beds, midafternoon chick-a-dee song, the mournful call of the
loons at night, the glistening of mussel shells at low tide, all graced
my childhood summers in Maine. They were more embedded than I
realized until I read Hannah's words about memories she carried from
the place where she belonged, the land where her feet were. I never
gave much thought to where I belonged until I faced the prospect of
selling my parents' house. News item (a Hannah-ism): I was learning
that I needed to pay attention to where my senses were most alive.
In my childhood, the closest I came to Hannah's Aunt Hannah was
Ola Winslow, a friend of my father's family, a connection made when
summering in Sheepscot, Maine. Ola, like Aunt Hannah, had no
children. She was an historian, professor and author, winner of the

Pulitzer Prize for her biography of Jonathan Edwards. Petite and soft-spoken, she had a warm, welcoming smile, and wore her grey hair in braids around her head.

Each summer when we arrived at Ola's weathered Cape nestled on a hillside near the Sheepscot River, she would take my hand, lean down and in a hushed voice, say, "Let's be very quiet." She would lead me down her stone path bordered by a carpet of moss, past her stone wall into her flower garden. With peanuts in her pocket, she made a quiet chirping noise and a chipmunk appeared. I was in awe. Standing amid the mosaic of garden colors, she made her offer. If I sat quietly in her kitchen while she and my parents talked, she would make a hollyhock doll for me. There was no way to turn down that offer. She put me in charge of selecting the hollyhock. A bud became the head and several opened blooms turned upside were the body. Another bloom became the hat. I watched as Ola's gentle hands attached all together with a toothpick. Once the doll was mine, I did as was instructed and sat quietly, handling the doll with care, imagining scenes for the doll, while hearing Ola and my parents' voices in the other room. A clock on the kitchen wall ticked away more time than was my custom to sit still, though I honored her offer and sat in the upright wooden chair, the aged linoleum floor sloping away from her wood cookstove, my blue Keds with rubber toes waving back and forth. I dared not make a sound. The fragile doll too prized. Ola was "that feeling."

Hannah's connection to her land was interwoven with her people. She grew up with extended family nearby in southern Indiana and Kentucky. Generations influencing generations. Hannah's mother, Fanny Rose, lived in Evansville until her death, as did four Hubbs aunts and uncles. Six of Hannah's Stevenson aunts and uncles called the area home. Two of her husband's siblings lived in Evansville and all fourteen Trimble and Hillyard aunts and uncles were Indiana residents. None of my relatives lived close by for easy visits and connections. My people and place weren't rooted together. A passage among the many I've collected since my teenage years was about a sense of belonging, a clue that belonging meant something to me well before my divorce.

Wallace Stegner, "The Sense of Place" 1992.
Back to Wendell Berry, and his belief that if you don't know where
you are you don't know who you are. . . . He is talking about the
kind of knowing that involves the senses, the memory, the history of
a family or a tribe. He is talking about the knowledge of place that
comes from working in it in all weathers, making a living from it,
suffering from its catastrophes, loving its mornings or evenings or
hot noons, valuing it for the profound investment of labor and feeling that you, your parents and grandparents, your all-but-unknown
ancestors have put into it.

Since my childhood, my father planted the seed that I belonged in
New England and the Midwest was a place to exit. We made yearly
pilgrimages to New England, checking in with his parents or sisters.
My mother kept quiet about the Midwest, except to defend it when
he claimed the Midwest grew cow corn while New England's was
sweet and delicious, or when he claimed the people in the Midwest
were friendly because the flat, uninviting landscape made people turn
to each other for relief. Looking back, I'm puzzled that my mother
never took me to Evansville, a mere seven-hour drive from Detroit.
While she spoke fondly of her roots when my father wasn't around,
maybe she decided advocating for a trip wasn't worth it, acquiescing
was easier. I regret not having witnessed my mother and grandmother
in the place that held their hearts.

Growing up, I took pride telling my Midwest friends that I was born
in New Hampshire. Michigan's Lake St. Clair, a swim forbidden once
pollution levels rose, was no match for my summers at a camp near
the White Mountains, breathing in balsams and swimming in what
was claimed to be the cleanest lake in New Hampshire With my life at
a crossroads, I knew I didn't belong in California, the place where my
senses rebelled with parched summers and moldy rainy winters, the place
where it appeared I was in the one percent of the women who didn't dye
their hair. Other than my children, I had no family nearby. Even with my
"back east" looking California home, even having steadied myself from

my divorce, I wasn't anchored. I was perched on the edge of discovering where I belonged, and Hannah with her clarity lent me some.

~

My sister had made clear she had no interest in ownership of the Maine house. She lived there after her divorce and was fine letting it go. Not so easy for me. Giving up the house meant no East Coast roots which I couldn't fathom. Wendell Berry, Kentucky writer, whose feet were planted not far from where Hannah and my mother grew up, summed up the importance of place in knowing oneself: "What I stand for is what I stand on." I sensed where I wanted to stand, and it was Maine. My daughter added to the chorus: "How could you sell Grandmama and Pappap's house?" She knew the connection to our colonial ancestors and was incensed that I even considered selling.

I bought out my sister's half of the house, a crazy decision on my part, living as I did all the way across the country. I decided to let things "play out." I reassured myself, my children and my California friends of almost twenty years that I wouldn't "up and move" to Maine full-time. I loved my "Maine cottage in Marin." My work mentoring parents of children with disabilities was rewarding and well known. Advice I'd tell my clients to lighten challenging situations, "Take my advice, I can't use it." I listened to my daughter's advice and used it. I became the owner of the 1798 Cape with remnants of its original barn, farm tools hanging on the wall and an outbuilding with a workshop, an area for a car and an upstairs full of spiders, mice, and bat droppings. Reflecting on the year I put in a Maine mooring and my actions since, I couldn't escape facing that I had a more-than-typical attachment to the past.

After taking ownership of the house and dividing up the contents with my sister, I inventoried the silver in the kitchen drawer, and there was Hannah. In my possession were eleven forks and four serving spoons engraved with "Hubbs," the married name of Hannah's grandmother, Sarah Ann Basnett. The forks had a beveled edge and a simple leaf-like design on the long oblong stem, leaving plenty of room for the engraving. There was one elaborate cheese knife with Sarah Ann's initials and four coin fiddleback teaspoons, two engraved with Hubbs and two with Basnett, the handles shaped like the top of a heart. Fiddle faddle, I imagine Hannah would say. The odd assortment makes me wonder why the forks didn't stay with the knives and spoons. Someone ran away with them, all except the one cheese knife which somehow ended up with Hannah. When I attempted to match up family wedding dates with the years these silver makers were in business in the 1800s, none aligned. The initial owners and who gave what to whom remain a mystery. Fanny Rose was the youngest of Sarah Ann's ten children; any of her siblings could have taken some, passed some to Fanny Rose, who passed them to Hannah, who passed them to my mother, who passed them to me. Mothers across time passing things along. My impression is these women valued their silver.

During each of my four annual pilgrimages to Maine, I made a dent in the process of keeping or discarding items my sister didn't want. Having already noted how many items from Hannah's I had in California, I took stock that many items in Maine originated with Hannah or Fanny Rose. Fanny Rose's three-quarter bed was in a guestroom and her upholstered rocking chair in the family room. The cupboards were chock full of plates and serving pieces that were from Hannah. The blanket chest was filled, not with blankets but with linens representing eras well before the 1940s, linens I never remember being used. All the rooms in the house but one represented my mother and her family. My father's room included a farm table from his parents, a collection of antique tools, a weather station, a model he built of the USS *Hailey* destroyer and books related to his life and medical career. Unlike some California homes where a designer picks out everything for the owners, new and matched with nary a personal effect, I belonged to a family of keepers. Items linked us, kept memories alive, reassured us who we were, where we came from and what we stood for.

∼

Information about past generations uncovered influences shaping Hannah, leading her to pass along what she did, express herself as she did, think as she did, raise my mother as she did, write to my father as she did and influence me as she did. This realization arose out of quiet weekends that offered time for reflection and some regret. Gone are opportunities to ask those who came before me questions I only now know to ask. I put Hannah's letters aside and stepped back in time losing myself in online research. I alternated cozying up in my office nook, printer behind me, to spreading out papers on the dining room table. Green binders held Hubbs and Basnett information and a fat orange one held Stevenson. My girlfriend was collecting information on men met on Match dates, and I was collecting information on family, anchoring myself, getting better acquainted with myself through the past. The story of Hannah navigating her life and me navigating mine begged for historical landmarks, and Hannah's family had many.

My research started with the Quaker roots of Fanny Rose Hubbs. While this may be a tale which may make Hannah say fiddle faddle, her great-grandparents, Charles Basnett and his wife Hannah Voris Basnett, with their where-with-all in silver, set the standard for generations to come on how life should be lived. Other evidence was found in the census and newspaper ads from the 1800s. Charles W. Basnett was a successful "Hatter" with real estate holdings. In 1850, he and his wife provided the home for his wife's seventy-eight-year-old mother and his only child, Sarah Ann, her husband Benjamin Hubbs and their seven children. Their daughter Fanny Rose and son John had not yet been born. George W, fourth-born child had died at six months of age. Sarah Ann, highly valued only child of the Basnett's, lived with four generations. Heading back to the silver in my kitchen drawer, if Sarah Ann's mother, Hannah Voris Basnett, was the initial owner of the Basnett coin silver, she may have made sure her daughter's substantial silverware was a step up. Along with the silver, being in good standing has been passed down the generations, a possible offset to the many tragedies in the family and the fear each generated. Remnants of fear flowed into Hannah, showed up in her letters, cascaded down to my mother.

The tragedies started with Benjamin, challenging the Basnett's notion of being in good standing. Benjamin's business skills were questionable. He incurred debt and received a bailout from his father-in-law. A few years later his dry goods store was consumed by a fire, supposedly "to have been set by design. "Benjamin's in-laws couldn't have been happy. When Charles Basnett died in 1852, Benjamin was still in debt. More trouble followed: The 1853 Indiana Supreme Court case, "Hubbs and Others v. Bancroft and Others," questioned if:

> . . . . a deed made upon a valuable consideration is fraudulent or
> not . . . On the 6th of March, 1836 Basnett, by deed in fee, conveyed
> the lot in question to Benjamin Hubbs, who was his son-in-law,
> the husband of his only child . . . Benjamin had an extensive credit
> in the eastern cities; and the firm had contracted a large amount of
> indebtedness . . .

Many transactions and court judgements followed. Good thing Charles wasn't alive to watch this go down. The question became "whether the deed from Hubbs to Basnett was made with intent to hinder, delay or defraud creditors." While the bill was dismissed, I wonder what Sarah Ann's mother said about her daughter's circumstances.

In 1859, Charles, the first born son of Sarah Ann and Benjamin, made news in Indiana and Kentucky:

> Suicide. December 20 – Charles B. Hubbs committed suicide last
> night by taking laudanum. He left a letter, in which he stated that
> life to him had become a burden and a failure.

Charles was twenty-eight, leaving a wife and two children. Bleak times. Hannah's mother, Fanny Rose, the youngest of the ten children, was one. A rose in the family amid all this bleakness, black mourning clothes and grief. Hannah's mother started life with dramatic life-shaping-events and a grieving mother, a young child absorbing the emotions of those around her.

In 1860, Benjamin left his struggling dry goods business and moved the family (mother-in-law included) to Terre Haute, Indiana to run a hotel. A harrowing experience followed for little Fanny Rose. Hannah's words:

> When your grandmother's mother was a little girl she lived for a
> while in a hotel in a city called Terre Haute. Her father owned the

hotel. In those days, Indians sometimes stopped at the hotel. Your great grandmother had red cheeks and long very black hair. Once an Indian came and wanted to buy her. He offered several ponies and beads instead of money. Her father said no and hid her until the Indians were gone.

What child wouldn't be terrified when whisked away and hidden? What mother and grandmother wouldn't be terrified? I imagine the women bemoaned that Benjamin took the family from their home in Madison. More seeds of trauma and fear were sown for Hannah's mother.

In December 1865 Fanny Rose's father, Benjamin Sr., committed suicide. The news of these two suicides never made it to my generation. The *Madison Courier* headline: "Ben Hubbs shot and killed himself." Excerpts from the *Evansville Daily Journal*:

> SAD – Benjamin Hubbs, well known in this city, Terre Haute and Indianapolis, laboring under a temporary aberration of mind, shot himself in the head . . . The unfortunate man went to the barber's, was shaved, had his hair dressed, and returned to his home....and there committing the dreadful deed . . . No man enjoyed a larger acquaintance or was more highly esteemed than Ben Hubbs . . .

Tragedy swirled around Fanny Rose, her mother and grandmother again. Women wore black mourning clothes again as evidenced in old photos in my sea chest. Fanny Rose was seven, an age when a parent's death, a suicide no less, would be seared in her memory, carried within as she married and raised my grandmother who raised my mother who raised me. Epigenetics: trauma leaves a chemical mark, alters the DNA passed onto future generations. The Hubbs family had no shortage of trauma.

Trouble wasn't over. In 1868 Benjamin Jr.'s wharf boat burned, a loss of over $4,000. A few months later, he made the news again:

> Mysterious Disappearance – Much anxiety and speculation was produced in the city yesterday by the mysterious disappearance of Mr. Ben Hubbs . . . The circumstances attending the disappearance are

of such a character as to give rise to the gravest apprehensions. There are thousands of rumors afloat . . .

Many words later:

. . . Hubbs took a skiff, crossed the river and returned.....and went to bed....Hubbs coming down, on the shore side, in a state of nudity almost, having only his under shirt on. This is the last that was seen of him . . . several theories respecting the case prevail. One is that he went upon the guard of the boat to answer a call of nature, fell overboard and was drowned. A second, is that he premeditatedly drowned himself while laboring under temporary aberration of mind, and a third is that, overwhelmed by financial embarrassments that he has left the city in order to evade pecuniary obligation . . .

By age eleven Hannah's mother had been alive for her father's and brother's suicides and now a brother purportedly drowned. Fanny Rose, with that sweet name of hers, witnessed trauma and lived with her mother's and grandmother's mountains of grief in a small community that knew all about it. My research left me stunned. Never a word had been mentioned about this family history which my grandmother would have known. Silence. Emotional times buried. Mental illness buried.

Fanny Rose was thirty-four when the Indianapolis Journal and papers far beyond Indiana reported that Benjamin Jr. had not drowned after all. My grandmother was twelve, old enough to sense something was amiss, she couldn't have escaped knowing. Family history kept under wraps was before me in lengthy details in multiple papers. Excerpts:

"Benjamin Hubbs Mystery: Veil Lifted from a Supposed Hidden Crime in Evansville in 1869 – Insurance Company had paid $5000 for His Life, But a Letter from California Shows He had Begun Life Anew in the West."

. . . there lived in this city a well-known family, consisting of Benjamin Hubbs and wife, five sons and three daughters . . . The family was a fated one, and it was held by some that it was tinged with a vein of insanity.

. .. the letter referred to at the head of this item . . . is written by one who claims to be his wife, who says he is dead, and desirous of securing a pension. It also develops that Hubbs was at the head of a large and influential family in San Francisco.

Life-shaping events did bring intermissions with good news. On January 28, 1880, at age twenty-two, Fanny Rose married Thomas Burke Stevenson, Jr. in a wedding dress made of "the choicest materials and lace" provided by her brother John. After their father's suicide, John left school at age twelve and went to work. Unlike his father, his dry goods enterprises prospered, and he bestowed his resources on his beloved little sister, Fanny Rose. In 1880, close to a year after she married, Fanny Rose gave birth to twins, whom she named after herself and her mother. Twins Sarah Ann and Fanny Rose died almost eight months later of cholera. Tragedy again. When I look at Fanny Rose's rocking chair in my guest bedroom, I envision my great-grandmother with a string of life's tragedies, rocking to comfort dying babies, rocking to comfort herself. Five years later in 1885 when Fanny Rose was twenty-seven her mother died. By then Fanny Rose had two children, Thomas Basnett (otherwise known as Basnett), age one and Lulie, age three. Hannah arrived in 1888, followed in 1889 by Frank.

The tragedies continued. Fanny Rose's brother William returned to Evansville, divorced. He died when Hannah was fourteen. His death certificate: "Immediate cause: exhaustion. Chronic condition: mania, Marital Status: divorced." The year before, Fanny Rose's brother Samuel had died in Evansville. Cause of death: alcoholism. Could teenage Hannah not have noticed her Uncle Samuel's alcoholism, her Uncle William's mania, both living just a short hop from Hannah? Doubtful. Could Hannah not have been impacted by all the tragedy, by how her mother coped? Doubtful. Could her early life not have shaped how she raised my mother and my mother me? Doubtful. My thoughts returned to Hannah's letters with florid, vivid images of beauty and love, all pushing back fear.

I kept waiting for tragedy to stop. It didn't. In 1919 the thirty-five-year-old daughter of Fanny Rose's beloved brother died. John's daughter was named Fanny Rose. Cause of death, pneumonia. This was the third Fanny Rose in the family, and the second to die prematurely. Hannah was thirty-nine. Once again, how could this not affect my grandmother? How could Hannah's mother be anything but numb? How could Fanny Rose's journey through sorrow not spill onto Hannah? A trail of tears and tragedy which would have remained locked in newspapers and town clerk records if my father had not directed me to do something with Hannah's letters. My mother never spoke a word about this part of the lives of her mother and grandmother, stone silent. I was stunned. Maybe she didn't know. Maybe Hannah kept all this under wraps. Maybe they both knew and boxed up the untidy and then continued to work on being in good standing.

What four generations of Hubbs women endured put the unraveling of my marriage and "how could this be happening to me" thoughts in perspective. My suffering was nothing in comparison. Early in my separation, my soon-to-be ex continued coming to the house unannounced to pick up more of his things or do his laundry. Filled with anxiety, I would lock myself in the bathroom, put on Gregorian chants and take a bubble bath in the "Tea for Two" bathtub, which was never used by two for tea. When answering a phone call, going numb with news that my son was in teenage trouble, with no capacity to stay upright, I curled up in a ball on the floor. No partner to rely on. No family close at hand. I called a girlfriend who came over, no hesitation. I had pulled her into a lifeboat when her son was in trouble, and now she pulled me in. Before she left, I shared a childhood memory, seared with significance. I had asked my mother where my father was. Her answer: "He went to pick Mary up off the floor." My mother's friend, a woman on the floor, was overwhelmed with children and husband. My father probably took his black house-call bag with a sedative inside. The day I was on the floor, I understood. When women suffer, friends and family can be saviors.

∾

While Hannah's maternal family had notoriety for being ill-fated and plagued with tragedy, her father's side of the family had notoriety on the other side of the ledger, and that I knew. In true form, while never bragging, never excessive, my mother's comments about her great-grandfather made clear he was esteemed. Also telling was his exquisite inlaid writing box which held a place of honor atop our living room Victrola, a pedestal of sorts. Once I was old enough and allowed to look inside, I sensed its uniqueness. When opened flat, inkwells and a pen tray topped the deep rose-colored felt writing surface, which when opened further revealed a storage place for papers—Hannah's writings. When I learned my mother gifted the box to my sister, I kept my disappointment quiet. I was gifted the contents. Dividing up who gets what, whether in divorce or death, has its impact. Two years out from the estate dividings, my feelings were muted that the contents didn't come with the box. I was nestled in with Hannah's writings and where they were leading me. A woman in a support group I attended shared that we might learn the most about ourselves and relationships when they end, and I was. With deceased generations before me, their impact on my grandmother's life and my life was coming to light.

Hannah's grandfather, Colonel Thomas Burke Stevenson Esquire, was a well-known orator, newspaper editor, lawyer, and close friend with Henry Clay, Senator from Kentucky, former Secretary of State, and presidential candidate. As a Whig supporter, Stevenson's views, activities, and whereabouts made the newspapers from Detroit to New Orleans and many cities in between. He wrote editorials, made speeches, participated in debates, and maintained an active and intimate correspondence with Clay. Hannah must have relished his prominence, and in turning the mirror on myself, I did also. Two lines in her article, "We Learn to Read" in *Childhood Education*, 1938, provided a clue about the value of stature. "We ourselves, like to feel important. We must succeed to sustain this feeling." Success and perseverance are deeply rooted within my family. Many times when reading about my great-great-grandfather,

I paused with the realization that I married someone with those two traits; Hannah, my mother, and her sister had done the same. I spent hours plowing through online newspaper clippings about Stevenson. I was blurry-eyed, my printer ink needed refilling often, my binder on him was filling up fast. I would tell myself to stop, that I had the picture of his success, but I persevered through the lengthy verbose articles he wrote, or others wrote about him. Vicarious escape. Now several years out from the "D"s in my life, I hadn't the energy to put into another relationship. Not to mention I hadn't sorted out what balance I needed between kind warm hearts and success.

Shoring myself up with the lives of those who came before me, I saw that Thomas Burke Stevenson did more than "succeed to a degree" as Hannah wrote, he excelled, holding editorships at five Midwest newspapers. Using his way with words, Hannah's grandfather pushed his opinions without reserve, nothing half-hearted. Reading example after example of his writing along with praise from others about his skill, there was no denying Stevenson's facility, ability, and proclivity to share opinions and pen words settled nicely into his granddaughter.

The Editor of *Ladies Home Journal*, November 16, 1950

What you said and, even more, the way you said it has stayed in my mind. Ever since reading your article I have been thinking that a person who can write like that <u>must</u> have more to say.

The Editor of Westminster Press, 1948

Have you ever thought of writing a book? If not, I hope you will, because we'd be very most interested in considering it for publication.

The Southern Literary Messenger, June 15, 1943

I wish you would write a book. This is only the second time in five years that I have written that line. My line usually - - -politely --- suggests that maybe some other field would be of more advantage than writing.

The New York Times, January 9, 1951
   You have my full permission, and that of the Times to go ahead and write a book. As far as The Times is concerned, we pay for only what are called first rights in any manuscript.

J.B. Lippincott Company, managing editor, November 13, 1950
   I read with much interest your article in the New York Times magazine yesterday. I wonder if you have any ideas for expanding that material into a full-length book.

To add stature for Hannah, Stevenson was appointed by President Buchanan to a Federal Judgeship in the territory of New Mexico. Hannah had to have beamed. I confess to feeling uplifted.

The Louisville Daily Courier, January 11, 1858
   "How They Howl!" -
. . . the announcement of the appointment of Col. Thomas B. Stevenson of Mason, to an honorable and important Judgeship in New Mexico . . . Col. Stevenson richly deserves the honors conferred on him . . .

A short-lived honor. A few months later:

Times-Picayune of New Orleans, Sunday, April 18, 1858
. . . . The Maysville (Ky) papers state that Thomas B Stevenson Esq, has resigned the office of Associate Judge of the Territory of New Mexico, to which he was not long since appointed. The inadequacy of the salary ($2,500) is assigned as the reason.

Money wasn't the only reason he turned down the judgeship. According to my cousin Tom (namesake of Thomas Sr.), Stevenson's wife, Sarah, had a fear of Indians and didn't want to move to New Mexico putting their nine children in danger. Stevenson wrote a tender letter to his wife while waiting to deliver his message to President Buchanan that he was declining the offer. Excerpts:

Feb 17, 1858, Wednesday, 2 pm from Washington

My Dear Wife,

My feelings today are more tranquil; though I am still anxious about
the future. I wrote you yesterday about the kindness of Mr. Baker....
He waked me up last night and told me he had talked my case over
with the President, who manifested great kindness and sympathy,
and said if I found it impractable to go to New Mexico, or injurious
to the interests of my family to do so, he approved my declining and
would endeavor to give me some other place more advantageous to
the interests of my family.

Having been confirmed by the Senate to an office of high rank and
dignity, I am content on that score, and now only wish to promote
your future comfort and happiness . . . I am now hopeful of being
satisfactorily placed hereafter and satisfied also that my long deten-
tion here, unconvenient as it has been, will be more than justified by
the event, and will receive your approbation in the end.

. . . love and kisses to all. Your Affectionate Husband, Thomas B.
Stevenson

My great-great-grandfather held his wife's comfort and happiness as
his only desire. Ambitious men in my family put love over career. That
value carried on to the next generation. In a photo of Hannah's parents
late in life, Thomas Jr. and Fanny Rose sat side by side on a glider, she
is leaning into him, her "I am cared for" smile told the story of love and
caring. After my mother's stroke, sixty plus years after they married, my
father put his wedding ring back on. I would not be honest if I didn't
admit to a tinge of envy. Generations sustained love well into old age.
I sighed. Gazing out the window from my dining room table, laptop
in front of me with the letter on the screen, a long pause ensued for
reflection and regrets. I married a man with one of those traits and
lacking in great measure, the other.

While Hannah held her grandfather in high regard, not so her father,
the first son, namesake and eighth child of Colonel Thomas Burke

Stevenson, Sr. Carrying a family name casts a shadow, and the shadow of Thomas B. Sr. was a large one, almost impossible to match. Hannah's father made his living as a traveling salesman, not the stature Hannah seemed to expect. Shortly after Hannah's death in 1972, her brother, Frank, made clear to his niece, my Aunt Ann, that Hannah's negative view of their father was unfair. Excerpts from Frank's letter:

> November 18, 1972
> Dear Ann,
>
> It is interesting . . . that two people who know a third more or less intimately, reach very different pictures. I think that Hannah's view of our father was the major initial basis of friction between my brother, myself and Hannah. I have always been both deeply hurt and resentful of my sister's view of our father . . . To me, if he had a fault, it was that he was too indulgent and far too concerned with regret and self-blame that he couldn't give us everything we wanted or that he thought we might want.
>
> My mother (Fanny Rose) was as you pictured her. Kind, loving, indulgent and tranquil, but she was never any effective help. I do not remember ever seeing Mother read a book, magazine or newspaper. She was lost in any conversation other than trivia about her acquaintances, but she did manage to spend every dollar Dad made each month. As for Dad quitting work as soon as Mother received an allowance from Uncle John's estate, your mother (Hannah) simply has her dates wrong....
>
> I have not detailed this in any way to criticize your mother. Probably she never knew these things. My father's generation didn't believe in discussing business matters with women. It is just that it hurts me that you should have a low opinion of your grandfather.....

Ann wasn't done. Before sending Frank's letter to my mother, she penned her opinion in the margin:

> I think mother looked upon Uncle F as the younger spoiled brat of a
> brother. He has her mind and gift as a writer.

A dig at her Uncle Frank and a compliment. Ann cut off the bottom
third of one page, removing what she didn't want my mother to know.
If I were to put a comment in the margin of Frank's letter, it would
be a reminder of the tragedies his mother endured. Be gentle. Be
understanding. Frank's description of Fanny Rose as tranquil, lost in
conversation, and indulgent may have been how she coped. Disassociation
wouldn't have been a bad strategy. If Thomas Jr. indulged his wife, Fanny
Rose may have needed it. Hannah couldn't keep her opinions about
her father from Ann, and Ann couldn't keep her thoughts to herself at
her mother's funeral. My mother, with restrained traits like her father,
would have held back. If Ann spouted off near my mother, she would
have said with the tone I heard often enough when together with the
two of them, words said with exasperation and a dose of shame sprinkled
on top: "Oh, Ann." Opinionated and restrained. I am grateful for traits
which may temper either of those.

How could Hannah not compare her father to her grandfather
Stevenson? She may have overlooked family circumstances. Thomas Jr.
was eleven when his famous father died, and with six older sisters, two
younger brothers, and a younger sister, at age eighteen he went to work
as a store clerk. Further schooling wasn't to happen. His education status
in the 1920 census indicated: "Attended School: NO." Any ambition was
short lived. Family needs dominated. Sometime after the death of his
father, Thomas Jr. and his younger brothers John and Horace along with
his three sisters and mother left Indiana for San Francisco as evidenced
by the 1875 San Francisco Voter Registration. I was shocked my mother
never mentioned relatives who settled in San Francisco, a mere twenty
minutes from my Marin home. The Stevenson family went west to put
loss behind them. My grandmother's decision to head to California
in 1929 after Arthur's death now made more sense. I was mulling over
whether I should leave California to go east to begin anew.

Thomas B. Sr. died before Hannah was born, a grandfather whose
lap she didn't sit on, whose tales of his professional life she only heard

secondhand. He left rich material for young Hannah's imagination and aspirations. I picture young Hannah with his book in her hands, *Correspondence of Henry Clay 1848-1851*, reading what Stevenson wrote to Clay, making note of her favorite phrases. A book with pages and pages of eloquent words, lofty thoughts, and passionate ideas. Two of his letters were about the early death of his fourth child, Louisiana, after whom Hannah's sister Lulie was named. I zeroed in on loss in my family. My great-grandfather's words were touching and heartwarming, filled with rich images of Louisiana, age five, fading away beside her tender grieving father. Instructive lessons for Hannah whose life would hold its own heart wrenching moments.

Thomas B. to Henry Clay regarding the death of Louisiana, age five, fourth of his twelve children
Frankfort, Kentucky, August 29, 1848.

My Dear Sir—The worst apprehensions in regard to my daughter, expressed in my last, have been realized. She is gone whither… it is the greatest purpose of my life to accomplish a preparation to rejoin her . . . yet, of all the afflictions I have experienced—and many of them have been recently concentrated in bitter draughts—this is the bitterest cup of all. She was so beautiful, so intellectual, so purely amiable, and, withal, so romantically tender in her love of me, that I feel as if a part of my existence has gone out from me, and that I can never more think of her without a pang. Though I should not obtrude my grief upon others, you, who are a father and have lost beloved children, will appreciate and excuse this un pre-meditated mention of it.

Henry Clay to Thomas Burke Stevenson regarding the death of his daughter
Ashland, September 4, 1848

My Dear Sir . . .
I tender you cordial condolence on your late great bereavement. My own heart has so often bled from similar afflictions, that I can easily comprehend the poignancy of your grief, and heartily sympathize

with you. Time alone, my dear sir, and your dependence on Him who, having given her to you, has seen fit to take her away, can mitigate your sorrows . . .

Yours truly,

Henry Clay

Lessons in loss continued. Stevenson supported Clay one year earlier with the task of procuring what was common in Victorian days, jewelry with the hair of the beloved within. A memorial to wear.

> *Biblical Recorder*, Raleigh, North Carolina, Saturday, September 18, 1847
> The Honorable Henry Clay . . . directed Thomas B. Stevenson, Esq. of Cincinnati, to procure a Gold Ring set with a precious stone, enclosing a braid of the hair of his lamented son, the late Lieut. Col. Henry Clay Jr . . .

After reading the above passage, I dug out and wore the gold hair ring passed along to me, which I imagined held Louisiana's hair. A broken prong snagged my clothes, ending that attempt to wear the past. Acknowledging my sentimentality, the ring now sits on my dresser, next to a hair brooch, the center of which rotates, fine baby hair on one side, braided hair on the other, a memorial to Fanny Rose's twin daughters, Sarah Ann and Fanny Rose.

I am a keeper of family, a keeper of meanings, of messages and passages that anchor me. I search them out, copy them down when they show up. One such passage appeared when reading *The Underland* by Robert MacFarlane.

> So these scenes from the underland unfold along the walls of this impossible chamber, down in the labyrinth beneath the riven ash. The same three tasks recur across cultures and epochs: to shelter what is precious, to yield what is valuable, and to dispose of what is harmful.
> Shelter (memories, precious matter, messages, fragile lives).
> Yield (information, wealth, metaphors, minerals, visions).

Dispose (waste, trauma, poison, secrets).

Into the underland we have long placed that which we fear and wish to lose, and that which we love and wish to save.

Colonel Thomas Burke Stevenson, Esquire, died on November 13, 1863 in Maysville, Kentucky, the same place where he began life fifty-four years earlier. His obituaries were effusive. I wonder if Hannah took note of his traits and recognized herself. Excerpts;

The Dollar Weekly Bulletin, Maysville, Kentucky, November 19, 1863
He wrote with singular ease, very forcibly . . . His faults were those of a temperament too sanguine and impulsive for his own success . . . He was a kind and affection man in his family, by whom he was dearly loved.

Maysville Weekly Bulletin, Nov 19, 1863, Death of Col. Thomas B. Stevenson
His quick perceptions, made him a formidable antagonist to encounter in debate . . . in his private relations Col. Stevenson was one of the most amiable of men, kind and affectionate in his family ardent in his friendships and generous to a fault.

Hannah's grandfather, flush with accomplishments, made a name for himself. A name passed along the generations, first to his son, then to his grandson Thomas Basnett Stevenson, then, a skip-hop over a generation as Hannah had no sons. If Hannah had had a son, I am certain she would have named him Thomas. I am certain she smiled when Ann named her firstborn son, Thomas. The trials of the "ill-fated Hubbs family . . . tinged with a vein of insanity" and the prominence of Hannah's grandfather Stevenson may have been a factor in Hannah's desire to push back fear and strive for success.

Family

Richmond Smith and Margaret
Trimble on their wedding day

Hannah Trimble

The destroyer, USS *Hailey*

Thomas Burke and
Sarah Combs Stevenson
Hannah's paternal
grandparents

Hannah Voris Basnett
Hannah's maternal
great-grandmother

Sarah Ann Basnett Hubbs
Hannah's maternal grandmother

Fanny Rose Hubbs Stevenson
Hannah's mother

Fanny Rose's Wedding

Fanny Rose and Hannah

Hannah (ctr) with her siblings,
Thomas and Lulie

Hannah

Fanny Rose and Thomas B. Stevenson
Hannah's mother and father

Chapter Ten

Child Is Mother to the Woman

My childhood kept reappearing as long-forgotten Hannah memories surfaced. Books among them. When our parents were clearing out the Michigan house for their move to Maine, my sister and I had to face the basement playroom shelves filled with children's books—many, gifts from Hannah. The task, an emotional one for me, was to decide which books we each wanted. I was in college, and the sale of my childhood home and dividing up what I wanted to bring into my adult life wasn't easy. Being the youngest by six years, I had enjoyed books given to me and books given to my sister. I knew that I would have to part with some of the ones she wanted. On this rare occasion when we were together, our mother insisted it was time to sort this out. I imagine she said, "Do it now so there won't be issues later." Having "issues" was a deadly family sin. I had learned from childhood how to navigate them with silent fortitude and sometimes grace.

With the books Hannah inscribed to one or the other of us, issues were avoided. Her large flowy handwriting, full of curlicues, often took up most of the inner cover: "To Dearest Stephie, Lovingly, Grandmother," or "With all my love to Cecily, Grandmother." Hannah's words were tender, her handwriting effusive.

Inscriptions that were only "Lovingly, Grandmother," required a decision before we claimed a book. I pulled *900 Buckets of Paint* off the shelf, held it up and looked at my sister, questioning, "What about this one?" I was sitting cross-legged on the floor in shorts and could feel the cool linoleum on my legs. My sister was next to me on one of the rush-seated children's chairs grandmother had given to each of us. Above my sister, the playful orange curtains from our childhood, edged in ball fringe and covered in a pattern that looked like oval eyes outlined in black, red dots in the middle, cheered the room. Hannah had proudly noted in an essay that the curtains were her doing. Staring at the curtains was a wee distraction from the anxious feeling in my stomach. Another distraction was a broken c-shaped piece of reed edging on the arm of the couch behind my sister. I remember picking at the arms when sitting next to a boyfriend knowing what we might do next: a "one thing leads to another" memory.

Lots of memories accompanied my longing to have *900 Buckets of Paint*. There was no inscription making clear whose book it was, and I had already acquiesced on several books, and this one I wanted with a passion. As a child, I pored over the map on the inside leaves which showed each house an old woman lived in on her journey to find the ideal home for herself, her donkey, cat, and cow. Looking back, my attachment to this book reflected my early need to feel at home. Other feelings centered on being fair in splitting up the books and my guilt about having teased my sister when we were children. Asserting myself brought all that up. I had been horrid at times, so much so that my mother made certain I knew the nursery rhyme: "There was a little girl and she had a little curl, right in the middle of her forehead. And when she was good, she was very, very good, and when she was bad she was horrid." All true, except I didn't have a curl. My bangs were cut straight across my forehead. I knew I should be generous and not finagle this book. I already had a pile next to me. The better side of me lost, and I ended up with *900 Buckets of Paint*. My sister was more than generous, but maybe not so understanding. We often heard, "The least you two can do is be civil with each other," another less-than-positive mother message.

The carefully curated books Hannah bestowed upon us, wittingly or not, told part of her story and chapters of mine. Books filled with idyllic romantic images stemmed from her dreams and fed my thirst for the same. Parting with any of them revealed the strong hold her books had. Hannah's delight, as she put it, in "the choicest" books was contagious. My shelves are testament to that, several are dedicated to children's books, many of which are collectible first editions. I have almost stopped myself from acquiring any more, except for new choicest ones for my grandson. In her essay, "A Daughter's the Daughter the Rest of Your Life," I note more than a little pride in heaping joy on Bubs, aka, me.

> Bubs had a playroom all for herself. Her father, who was a doctor, had gone without a study so that this could be accomplished. He painted its walls and made shelves from planks he found in the base-ment. On the shelves I heaped presents for Bubs. They were chosen with care. I knew which books were good and which ones were not, and I bought the choicest editions. I also knew about toys that are called educational. I bought those too.

Opening a book from Hannah, her scrawled inscription dancing on the page, conjures up thoughts of the postcards she sent and I've saved, her loving words taking over the back: "Thank you for the sweet valentine. Keep the hug for me and I'll collect it. Lovingly, Grandmother." Messages for my five-year-old-self included, "I don't know where I'll fit all my coffee pots in my new house – HELP! Lovingly, Grandmother." The formal Hannah I knew when she visited doesn't jibe with her loving words on the dreamy ethereal postcards she sent of German Sulamith Wulfing's art. Her handwriting on these postcards was as flowing and floaty as the images on the front. Images to escape into. At an early age, Hannah transported me, swept me into Wulfing's spell and into books rich with nature and dreams. The best of her childhood burrowed all the way down into mine. The worst, she inflicted on my mother and her sister. Excerpts from "That Inner Me," an unpublished essay:

Once I was very little, very shy, wanted most ardently to be a rubber stamp. My mother one dreary summer day chose a bolt of blue satin and cut three dresses for me from the same dull Butterick pattern. I loved my mother, so could not speak of that empty feeling. What is that empty feeling? My mother liked to have us play in the back yard. My brother led the assault up the ridgepole of the stable to spit into the chimney. The last to spit was 'poison'. I was always 'poison'. Inferior and lonely even in spitting. Then I grew up to be six and went to school. Stood and stood and stood in a cloakroom for something I did not do. In semi-darkness, among wet coats and overshoes. A nameless horror. Why did I take the blame for some- one else? When I grew up, married and had children, I never let my daughters wear butterfly skirts in school when it was the thing to do to wear butterfly skirts that swirled like wings of delicious colors. Instead, they had to wear Best and Company tight blue sweaters with three red lines around a high neck when young breasts were bursting. …..They never held it against me that they could not have bras but went to my corset lady to be fitted with a confiner when there was ample to fit. Nor would I let them wear silk stockings to school . . .

I remember one day in the country at an auction, my father bought for me a dozen pair of round-toed, buttoned shoes. My friends wore Trilbies. Trilby shoes laced up in front. What a devastating solitude. I was lonely.

But I was lucky. A game of hopscotch quickly dissipated any chill from drifting clouds when a little girl. Adolescent loneliness came and went protected by pride . . . Now that I am what the young call old, I am less lonely. When I am really old I will expect the waves of torment to have tossed and broken.

Waves of torment as a child, lonely feelings remembered and reported on when middle aged are telling. In one line from her 1950 article, "An

Old Woman Refuses to be Aged," *New York Times Magazine*, Hannah reflected once again on her childhood and put forth a theory about herself: "Perhaps I suffer from inadequacies rooted in my early life?"

My grandmother feeling inadequate was a disconnect. I felt intimidated in her presence, searched for signs from her that I was behaving as expected. Her sturdy and commanding stature gave no hint of insecurity or a nary-a-care, throw-it-all-to-the-wind approach. Never had I imagined how sensitive she was, how deep her feelings were. The persona she wore belied what churned within. There were clues, though I was too young to recognize then. My emerging understanding of Hannah warms and softens my view of both her and my mother, and may soften my view of myself.

With childhood feelings of loneliness and inferiority, why did Hannah make parenting choices that set her daughters apart from others as she felt her parents had done to her? Despite how hard any of us try to not repeat our parents' actions, it may be inevitable that some show up. For my mother, as a counter-reaction to her mother insisting upon clothes which set her apart, she did the opposite with me. She bought clothes I wanted, clothes which were popular, reinforcing generational values: clothes and style mattered. My mother made sure I had saddle shoes when they were the norm and penny loafers to replace them when the style changed. I had sweaters that complemented skirts. When I came home from school after wearing a new outfit, she asked if the kids liked what I had on. That question felt intrusive. There is a point-counterpoint for some in raising their children, and for others, what was tolerated for the parent can be tolerated for their child. I know I am guilty of both. I tried to control my children's clothing choices and rarely succeeded.

I am contemplating how Hannah's and my mother's choices affected my choices. I am indebted to the two of them, along with Valerie coaching me in their absence, her dog Poppy on the store floor watching my confidence grow. I wore a proud smile at the first holiday party I attended in one of Valerie's Prada dresses, a single woman who had cast off her bland look, and was greeted by "Wow, you look great."

If Hannah suffered with insecurities rooted in early life, from not having what other children had, from feeling separate, from brothers who beat her up the ridgepole, all was not horror and torment. Her mother and Aunt Hannah were as she described, "a feeling," giving her "the stuff dreams are made of." Coupling this with threads of childhood insecurity, all may have contributed to her astute understanding of the inner world of children and her passion to teach and reach them through creative writing. Her unpublished essay, "Whatever Miss T Eats Turns Into Miss T." offered up another window into her childhood and what drove her to influence the children in her life as she did. Those children included me.

I was once a dreamy child. To daydream, for some children, is as unconscious as their breathing. Such dreams are like iridescent bubbles, held for an instant on a finger-tip before they are forgotten. They were, for me, my most "fun-riding" thing. I almost, but not quite, dreamed myself into curls for Sunday school. In dreams I moved from long-sleeved, tailored aprons made of linen crash, into dotted Swiss, with sashes. I endured my round toed, low heeled shoes only because I thought of them as Trilby kids with tooth-pick, patent leather tips. My dreams never sprang from long-term idleness. Every day I dried the dishes, made my bed and swept the sidewalk. If I did a sloppy job, I had to do it over. There was no poison in my dreams. I needed no defense. I was not a solitary introvert. I was not neglected. I most certainly was not trying to attain a place in the sun without having earned it. I didn't even want a place in the sun. I was experimenting. In my dreams I sampled ways of being happy, sifting and discarding values as they failed me. In the doing, some receiving apparatus of my senses became more and more selective.

My mother, watching this, moved to meet each step I took, without my knowing it. I never really knew my mother, as a person, then.

She was a feeling: an apple on my pillow when I went to bed, molasses candy bubbling in an iron pot . . .

There were other, less tangible emotions which children feel and out of which both they and I made little singing dreams. Only happy children sing them. Sometimes they are soft, like bird sounds, with no words. Sometimes they have wonderful words with no meaning. I sang them as I set the table and when I buttoned on the dresses of my dolls. I sang them when, with backward flying hair, I ran down the hill to get letters from the mailbox.

A doctor might say that they were evidences of mental activity from one of the multiple levels of consciousness. "Bio-chemical," he might add. Nonsense! They were dreams—an essence of pure happiness, distilled from an integrated child's response to a home where love gives immunity to fear. I would have had none to sing had I not known that I was a satisfactory part of such a home.

My mother offered me the stuff dreams are made of. It lay all about me . . . My dreams were highly improbable, wildly exhilarating, but left me with no hangover. Maybe I was just lucky.

Hannah was lucky to be able to escape into nature, into the world of dreams. Despite all of her mother's trials, the endless waves of grief and tragedy, Fanny Rose offered her daughter "the stuff dreams are made of." What better escape from the ill-fated family? The world of make-believe and the beauty of the natural world are antidotes to the tough stuff. Fostered and encouraged, young Hannah submerged herself in the sublime, fortified herself against insecurities and ventured out in the world. At age eight the *Evansville Journal* reported she was one of several attending a party. Her newsworthy activities continued with frequent mention of her artistic skills of "dainty pen and ink sketches." In her teen years, she was cited as a hostess for parties offering up "a sparkling repartee" while also receiving notice for her serious endeavors as assistant editor of her high school newspaper and member of the Arts and Crafts Society. Newspaper searches brought up so many mentions I was stunned. Uncovering the childhood roots to her later life was a thrill.

As a member of Evansville's literary Clio Club, young adult Hannah was in her element, attending, presenting and hosting meetings in her home for an intellectual group of women. Hannah on stage with an audience, a clue for the future.

> *The Evansville Press*, Tuesday, May 23, 1911
> The Clio club met Monday . . . American Art and Artists was the subject . . . Miss Hannah Stevenson read a paper on "Modern American Woman Sculptors."

Formed in 1874, the Clio Club was led by Hannah's friend Carrie Akin Clifford. Hannah's other lifelong friends Hazel McCurdy and Josephine Foster were members. These were young women I would have been fascinated to know. Each grew up in families with stature. Hazel's father, reported to be a millionaire, was president of Old National Bank and owned the Evansville Hercules Buggy company. Josephine's father was a Vanderburgh County superior court judge and was elected to the US Congress in 1905. Josephine's great-uncle, John W. Foster, was a former United States Secretary of State, diplomat and lawyer. Carrie's father, William Akin, was a businessman and mayor of Evansville. Hannah's brother reported that their mother Fanny Rose was lost in any conversation other than trivia, and was never seen reading a book. That description didn't fit Hannah. Besides making the news for her literary activities, social news about Hannah was telling. Hannah made sure she was noticed.

> *The Indianapolis Star*, August 21, 1913
> Miss Ellen Zaring's 500 party of yesterday . . . one of the prettiest affairs of the week . . . Miss Hannah Stevenson and Miss Ada Norton of Evansville were the guests of honor.

Child is Mother to the Woman

The Evansville Press, March 2, 1914

Miss Frances Leich, daughter of Mr. and Mrs. Carl Leich, gave a matinee party at the New Grand Saturday . . . entertaining 18 young friends. The party occupied two boxes and was chaperoned by Mrs. Leich . . . and Miss Hannah Stevenson . . .

The Leich family founded and ran an Evansville wholesale drug business, and featured prominently in Hannah's life. Evansville history detailed the family's "unquestionable loyalty and civic eminence."* The Leichs traveled and studied in Europe and lived in the Riverside district claimed by leaders of Evansville civic and business affairs. Hannah's dear friend Frances Leich married Guatemala-born Richard Hansen, and was high up in Evansville's ranks. Friend Josephine Foster married a Leich. Young and single, Hannah connected herself with a cosmopolitan group and was not sitting on the sidelines even while holding down a teaching job. Something lured her to others who were accomplished. Did her sense of esteemed lineage through her Grandfather Stevenson build confidence to connect with others of stature? Was she determined to offset her father's lowly career, or to wipe away remnants of the Hubbses failures and reputation?

Hannah's kinship with those of stature and her dreams of a dashing knight led her to say yes to the man who asked her to marry him. George Arthur Trimble, age thirty-seven, ". . . an interesting example of the value of persistence and fidelity in the winning of success . . . industry, ability and loyalty,"† proposed to Hannah, ten years his junior, in 1916. No surprise, the news made the papers.

Teacher Resigns – Miss Hannah Stevenson, 1237 U. First Street tendered her resignation as teacher at Fulton Ave school and on January 24 will become the bride of Geo. Arthur Trimble, assistant manager of the Vulcan Plow Company.

---

* *Indiana Magazine of History*, 1974
† *History of Vanderburgh County*

Arthur was a unique match for Hannah, a man whose photos show him ready for business, buttoned up with starched collars and ties. His father, Arthur, came from Northern Ireland in 1847 and died two years after his son's birth. His mother, Alice Hilliard Trimble, then age thirty-six, moved her five children from the farm in Kirksville, Missouri to Evansville. Arthur, the youngest and the only boy, had a role to play in his family. Ann had the following to say about her father's sisters:

> They were so controlled with no show of emotion I used to curl my
> toes in my shoes when taken to church Sundays with my feet on
> stool . . . One married . . . I am sure my mother had a rough time
> with them, for they did not want my father to marry . . . he had
> cared for them, and put two through University.

If the stern visage in the photo of Arthur's unmarried sister Alta was any indication of personality, Hannah, warm and dreamy, was quite the contrast.

Maybe in part because she was not like his sisters or mother, Hannah found her way into Arthur's heart. His close friend and Vulcan Plow colleague, Adolph Volderauer, signed their marriage application, stating, among other facts, that it was true that neither were "an imbecile, feeble-minded, idiotic or insane, or is under guardianship as a person of unsound mind." Hannah had to have been thankful that the Hubbs mental illness hadn't landed in her. Hannah would not have known at the time that Adolph, Arthur's faithful friend, would be in her life well into old age.

With divorce fading into the background of my life, family weddings fascinated. While Hannah's mother had a formal wedding announcement, nothing of the kind did I find for Hannah. What she had was what her mother had, a portrait wearing her mother's wedding dress. Anyone seeing either the photo of Fanny Rose or Hannah in the dress draws in for a closer look. The skirt is scrunched-up satin, the bodice tight, the collar cradling the neck. Both the dress and overskirt with a satin brocade train are finished off with lace at all extremities. Years later the dress merited a newspaper photo with my mother as the model. Three generations in the same dress, Fanny Rose, Hannah, and Margaret. The dress, an heirloom that survived over one hundred years, is in my possession, a dress which conjures up visions of a regal romantic wedding which Hannah full of dreams had to have imagined:

> Toward sundown I buttoned on two stiff petticoats, with dust ruf-
> fles, and came down to the front porch, where I waited for romance.

I wallowed in my image of Hannah wearing her mother's dress for her wedding until my newspaper article searches jolted me to a new reality. *The Evansville Press,* January 25, 1916 headline: "Stevenson-Trimble Wedding Monday":

> Members of the families were the only witnesses to the marriage
> of Miss Hannah Stevenson, daughter of Mr. and Mrs. Thos. B.
> Stevenson and George Arthur Trimble, son of Mrs. Alice Trimble,
> and assistant manager of the Vulcan Plow Works which took place
> Monday evening in the pastor's study of Trinity M E church. Rev.
> M.P. Giffin officiated, using the ring service.

> The bride wore a tailored costume of dark blue gabardine with black
> and white hat and corsage of bride's roses and white sweet peas.
> After the ceremony Mr. and Mrs. Trimble went at once to their new
> home, 312 Parrett-st, where they will be at home after Feb. 15.

Hannah, who overflowed with dreams and romance, wore dark blue gabardine. The notions I had of her wedding day vanished. I uncovered nothing that explained the tailored costume of gabardine with a black and white hat. Hannah was not pregnant. Ann was born thirteen months later. While WWI was underway in Europe, America had not yet joined in. There were no deaths in the family that would have made a traditional wedding dress inappropriate. Facts aside, the photo of Hannah in her mother's wedding dress keeps me wedded to imaginings of a bride decked out on behalf of beauty, on behalf of the marriage.

Ann's birth in February 1917 was a newsworthy event. Margaret followed in February 1918, once again a news item for the residents of Evansville. Not one to sit still, Hannah was up and about two months after my mother's birth, hosting a Clio Club meeting in her home. The Trimbles' summer whereabouts also needed a newspaper announcement as did their hospitalization due to the 1918 pandemic, noting that Fanny Rose came to the rescue to watch her grandchildren.

Old newspapers, which I spent many hours devouring, filled in many gaps about Hannah's life. Even when busy with her children and social comings and goings, her doings included intellectual pursuits. A 1919 newspaper reported she enrolled in an Evansville college extension class studying contemporary literature with the detail that the class met each Thursday at 4:30 pm, raising my curiosity about who was taking care of Ann and Margaret. I pulled up the 1920 census. Alma Schumacher, age twenty-four, was listed as their live-in maid. Hannah had the life I imagine she desired: handsome successful husband, two children, household help, intellectual pursuits, social connections, and a summer getaway spot.

After reading a news clip that "Mr. and Mrs. Arthur Trimble and children left Wednesday for an eastern motor trip," there was no denying that Hannah needed to be on the move even with baby and toddler in tow, making certain others knew about it. One has to work at making the news, making connections, being seen and noticed. That merited a moment or more of reflection about the inferiorities she claimed feeling at an early age and whether seeking public acceptance and a successful partner were offsets, which led me to benchmark myself against my grandmother. I've never had a desire to be in the public spotlight, though as with Hannah, my mother, and my aunt, I selected a partner destined for success. I was oblivious to the limited emotional bandwidth of the man I married and my need for depth in that area, a possible side effect of growing up in a family that kept feelings under wraps. My impulsive answer of, "Yes, I will," coupled with notions of a romantic wedding, led me down the aisle.

Pushing aside my limited awareness when I married, I turned instead to reveling in the trove of family photographs, many of which were taken by Hannah, most of which were of my mother and her sister. When cameras first became available in the early 1900s, Hannah stepped right up. She wasn't content with the Kodak Brownie camera introduced to the masses which took two-and-a-quarter inch square snapshots. Hannah's camera took rectangular photographs and may have been the American Tourist Multiple, an option for those who could, in 1913, outlay the equivalent of one hundred and seventy-five of today's dollars. In photo after photo, her observant eye and creativity captured a magical view of childhood; whether in candid shots or in ones she posed, she captured the essence. In one, Ann and Margaret in white dresses, knee socks and shoes are perched in the crotch of a large tree. In another my mother, bob haircut with bangs, is poised, parasol in hand. Several photographs shout out the playful delight of children: a group beaming in wet saggy bathing suits, another of my mother and her best friend hiding under an oversized birdbath, and yet another of my mother and her sister lying on their stomachs side by side on the grass, hands under their chins, faces saying, "Look at us."

Hannah's photographs reflected what she valued:

> We can offer children the stuff that dreams are made of. They come more surely in quiet places where time is not measured in hours, where chipmunks live in acorn trees and toadstools are knee deep in moss. They wait in meadow grass where, under the blurred wings of insects, sun enters the brown earth without a sound.
>
> But few of us have a chipmunk tree and almost none of us prepare ourselves for a dream of lying flat on our backs in a meadow. So children must dream dreams where they find them.

Hannah artifacts confirmed a theme that flowed from one generation to another. A childhood shared with dear friends, bosom buddies as my mother called them, sprinkled with simple delights and quiet moments, nurtured the imagination, captured the surrounding beauty and fostered a sense of security. Hannah told it best in her undated essay "Anyone with Half an Eye Can See."

> I watched her bend and touch, with shivering attention, a cobweb, wet with rain. The cobweb, although she didn't know it, would become a dream. She will never really forget it. She could not tell - - not then - - how her senses responded to the cobweb, but the imprint of its beauty will remain a part of her.

> It was my job to show them how to make this beauty ever into dreams. I don't mean those dreams which are not more than static sense impressions. I mean those that come alive, as action . . . "Who lives with beauty hath no need of fear."

On dark days, I told myself, "Take heart," those values Hannah instilled in my mother as a child, are instilled in me. I grabbed onto the word security, and was starting to believe I would come out the other side of a challenging marriage and subsequent divorce with values to sustain and guide me. I was comforted with the discovery that my grandmother had insecurities, and I was becoming mindful of how insecurities can work for or against us.

Chapter Eleven

Married Life

Piecing together Hannah's life, I returned over and over to the trove of photos I had dug out of the chest in Maine. I took photos of the photos for easy storage on my phone, handy access when needed, and I had copies made so that there was a box of photos both in Maine and Marin, perfect for my bi-coastal life. I was in no rush to put my grandmother aside, which indicated something about me, as it had already been three years since I started transcribing her work. Scouring over photo after photo, stories about her emerged. One theme became obvious, Hannah bought hats and wore hats, many of them: hats scrunched flat atop her head; hats covering her head with her face peeking out from under flowy fabric; hats sitting rakishly askew, flowers akilter. Each image revealed a woman at home in a hat. Hannah had pizzazz. In one photo she had a fern tucked into the belt of her dress, her hat looked like a smooshed marshmallow, strands of hair had fallen down her face. Her smile beamed. In another, she stood in a tent near a table and had what apeared to be a tablecloth around her, pinned at the neck. The stripes on the edges of the table cloth gave it away. Her smile and the words she scrawled on the back of that photo, "If this don't beat all," showed she knew it did. Even when well into the years when hats were no longer fashionable, Hannah wore a hat.

Hannah had hats, Arthur, her husband, had ties. In almost every photograph, he was wearing a tie. In the "can you believe it department," there he was in a canoe in the middle of Lake Leelanau in Michigan, wearing a hat, a v-neck sweater and, yes, a tie. Not to be overlooked, a German Shepard was in the canoe with him. How about a tie, suit and vest when he was sitting on the grass with my mother and sister, a baby in his lap, a hole in the sole of his shoe? I am grateful for that hole, a sign of something not tended to. I am grateful for the baby in his lap, a proof of caring. Even posing on his farm, he wore a tie. The only photo without a tie was one in which he was wearing a full-body bathing suit standing near the dock in Lake Leelanau. That stands to reason. Now a word about his starched collars. One was about three inches tall and made you wonder how he could swallow. All photos portrayed him as formal and stiff even when considering the style at the time for businessmen. My sister found a photograph of him at the historical library in Evansville, a wow photo, handsome beyond handsome. His eyes, deep and penetrating, combined with a slight upturned mouth made me sense a slight glint of softness, a warmth in that stiffness. I may be creating a story about a grandfather I never knew as Hannah may have done about hers. When he looked at Hannah with those eyes, oh my. What a duo they were.

With caution, I told myself not to get wrapped up in future thoughts of a handsome man in my life, with a warm glint in his eye like my grandfather. My inner me knows my potential for daydreaming about romance. A photo of my mother and father, side by side, young and in love: a handsome man, a beautiful woman, and the stage is set for that unexplainable chemistry of physical attraction.

The man I married didn't match these portraits of warmth and love, but he was, like my grandfather, a man dominated by strivings for success, a man with many ties around his neck for business. Besides ties, my grandfather also had positions, many of them: Manager and Treasurer of Vulcan Plow, Vice-president of D. Roderick Lean company, President of the Hayes Pump and Planter company, Vice-president of

Peoria Drill and Seeder, Secretary and Treasurer of the South Bend Chilled Plow company, and a Director of Old National bank. Unlike the man I married, my grandfather actively supported social causes and gave back to the community.

With the need to pull my grandfather close, I searched and became the owner of a rusted plow seat from Vulcan which I propped up in the mudroom of the house in Maine, a symbol of family loyalty. Established in 1847 as Heilman Plow works, the company was renamed Vulcan when a friend of my grandfather's father, Albert Rosencranz, took over from his father-in-law William Heilman. A story, one of the few from my paternal grandfather's side of the family, was that my great-grandfather Arthur Trimble formed deep bonds with Major Albert Rosencrantz during their days together in a Civil War prison camp. Their sons grew up together and carried on the Trimble/Rosencranz loyalty which secured my grandfather a minor position at Vulcan. By 1920, he became Treasurer, and by 1922 he was Vice President at one of Evansville's largest manufacturing companies shipping equipment as far as South Africa. My aunt added the opinion, true or not, that my grandfather led the business because "Uncle" Dick Rosencranz was a musician and hopeless as a businessman. Loyalty, an admired value. My ex was loyal to his father, working for him in the same profession for a time, until his drive for achievement overruled. I overlooked the intensity that drove him to leave his father's law firm striving for financial success above all. Money dominated. He hardened. I look at my grandfather's portrait and take in the glint of warmth in his eyes and wonder whether I am unrealistic to want both warmth and success.

Atop the Vulcan Plow building since 1889 was a metal statue, well over nine feet tall, of Vulcan, the Roman god of fire and forge. Riverboat captains, seeing the statue, knew they were rounding the bend in the Ohio River and were coming into Evansville. The mythological god Vulcan was imposing and strong as steel. His wife, Venus, the goddess of love, beauty, sex and fertility epitomized a female. While it may be a stretch, Vulcan and Venus conjure up Arthur and Hannah. Arthur, strong and prominent, and Hannah, a woman filled with desire for beauty and love. I imagine they were a team, meeting each other's needs.

Arthur's position at Vulcan and his service on the Old National Bank board, reinforced Hannah's connections with the wives of prominent Evansville men. If Hannah was out for success, she was succeeding. While on the Old National Bank board, Arthur sat alongside Mr. McCurdy, the father of Hannah's friend Hazel. Austin and James Igleheart, descendants of one of the founding families of Evansville, were also on the Bank board and family friends. Two of the Igleheart brothers founded Swan Flour, which later became part of General Foods with an Igleheart brother at the helm as CEO. Another Igleheart became CEO of Evansville's International Steel Company. Lockie Igleheart was a friend of Hannah's and the woman Ann and Margaret called "Tante." My mother and her sister passed many idyllic summer days at Lockie's house in Newburgh, Indiana overlooking the Ohio River. Hannah and Arthur's friends were cultured, successful and connected. All this was news to me and shed light on my mother and her sister's relationship with success and social standing in their communities.

As many midwest industrialists did in the summer during the early 1900s, Hannah, Arthur and the girls headed north for cooler weather. The destination was Leland, Michigan, a small fishing village on the shores of Lake Michigan. Weathered fishing shanties with nets strung along their sides dotted the docks. A short walk from Leland's Lake Michigan beaches is Lake Leelanau, a small quiet lake for swimming and boating. The Trimbles' connection to Leland was solid. One of my mother's friends who summered in Leland said others commonly referred to a grey, weathered house on the road leading into Indiana Woods (an apt reference given the number of Indiana families in Leland), as "the Trimble house." My mother had fond memories of her youth in Leland. Photos tell much of the Leland story. In one, when about eight years old, she was a passenger whizzing along in a motor boat with a Leland Swim Club logo on her bathing suit. Another featured my mother and her sister still wet from swimming posing with their father and the Rosencranz family, and another was of my mother as a young woman surrounded by young men on a sand dune.

When I was very young, my mother prevailed and we spent a few summers in Leland, until my father insisted we go to New England. He refused to be "a married in," the term for the spouse who married into a family that had summered in Leland for generations. When my children were very young, I insisted we spend a summer vacation in Leland. One of my mother's friends used her connections to find a cottage for the "Trimbles' granddaughter." Examples are piling up that even when married, I searched for what Robert MacFarlane, in his book *Landmarks,* referred to as "the mutual relations of place, language and spirit – how we landmark, and we are landmarked."

Leland was imprinted on me, and returning to a place full of my Trimble lineage gave me a sense of belonging. My husband was accommodating as I pulled him into the Leland community. Hannah didn't seem to mind being Mrs. George Arthur Trimble, "married in" wife of a prominent Midwest industrialist, and relished being a proud member of the Leland community all her life. Summers in Leland, a handsome husband who was a pillar of the community, two young daughters and a network of friends, Hannah had the package many women of that time might have dreamed of having. That package eluded me.

During her married years, when with her children and too happy to spend time in the solitary activity of writing, Hannah's creativity found an oulet in taking photographs to capture the full life she lived. I once again scoured over boxes of photographs and more newspaper articles about the Trimble's social activities. If I couldn't read her words, I was content creating my own story from the dreamy photographs she took and reading between the lines of the newspaper articles. I insist on believing the contrast of starched upright Arthur and Hannah with flair and her "if this don't beat all" attitude was a partnership that worked. Opposites who complemented each other. He may have given structure to the one with a flower in her belt, the one who may have pulled laughter and frivolity out of the one tightly wound. Both were determined, striving after what they valued. Each in their own domain, one with creativity and dreams, the other with structure and order. The trick must be in admiration and appreciation for the traits of the other coupled with a shared vision. Appreciation that each may expand the world of the other. Admiration and not frustration. Admiration and not disappointment. Easy to project this hypothesis when the marriage wasn't the one that was mine.

What happened on Monday, November 25, 1929, three days before Thanksgiving, a little less than four weeks after the stock market crash, redirected Hannah's life, influenced my mother's, and while diluted, flowed on to influence my life. The past is in our present or maybe it is better to say the present emerges from the past. My mother never said a word to me about the specifics of that day, and my heart skipped more than a beat reading what *The Evansville Courier* spelled out in great detail about what happened to forty-one-year-old Hannah sometime after two o'clock. Hannah was away from home, and upon contacting Arthur's office after lunch, she learned he left not feeling well and she went home to check on him. Odd, she must have thought, for him to leave work, as he had been reported to be in good health in the morning, attending to his duties as usual. With his work ethic, even when not feeling well, he would have pushed through. When Hannah returned home, I imagine she saw him, not lying down, but leaning back on the couch, feet straight out in front of him on the floor, tie loosened and stiff collar unbuttoned, both signs the upright and buttoned-up man wasn't well. George Arthur, the Vulcan man, was measured, strong and stable. Hannah flirted with being spontaneous and fun-loving, but as a former teacher she knew how to call a situation to order, taking charge after learning Arthur had called the physician who said the trouble was not considered serious.

Evansville Courier, November 29, 1929

Mrs. Trimble . . . arrived shortly after her husband had when she was told at his office that he had gone home not feeling well. She immediately saw that he was seriously ill, and again called the physician. By the time the family physician arrived at the home, Mr. Trimble's condition had become so bad that there was no possible aid for him and he died soon after.

Hannah had to have been in shock. Margaret and Ann, ages eleven and twelve, were either home when their father died or returned from school shortly thereafter. Either way, seeing their father dead in their home would have been traumatic. With Hannah's mother and father living around the corner, she would have called them immediately. Fanny Rose, whose life since childhood had been filled with unexpected death and tragedy, once again faced the unthinkable. Death was at her door along with the grief of her daughter and two granddaughters. Life for them changed in a few short hours. The depth of grief some say is in proportion to the depth of love.

If it weren't for the lengthy obituary in the *Evansville Courier*, full of storytelling details, I would be in the dark about what happened on November 25th. My mother never talked much about her father and never about the day he died. She did make vague comments about going to "Dad's farm" when she was young. The most information she shared was relative to his career at Vulcan Plow, a story of success and loyalty. An obituary confirmed: "Men of his caliber are not easily found. It is too bad to lose them."

When the stock market crashed, Arthur had leveraged his life insurance policy to keep Vulcan Plow Company afloat, a fact that Hannah didn't learn until after his death. What a shock. No husband. No life insurance. Two teenage daughters. It was the Depression. Hannah was forty-one and on her own. The protected and idyllic life she had as a dreamy child on the banks of the Ohio River, as a young wife, mother, and woman of Evansville and Leland was altered. Words from "Round Trip," her unpublished essay:

> It is not surprising that I was unprepared for the life I must now
> begin at forty.

Unprepared for life at forty. How could anyone be prepared for what she faced? A friend in a condolence letter shored her up, reminded her that she had what Arthur had: "clear-sighted courage, the same ability as a manager."

Thank God for friends who remind us of what we may have forgotten about ourselves. Thank God for the stack of condolence letters tucked into the Maine sea chest with a note wrapped around with the words, "Letters to Hannah," letters that gave me a glimpse into my grandmother's heart-wrenching loss. I teared up reading the word "sorrow" over and over, a word not often heard today. Sadness yes. Grief yes. Sorrow is a deeper, darker well of sadness and desolation. Many powerful words stood out in these condolence letters: assuaged, solace, platitudes, bitterness, destiny. Sadness swept over me for my mother who didn't experience a long rich life with a father.

When I was in my twenties, something made my mother open up in a letter:

> At the age of eleven my security was in one day swept out from under me, tho at that time I think I was so naïve and oblivious to the adult world, and so unquestioning about whether anything would turn out all right, that I don't remember being demolished by my father's sudden death - - - I do remember for years afterwards crying to myself at night, but as you know, Grandmother was a very determined woman - - very emotional, but very determined, and she set out to see that we had opportunities she thought we ought to have. For her teen years, Ann took it quite differently and as I remember was very difficult, for she blamed G-mother for his death - - how, I don't know.

The contradiction in her analysis was puzzling. Not being devastated yet crying herself to sleep for years? For the first time, I gave thought to how her father's death might have affected my mother. I needed multiple losses of my own, her death, my father's death, my divorce, to wake up to what may have shaped my mother's life and mine. Loss and longing, fear and loneliness. The day I read over all the condolence letters, I sat on the floor, as I did the day I found my parent's love letters. I sat on the floor for a long time flooded with emotions, alone.

Married Life

Hannah in her mother's
wedding dress

George Arthur Trimble

George Arthur with daughter Ann

Ann and Margaret

Leland, Michigan: Arthur on the right, Ann and Margaret
in the middle, Joe Iglehart, family friend, far left

Ann and Margaret

Hannah in Pasadena after
Arthur's death

Chapter Twelve

Facing Life on her Own

Hannah was beginning life without a spouse, and I was doing the same. Middle-aged single women forging ahead, taking stock of our lives, taking stock of ourselves. Hannah's mother was around the corner as a guide. I didn't have mine. On my own, I faced the need to look at myself with total honesty. What was it about me that led me to this juncture, divorced? What did I have within to face my new life, push back fears, embrace knowing myself better, and work on what needed work? An inside repair job was before me, and Hannah had the potential to be my guide. In the few years since her letters were in my hand, she had expanded my awareness of how my family marched through challenges. I hoped she left more bread crumbs.

After Arthur's death Hannah gathered up Ann and Margaret and headed to Pasadena for six months, a dramatic decision. My mother never explained why Hannah up and went west, a move which I now understand. Both Hubbses and Stevensons fled to California to escape tragedy. Hannah followed suit. November in Indiana meant grey, cold and dreary days. Pasadena would be warm and sunny, a backdrop for healing as Hannah sorted out her next step.

Pasadena, dubbed the Indiana Colony of California, had lured many from Indiana. Come west was the message from her relatives. Beauty lured. Her future before her, Hannah posed in a photo in front of the Pasadena house she rented, hands behind her back, gazing off into the distance, wondering what will come next. Rare for her to not look directly at the photographer. She was dressed in a white sailor top, skirt, and tights. No black mourning clothes for Hannah. She was ready to step up and tackle the challenge.

When Hannah returned to Evansville, the Depression was underway, and the reality of supporting herself and two daughters was before her. Vulcan Plow was being held together in part by Arthur's life insurance funds. Hannah needed a source of livelihood, and she rationalized her decision on what to do in her article, "Gladly Teach," *Southern Literary Messenger*, 1943.

> When in a day which now seems long ago it had become necessary to separate my assets from liabilities in order to earn a living, I discounted accounting as the Job. I had never even counted my laundry, preferring to lose a sheet now and then. I could not play with the idea of becoming a statistician, nor had I built up a past which would recommend me as an executive's secretary.
>
> Those legal documents which had punctuated my life gathered dust in unused sugar bowls, and even wishful thinking could not locate the gas bill. I dropped grocery slips into the garbage can and made no mailing lists for my Christmas cards. I lost my car keys, forgot my family's birthdays and confused my friends' addresses. I never read my insurance policies.
>
> But I was very happy, and I felt at home with little children. This was not strange for that was exactly where I had been for fourteen years. In the end my friends decided for me. I could teach.
>
> Before I went to see the Superintendent, to whom I was not a stranger, I had the heels of my shoes straightened. "I'm pretty old," I said. "Nonsense," he answered robustly.

So, I went to college again and took what was called
"Education." There was more to it than met the eye . . . I
was given an Intelligence test. When I asked my department
head what ailed me, he said I had a bad sense of inter-spatial
relationships. I could not deny it.

By this time, I had discovered from my psychology books
that I had gone out of style, so when I was again given sheets of
questions which I suspected would diagnose my temperamental
weaknesses I was ready. I put crosses by the right answers and
emerged a dyed-in-the-wool extrovert with aptitudes.

But my twos, when I was forced to add them, still failed
to make four. It was plain that I did not have a mathematical
mind. How the Gods must have laughed when I became part
of the Public School System!

Hannah's liabilities were Arthur's assets. For him all must be tidy,
in order and accounted for. If her self-described disorganization was
present in her married life, the dynamics with Arthur would have been
intriguing. Liabilities aside, with assets in spades, she became a self-
proclaimed renegade teacher and earned a reputation writing about it.

"Milk Can be Homogenized but Not Children," *New York
Times Magazine,* May 2 1948.

I am a well-greased cog in the machinery of a public
school . . . I have become a Grade A teacher (not Government
inspected). But I have subversive leanings. I cannot bear to see
a creative child like Bill conform to the mold which I must
offer as a group pattern . . . he (Bill) was coming down with
the disease which is endemic in overcrowded schoolrooms. He
was becoming introjected. That means that without conscious
choice he was soaking up his background as a piece of bread
soaks up gravy. He eventually would disappear into it. It meant
he would lose the flavor that made him Bill, or else he would
mistrust it and hide it away. It did not make me happy to be a
party to this crime.

Similar to her grandfather Stevenson, Hannah's message was effective, astute and filled with creative metaphors. Her opinions were like gravy to bread, freely poured out for others to absorb. I suspect her insight into the inner world of children and ways of reaching them was the convergence of childhood fond memories and disappointments, her highly sensitive nature, a penchant for flirting with what was outside the norm and an ability to see what lay beneath the surface. Her mother's role can't be discounted. Mothers influencing mothers.

Hannah's mother, the tenth of ten children, was the "baby" of the family, a position that often keeps childhood alive long after that age has passed. If that was true for Fanny Rose, she and her maiden sister Hannah Hubbs doted on little Hannah and set the stage for a childhood rich in creativity and imagination. Adults can tarnish or polish the delights of a child. Hannah's mother and her Aunt Hannah Hubbs were "that feeling," and Hannah wanted to be "that feeling" to her students. She succeeded and was witness on a daily basis to the secret fountains of delight which children provide, a certain distraction from her grief, a way to be surrounded with admiring faces.

Children give invitations to be spontaneous. They know how to reach hearts and whose hearts they can reach. Children sense when an adult has his or her inner child well and alive. They sense adults who understand and respect their world, a world that Hannah described as similar to hers. That similarity wasn't lost on Hannah and not lost on me when reading these passages in "Milk Can be Homogenized But Not Children."

> Creative children do not need to be set apart and tenderly nurtured. They do not have the delicacy of a pale moccasin flower in rain-wet woods, and their secret fountains of delight do not always sparkle with moonshine. They are often quite robust and speak as of the gutter. But they are not joiners – they suffer regimentation badly and they need time and overtime to ponder.

> Milk can be homogenized but not children. No two move at the same speed in the same direction. Each is altered by a very personal and sometimes accidental understanding of a teacher.

No matter how many degrees you have, you will have to do some quick thinking of your own when you face forty children – or maybe forty-five.

It is this renegade half of me that is allergic on assembly-line methods.

There never was a question in my mind about what career I would pursue. Hannah taught third grade. Before the war, my mother taught kindergarten. Both created a warm and magical childhood for me that I wanted to pass along. Teaching a class of ten or fifteen preschoolers when in my twenties, I marveled at middle-aged Hannah, intrepid as she was, teaching forty or forty-five children, most of whom came from tough situations. When in her prime, photographs revealed she had a magnetic presence which she cast out to draw in her students. Her writing confirmed she liked being "on stage," an orchestra leader for creativity. Good teachers are performers. Hannah's essays reflected a deep passion for her work with children. Never a grumble, though maybe a comment or two, about managing a large class. Children and Hannah were taken in by beauty, a way to dream themselves out of challenges, marveling in small discoveries, a way to push back fear. The same held true for my mother and was true for me.

> "Whatever Miss T Eats Turns Into Miss T", unpublished essay:
> For twenty years which are behind me now I worked with little children - - children we tend to call the underprivileged. Some were - - some were not. No child is really underprivileged until his thoughts are muddied by some social pattern. In each batch that came to me up thru second grade, there were sensitive, potential dreamers. There were also the tough guys. But no matter what the stamp of personality had laid upon each child, one thing was standard, like equipment basic on a car. That was a sense of beauty. They found beauty in the alleys, on a city dump, in railroad yards and in a muddy creek where, now and then, dead bodies floated. And, because I was,

to them,"that feeling," as my mother and Aunt Hannah were to me, they were not too shy to share it. It was my job to show them how to make this beauty into dreams. I don't mean those dreams which are not more than static sense impressions. I mean those that come alive, as action. "When I write stories," Betty said, "I don't feel lonely now." Adults would phrase that differently."Who lives with beauty hath no need of fear."

"That feeling" is elusive, hard to describe. In moments when angst crept in about my life after divorce, I pulled up that "feeling" of security, of being loved, and embraced beauty.

With the unimaginable loss from the early death of her husband, Hannah's decision to earn a living by teaching opened other doors for her. She became an advocate for children in an era when children were to be seen and not heard. Mrs. Trimble, third-grade teacher at the Fulton School, was making her mark beyond Evansville. Her scrapbook about her publications was filled with admiration letters from across the country. One admirer had seen what I was only now discovering and had written: "She looks down underneath things and finds out why."

Between 1938 and 1961, in addition to her *New York Times* piece about not homogenizing children, Hannah published ten articles on teaching and the creative process. She was a frequent contributor to *Childhood Education,* and published in the *Southern Literary Messenger*, the *Literary Cavalcade, Progressive Education, Family Circle, Parents Magazine,* and *Baby Talk*. The Library of Congress offered up articles I didn't know existed, several of which included the creative writing of her students, the needed antidote during her dark times and the dark years of WWII. Light entertaining voices of children were uplifting.

"How come I spell ilanoysentrul is because it aint hord," *Family Circle*, 1948:
  They're beauty in the eyes of young beholders, third-grade level. They're imagination. They are human documents,

relieving tensions. They're case records. And not one child
could or would have written one of them had he denied
himself the words he couldn't spell.

To translate, "ilanouysentrul" is the Illinois Central Railroad.

Hannah extolled the value of teaching creative writing long before
it was in fashion. That was "Oh, so Hannah." A woman on the leading
edge of the curve. The photograph of her as a young woman, hat askew,
tablecloth around her shoulders, her writing on the back of the photo, "If
this don't beat all," could have been her motto. Hannah was determined
to beat all, step out from the crowd no matter what she did. Her views
on teaching reading were also not the norm. While she acknowledged
the merit of regimented drills, delight had to be part of the mix, and
her delight in words and reading was contagious. She couldn't contain
herself. Her passion for words and stories made "gabbing" about them
a core part of her teaching. My admiration was growing, and I shared
her articles with my teacher friends.

> "We Learn to Read," *Childhood Education*, September, 1938:
> Here again I am old-fashioned. We have no library corner.
> We have no formal story hour. We just read and gabble about
> the stories because we can't help it. With it all we are learning
> to gather up ragged edges of time and use them.

> "Out of the Mouths of – the Third Grade," *New York Times
> Magazine*, June 22, 1947:
> Children are always busting to talk to you. Always they are
> being shushed. One day, in self-protection, I suggested that
> they write down what they had on their minds, and I prom-
> ised to read it. They supplied what every teacher's heart needs
> overmuch – constant replenishment from the eternal well of
> childhood. It is because the world today needs such replenish-
> ment that I pass them along as they came to me – completely
> honest, uncorrected unchanged, unexpurgated, revealing.

When I started looking for more material from my grandmother, I discovered an envelope, postmarked January 8, 2002, which I had shoved in a drawer. I have no recollection of paying attention to its contents when it arrived or why my mother mailed it. Inside were fifty-three yellowed cracked pages of words from Hannah's third graders which she had typed up. I retyped these handwritten gems and realized that she knew something I had discovered. Typing someone else's words transports you out of your world into theirs. Transporting out of the land of "too many days alone" was a healthy tonic for Hannah and me. It would have taken Hannah hours to type what she did, many hours lost in the inner world of children, seeding ideas in Hannah. Her creative use of words was enhanced by her students' words, and her creativity brought out the same in her students, reciprocity at its best. A few gems, third-grade spelling included:

> Them leaves over there in the baked bean jar on the windy sill looks like someones waving their hands to you.

> One day Mrs. Trimble's daughter got two twin boys. She got a telegram and when she went to the office to read it, and come to the door and said "pass." And she showed us a bean bag frog and she held it by the neck and dropped it and it layd flat on its body. And she said "This is how I feel."

> Mrs. Trimble give me a flower. It was a daisy. Before I could get home with it it's head just wouldn't hold up. It was just like when my mother starched my dress and after I wore it a while it just flopped down.

Reading her unpublished essay, "There you Have It," I tried to not let her words permeate and burrow within me, but it was futile. She percolated ideas, as old coffee pots percolated the sound and smell of coffee. I am guilty of stealing the word permeate, which then led to thoughts of coffee. I twitched the word out, to steal another of her words. There you have it. It is quite fun to play with the words Hannah played with, though I dare not try to emulate when she wrote about the sublime. That domain is hers.

> "They Call it Creative Writing," *Progressive Education*, February 1943:
>   My spirit is not colored by sunsets pierced by snowy moun-
> tains. I stand on a levee and look across a muddy river to see
> my sunsets, but that does not mean that my own word images
> do not feed my soul. Even with B1 added, we cannot live by
> bread alone.

Hannah was giving me early sprouts of confidence. I was digging down deep into the cool dark place within, a place a voice of mine told me to avoid. When meeting with a therapist during the divorce, when asked how I was feeling, my reply was, "I think I feel . . ." His reply to my reply, "I don't want to know what you think. I want to know what you feel." I was stumped. Being tucked in with Hannah's writing gave me burgeoning security in my voice as I marched into the world, a woman who smiled checking the marital status box on various forms, "divorced." Relief. A woman starting to use words about feelings.

~

Hannah grabbed hold of her assets and marched forward. A single parent with extended family close at hand, Hannah was determined to make sure her daughters had the opportunities she thought they should have. She made it possible for Ann and Margaret to attend sleepaway summer camp, an experience that I imagine influenced my mother's decision to send my sister and me to sleep-away camp. The experience, we were told, built character. It did. Hannah also went to summer camp, as a counselor to earn money when school wasn't in session. Her 1943 *Southern Literary Messenger* essay, "Round Trip," about this experience started with:

Even a dumb bunny could do anything in a camp, my college age daughter wrote me reassuringly.

And continued with descriptions of how her character was renovated:

. . . I was unprepared for the life I must now begin at forty. No-one can say that I have not honestly tried to learn what I could. But I was still a half-baked modernist when I became over confident and accepted a job in a SUMMER CAMP FOR GIRLS.

I knew nothing of camps, although of course I had sent my children. It was then the only acceptable thing to do. I had remained at home and had spoken sturdily to my friends of the beautiful simplicity of such a life – of sunrise in the Carolina mountains and of the spiritual benefits to a body unbound save by shorts and a halter.

My first discoveries were that I lacked confidence to climb into the upper bunk of a double-decked bed. I was not adept at collective bargaining for a seat in the John - - I did not penetrate crowded shower rooms with assurance, and a mental hazard prevented my stepping out of a sleeping garment before I rooted around in a bag to find something to wear to flag-raising. I did not care to begin the day with a song and I definitely prefer coffee to cocoa for breakfast. So, I avoided issues. While the sky was still grey above mist that clung to the lake, I wrapped myself in a dressing gown and sneaked past sleeping cabins to the shower house. Only a frog and a couple of snakes, or an occasional spider were there before me, cooling themselves among forgotten bits of yesterday's soap that dissolved in pools on the uneven floor. The shower offered sporting adventures. Sometimes the pump went off when I was making my best scenic effects with soap, and usually my swimming shoes parked outside the curtain, floated away with the discard.

Hannah's camp experience added to her realization that her life had plenty of comforts, and despite the hard times following Arthur's death, she was preparing herself for life after forty, alone. Her ending:

> Three days before the actual closing of camp, I knew that I could stand it no longer. I felt that I was ready to welcome senile old age. Without the help of a book, camp had taught me how to Live Alone and Like It.

Feelings about living alone, once not to her liking, changed when the camp experience didn't fit her expectation for communal living. Hannah debuted her streak of being more than particular about what suited her, and her writing offered more glimpses into her character, a woman who "wrote sensuously" and who worked herself "up to a sentimental climax." I smiled with images those words conjured up. I had been in a sensual desert for too long.

> One of my duties . . . was to publish a paper. I went off alone and sat under a tree where I felt I would be most sensitive to atmosphere and began. I looked at the lake which, as a matter of fact, was sluggish at the moment, and wrote sensuously,
>   "Sped by the wind from the river,
>   Rippling, dark green, shot with silver —"
> I began to suspect that I was leaning too heavily upon Mr. Longfellow, so I tried again.
>   "Have you seen the bobbing lanterns
>   On the worn path to the well?
>   Like fireflies underneath the trees, before the last light bell?"
> I worked myself up to a sentimental climax, entirely satisfied. My public did not comment. I come, however, of stubborn stock. I studied my background and substituted realism for sentiment before I wrote next Monday's issue.

I was ten when my camp experience toughened me up. Now I have a better glimpse into why I was sent to camp. My mother was sent, Hannah sent herself, and to follow suit, my sister and I were sent. Note that I wrote "sent" versus "went." My sister and I weren't asked. We were sent from Michigan to New Hampshire to an eight-week girl's camp with an Episcopal bent. Episcopalian was far from our Unitarian upbringing. Our uniforms were brown-and-white seersucker tops and brown shorts. For Sunday chapel we wore white, pleated skirts with sailor tops and brown satin ties, not unlike the uniform my mother wore in her camp photo. Our sneakers had to be unblemished white. The Saturday ritual was to whiten them with roll-on shoe polish. Each morning before breakfast, we lined up outside the dining hall, one in front of the other, put our hands out, and our fingernails were given a score. The score was recorded and added up all summer to determine if we deserved a "nail badge" to sew on our camp sweater. After nail inspection, we proceeded into the dining hall to be scored on table manners. Always cut your toast into four parts. Cutting it into halves was acceptable, best was cutting it into quarters. Our two-person cabins were inspected each day. No wrinkles in the blanket. Nothing on the floor except our camp trunk and shoes neatly lined up. All clothes folded just so. If none of our belongings ended up in "the pound," we earned a badge for not losing anything. At the end of eight weeks, we collected any badges our character merited. Each week at chapel, we recited the "Be Strong"* poem. If I am honest, that poem shored me up. I share only a bit, as a bit will do:

> Be Strong. We are not here to play to dream to drift, we have hard work to do and loads to lift, shun not the struggle face it, tis God's gift. Be strong, It matters not how deep entrenched the wrong . . .

The poem ends with,

> Faint not, fight on, tomorrow comes the song.

---

* "Be Strong," Maltbie Davenport Babcock, 1901

I learned to walk in formation by height, in silence, and to be strong as I marched through the woods to the chapel by the lake. I was short, always near the front of the line. Throughout my five summers at camp, I had moments of feeling inferior. A feeling Hannah knew. I didn't own the brown hiking shoes like the girls from the Main Line of Philadelphia. I didn't go to a private school as those girls did. I wasn't a tennis star as those girls were. There were clumps of Main Line girls. I was a singleton from outside Detroit. Even though Grosse Pointe could be seen as similar to the Main Line, I felt inferior. I wasn't raised to feel superior. My mother tried to find those brown shoes for me. No success.

My mother's best friend in Grosse Pointe went to that camp in the early 1900s and hated it. My mother sent my sister and me anyway. I sent my daughter to that camp. She hated it. She told me she felt inferior. I need to ask her if it built character. "Faint not, fight on, tomorrow comes the song."

~

There was no denying Hannah had a competitive streak, a drive to "beat all," to use, again, one of her expressions. In addition to her grandfather and husband, Hannah's cousin Gertrude Hubbs, who grew up in Evansville, was another inspiration. Gertrude, born eight years before Hannah, was the surviving daughter of Fanny Rose's brother, John. Counteracting the shame of his "ill fated" Hubbs family, John made sure his children had the best. Gertrude graduated from Wellesley, well-educated for a woman born in 1800. She married an Evansville man and went on to send her daughter Hanna to Vassar. Hannah no doubt took note. Gertrude rose up through education, and Hannah made sure her daughters would also. With Hannah's determination to seek the best, whether camp or college, she obtained scholarships for Ann and Margaret to Swarthmore College. No small feat. How they selected Swarthmore, a college with Quaker origins, or most likely how Hannah selected Swarthmore for her daughters, may have been linked to the Quaker Hubbses and Basnetts from the area around the time Swarthmore was founded. Faint not, strive on.

Ann and Margaret, one year apart at Swarthmore, fulfilled Hannah's expectations. The Swarthmore yearbook captured Ann's creative flair:

> With sphinx-like sang-froid and a riotous colour-sense, sloe-eyed
> Ann slashes her modernistic way through Sketch Club, designing
> and executing Little Theatre stage-sets, and turning out indispens-
> able and enticing decors for college dances. Confident in her own
> ability to pull through anything, quietly but definitely self-reliant,
> she also turns the battery of her concentration-power on a zo major,
> combining brilliant work with a heavy social schedule.

Margaret's yearbook tagged her:

> . . . the delightful paradox . . . determined and efficient, she will
> study seriously for hours, then be put out of the libe for laughing . . .
> at one time as serious as a church, at the next burlesquing modern
> dancing in the Freshman show.

Never having seen my mother dance, I can't connect her with burlesque modern dancing. The trajectory of the years changed her. As I launched after college, her letters included messages about life, not once but several times, messages about missing a good laugh and looking back on years being silly, loving to dance. I tucked these letters away, only to find her messages most instructive thirty years later with thoughts on how my marriage changed me.

I've read my mother's words over and over since I pulled her letters out of the drawer and reflected on losing my fun side. After my divorce, a friend who only knew me during the most stressful years of my marriage, commented, "I never knew you could be so much fun." I hadn't realized what I had lost until she pointed that out. Maybe my father saw my fun had gone and thought the humor in Hannah's letters would inspire me. He was right. Until reading her writing, I never associated fun with my grandmother. Somewhere along the way, like my mother, she too lost her fun. I don't need to carry on that part of the legacy. With that backdrop, I was relieved when a friend saw my fun returning. Released and far enough out from a tense marriage, I was relaxing into laughter. Hannah's comment about me which burrowed in at first reading, rose up: "She is turning out to be a hilarious extrovert—the only one in our blood stream." Yes, Hannah was helping my former self re-emerge. I was determined not to lose my fun again.

Chapter Thirteen

Hannah Steps Out in the World

Fear never seemed far behind Hannah. It trailed her like a shadow, as it did my mother. Hannah's approach was to face it head on, the way she did when trying to beat her brothers up the ridgepole, and the way she did when she moved to Pasadena. My mother kept her fear under wraps, but despite efforts to tidy up any signs of a woman not in control, evidence of it seeped out sideways. Both spent time in their heads where the land of worry and fear can grow at a rapid pace, especially when there isn't a someone or something to distract. Despite having days rich with relief that I no longer had to contend with an empty marriage, fear crept in when my financial advisor warned me that having two houses across the country was not sustainable in the long run. What the long run meant, I avoided asking.

My immediate worries centered on when my kids would settle. The remnants of divorce were hanging on longer than I expected. More than five years had gone by. Somehow I was deluded thinking once children hit age twenty-one, they would find their footing. Not true. I was serving as a ballast in each of their lives. Their father detached himself from day-to-day fathering, and I was, as my mother used to warn about single mothers, "the one left holding the bag." I was holding a bag brimming with love for my children. I couldn't imagine not holding each of them with care, but I knew the limits of what I could do and feared the impact of the divorce and parenting mistakes I had made. One of Hannah's outlets when fear approached was going to her typewriter. My solace was typing what she typed, gleaning whatever I could. I made no edits, no word changes, pure Hannah, unadulterated. Like reading a book I didn't want to end, I put aside my Hannah project for long stretches of time. When my life became lumpy, I pulled out my laptop and Hannah binder to distract myself from whatever my newest fear was. Owning two homes was a huge lump. Where I belonged was another.

Having worked my way through her war letters, Hannah anointed the next one, "Sunday Morning." The envelope, rare in that it was saved, was postmarked March 24, 1946. Hannah's jumbled thoughts required multiple readings as she packed in more than the paragraphs could carry, or maybe it was my jumbled thoughts commingling with hers. One thing was clear. Fear had reappeared.

> Margaret dear,
> . . . thank you darling for telling me. It wouldn't be something
> that you could understand until you are fifty eight, that in the
> forevermore of the verities of life, quick responses in words is not
> within my grasp. Instead with a pen in my hand, I sit and look at
> something that is not here. There is so much more to it than having
> someone else to love. Nature is very cunning when it leaves us unful-
> filled and empty without children. You would be – I would have
> been. Nature makes youth toss its hat in the air, unafraid and laugh.
> It makes you feel an important part of a place. A wonderful world.
> With a hand in mine! And it makes you, at 58, echo the same words,
> "Yes, a wonderful world had I been wiser."
>
> Please forgive me for talking so, but it seemed this or no letter, for
> there were not other things to say that did not sound artificial. I
> would have died if you had not had a baby, but to me now its like

looking into the face of God and feeling frightened. But it is also like waiting for an alarm clock to sweep out night thoughts – you roll out, snap up the blind, and go to work, facing the sun. I do that every morning. We all do. If I talked this way to Ann, she thinks me a melodramatic fool. You will not understand, but you will feel your way toward me without understanding.

I have more money within reach than I have had. I will keep it free – tell me when your savings need replenishing – and thank Rich too for writing.

Lovingly,

Mother

Could I maybe tell one person so that I can talk of you – Aunt Jess or Tante or Carrie – no one of them would break your confidence.

Margaret was pregnant, and Hannah was delighted and frightened. How could she not be? Her mother's first born twins died as infants. One of Ann's first-born twins died as an infant. Now Hannah was awaiting the birth of Margaret's first child. Sediments from the past were bubbling up, laying bare inner thoughts and feelings, many hard to comprehend. Her statement that there is much more to life than having someone to love, meant what? With many readings, her line, "the forevermore of the verities of life" became clearer. With age and life experiences, complexities bring a search for life's truths. I was at the same approximate stage in life as Hannah was when she wrote those words. Margaret, a new mother-to-be, wasn't far enough down life's timeline to understand what her mother was muddling about to explain. Without a husband, Hannah was alone with her thoughts, begging her daughter to let her share the news with her inner circle of friends. Without a partner, having conversations with oneself about the verities of life can result in thinking that loops and loops around. That I know too well.

Hannah brought up a topic that was on the list of what was not often talked about in our family: money. After almost two decades, Hannah was out from under financial strain. As her great-grandfather Charles Basnett did for his daughter Sarah Ann Hubbs, and as Hannah's Uncle John did for his sister Fanny Rose, Hannah was offering support for Margaret, who in turn did the same for my sister and me, and I have done the same for my children. Five generations helping with funds. My ex disapproved of that practice, a core value for me, one of several that widened the Grand Canyon gap between us that was impossible to bridge. Somehow when saying, "Yes, I will," to a marriage proposal, I overlooked the importance of shared core values.

Hannah came into money sometime in the mid 1940s. The source was never explained, another of those off-limit topics. Good guesses were that her mother left money after her death in 1946, that Vulcan reimbursed the leveraged life insurance policy, or that company stock Arthur owned had accrued value. With more money within reach and her daughters secure in their own families, Hannah, not one to be left on the sidelines, was poised to expand her horizons. Friends Josephine, Frances, Carrie, and Hazel had all traveled abroad. Josephine's son, John, had developed many international connections through an international affairs degree at Yale, a stint in Tampico during the Navy, and an assignment in the Foreign Service, serving as vice consul and third secretary in Gdansk, Warsaw, Munich, and Bremen. John was the likely inspiration for Hannah's first trip sometime before 1944 which she alluded to in a "Dear Rich" letter:

> (Josephine) . . . is going to Mexico tomorrow . . . I wonder what she will find for herself in Mexico - - it will not be in the wonderful, filthy markets which I loved to frequent - - or by way of the flea ridden buses . . . She is a dainty creature who moves about in compartments.

Without a photo of Josephine, I can't conjure up that dainty creature. Hannah was hardly dainty, and given what I was learning, I was not surprised that she loved filthy markets. Hannah moved easily between everyday people and those of prominence, between her third-grade students who lived near alleys in Evansville and those who made their homes in Evansville's prestigious Riverside district. Would it be surprising that Arthur would have been appalled by filthy markets and Hannah's desire to wander around them? Could I make a case that while Hannah enjoyed the benefits of being Mrs. George Arthur Trimble, she was a bit stifled?

Sleuthing out Hannah's travels was like sleuthing out her publications at the Library of Congress. It took some doing. During the evenings and weekends when I was alone and without plans, I searched online for travel manifests and newspaper articles and hit many jackpots. *The Evansville Press* and the *Courier* told of Hannah's two-month European trip with friends, confirmed by a June 15, 1949 ship's log of passengers on the Queen Elizabeth II, sailing from New York to South Hampton. Hannah was listed by passport #17891 with a length of intended stay, two months; occupation, teacher. Josephine had traveled on the Queen Elizabeth two years earlier, possible proof that friends spurred Hannah on. If Hannah had any fears about traveling, she pushed them aside, grabbed her friend Carrie, then newly widowed, and said, "Let's go." Or maybe they both looked at each other and said the same. Hannah and Carrie were off to Europe.

On her return to Indiana, Hannah submitted an article to the *Ladies Home Journal* about her trip. She had already published on a topic other than teaching: "An Old Lady Refuses to Be Aged," *New York Times Magazine*, November 12, 1950, and was on a mission to publish more, and the *Ladies Home Journal* seemed on a mission to secure these from her. The editor's request, November 16, 1950:

> What I am really hoping for is that you may have another piece
> either on the typewriter or in your mind which could be described
> by that sentence quoted in the Times, "This is a feminine and per-
> sonal outcry which excludes all problems of all men." If so, please do
> send it to us.

No further comment about my grandmother's proclivity to voice opinions and outcries, though I wonder what her feminine outcry was in 1950.

The *Ladies Home Journal* turned down her trip manuscript which was not the outcry they requested, though encouragement was clear to keep submitting. The editor knew Hannah was worth pulling into the Journal, and I join the editor in wanting more from Hannah on issues relating to women. From Laura Brookman, Managing Editor:

> Your manuscript about the trip to Europe isn't "a crazy thing." I read it with a lot of enjoyment and have asked some others on our staff to read it. I don't think it's quite a magazine article, (maybe I'm wrong) but I am more than ever convinced, after reading it, that you should be writing for the Journal.
>
> You said in your letter that you're not a writer. All right, so long as you "just write things," I'll settle for that. All we need to do, it seems to me, is find the subject you'd like to write about and there could be no better way to do this than to have lunch together. I hope that you will decide to spend Christmas in Boston, and stop off here en route. You are invited to lunch any day . . . but I hope it will be a Wednesday so that Hugh Kahler, who is our fiction editor, can join us. He is a friend of George Stevens at Lippincott's. I'm glad they're interested in turning "The Old Lady" into a book. If so, there is no reason why it couldn't appear in the Journal first; we work closely with all the publishers.
>
> Thank you so much for your letters and manuscript. I hope you enjoy your stay in Florida – but not too much because I'm looking forward to that lunch date.

A subsequent letter from the editor expressed disappointment that Hannah did not come to Philadelphia en route to Boston, though the letter included a "wish for the New Year that it will bring Hannah Trimble to the Journal." I was shocked that Hannah passed up an invitation that opened the door for her to publish a book, an opportunity confirmed by a letter from the Managing Editor at J.B. Lippincott. The Journal was not Hannah's first prestigious luncheon invite. In 1948. the editor of the *Sunday New York Times* wrote:

> Didn't you once say you were going to be passing through New York this summer? We shall ceremoniously take you to lunch at Sardi's or Schraff's or the Automat, or any other place of your choice.

Hannah would not be cavalier about such invitations. She pasted these invite letters in her scrapbook. Why not a scrap of information from her about why she did not go? As I read these clippings, I was growing more and more frustrated about my family's "Let's not talk about it" philosophy.

Unless there is an article hiding somewhere, Hannah never got to the Journal and never published a book, though one of her articles made it into *Background and Foreground: An Anthology of Articles from the New York Times Magazine*, 1960, in the chapter entitled: "Male, Female and Offspring." She was in good company with prominent men in that anthology: Albert Einstein, Bertrand Russell, Tennessee Williams, John D. Rockefeller, James Thurber, Russell Baker, and Ashley Montagu. As for well-known female company in the book, they were few and far between: Rebecca West, Phyllis McGinley. Now that should be an outcry, despite my pride that my grandmother's work was included.

Hannah made a name for herself. The Times wanted more from her: " . . . you might have an article in your head on Enjoying Bad Habits." How I wish she had written that one. Being one to do as she pleased, she grabbed hold of what captured her heart as she marched into old age. A sentence in her Sunday Times article on aging almost but not quite foretold the future:

> I have developed "mental resources" and in rarer instances, a sense of humor, which should succor my old age and entertain me even if I fall down and break a hip

Hannah was off and away, and I was deep into researching passenger manifests to document her travels. Next up: Pan American World Airways to Lisbon, Portugal, on March 27, 1952, a date confirming she no longer was teaching. On this trip, as with the last, she went with friends. My level of excitement reading about who joined her reflected my less-than-adventurous life. If Hannah vicariously enjoyed young love through my parents early married years, I was vicariously enjoying Hannah's worldwide travels.

There was benefit in reading, re-reading, and typing up her words, multiple opportunities to link Hannah to friends, a couple of whom popped up as companions on her travels.

> Ah-h-h . . . My little maid. When she says "Wee, wee, mushrar," she sings it – sounds just like a wood thrush on a twig. I know you feel "repugnant" (quote Alice Fraser]) to such thoughts so early in the morning, but I can't help it. [Paris, 1955]

> There is one from Hazel and from Bee, a fat one from Alice Fraser, [Edna Page, from Paris, on the way to Minneapolis. Austria 1955]

Edna and Alice are now on my list of the who's who of Hannah's friends, along with Josephine, Carrie, Tante, Jess, Hazel and Frances. Her cadre of compatriots was growing. I added in Bee, who taught high school with Hannah's sister-in-law Edith Trimble and who she called out by name along with Edna and Alice, in a 1955 Europe letter salutation, "Dear Everybody." Never ever discount female friends, I reminded myself.

Calling Alice and Edna: how did you two women from Minnesota come to know Hannah? Flour and mills may be the connection. Alice's grandfather, Francis Bean, started a flour mill which became the International Milling Company in 1910 when it purchased Robin Hood Flour. Enter Evansville's Igleheart family, owners of Swan Flour which, when merging with General Foods, appointed Austin Igleheart, a bank director colleague and friend of Hannah's husband, CEO. The Trimble – Igleheart connection had to have led to the Alice connection, and Alice led to Edna. Hannah didn't ignore what connections brought. The Swan Flour family socialized with the Robin Hood Flour family, and Hannah met Alice. To quote one of Hannah's Europe letters:

> In the bus were four Americans - - one, a woman from New Jersey sat next to me. We were instantly sympatica, like me and Alice Fraser. [Vienna to Nurnberg (Nuremberg), 1955]

Hannah and Alice were sympatica. Alice introduced Edna to Hannah, and they took off as friends.

This trio on that Pan American flight had several things in common. Each were widows: Edna age seventy-four, Alice age sixty-nine, and Hannah, the youngest, age sixty-four. These women were worldly, with families who had made their mark. Edna's mother, Martha, born in 1843, was among the first two dozen female physicians licensed in Minnesota, and was a well-known Boston suffragist and close friend with Lucy Stone. Alice's father was described as a millionaire Minnesota flour mill owner. How I wish I could have witnessed the conversation between Hannah, Alice, and Edna on their way to Lisbon. A dynamite trio. While reading and fantasizing about her Grandfather Stevenson and his influential network, I felt the way Hannah must have felt—proud. A pang of remorse set in. Feelings of pride were to be tamped down in my family. Striving for competence, yes. Glowing with pride, no. More than once I have brushed off a compliment from a friend, and each time friends suggested a simple "thank you" from me would be in order. I started a mental list of needed repairs to my inner workings while reveling silently in Hannah's triumphs. She had no trouble doing exactly that, though silent she wasn't. The least I can do is bow to my accomplished female friends, women making a mark in the world.

Knowing Hannah's flight landed in Lisbon confirmed that her third *New York Times* article, "Cherchez le Spring: A Tourist Tracks it from Morocco to Norway," March 7, 1954, was a result of this trip. In this article, Hannah let everyone know she ventured by car, bus, and plane to Lisbon, Lucerne, Tangiers, Morocco, Granada, the Alps, Norway, Sweden, France, Germany, and England. A sixty-four-year-old woman who, to quote her article, ". . . on impulse, followed Spring," was prolific and passionate, wrapped up in images of flowers and forests and not shy to broadcast it. Her words flowed with pure joy, sweeping the reader into the beauty she embraced. Restraint, if any, was cast off. There was a lot Hannah couldn't resist. She was seduced by the sublime. Whether on this spring journey across the Atlantic with her fellow widows or down the river in Newburgh, Indiana to the garden of Lockie Igleheart, aka "Tante," Hannah feasted on flowers. Her first few lines in "Cherchez le Spring . . .":

> My memories are splashed with colors of gardens I have not planted.
> I have loved them and left them – gardens of every sort . . .
> Collecting gardens may become a fever, like collecting stamps. The
> tail begins to wag the dog.

I have returned to this article multiple times, lingering over her rich fantastical dance with words:

> Spring in the Alps is a dab of forget-me-nots under an apple tree,
> pink-soft with blossoms. It lay for the looking, first in the valleys.
> Flowers starred the grass under clouds of white cherry. Then, shiver-
> ing, crisp wild narcissus, advanced up the slopes, drifting in passes
> where wind over melting snow, chilled the sunshine.

In addition to my collection of words Hannah wrote about herself, I have begun a collection called Hannah's passions: gardens, children, friends, nature, beauty, photography, literature, poems, travel, and writing. A collection of her sustenance, reflecting on mine. With the verities of life before me, there is no quick response as I consider her words: "there is much more to it than having someone to love."

Hannah Steps Out

CHERCHEZ LE SPRING

Tourist tracks it from Morocco to Norway.

By HANNAH TRIMBLE

MY memories are splashed with colors of gardens I have not planted. I have loved them and left them—gardens of every sort— vegetable, window sill, roadside and meadow, forest and dooryard. My pet is a little birch log, hollowed out and stuffed full of eidelweiss. It was nailed to 'a roof on the Jungfrau. Then there was a bus in Lucerne. Under its windows were boxes, bobbing with pansies. And everywhere I went it was spring.

Collecting gardens may become a fever, like collecting stamps. The tail begins to wag the dog. Last year I flew to Lisbon, crossed from Algeciras to Tangiers, drove across Morocco and then, on impulse, turned around and followed spring.

In the Moroccos spring is raw color, mixed in hot sunshine. It is wind over plowed fields, the smell of moist furrows, darting swallows' wings, lines of camels walking with awkward grace. It is sweet violets pinned to my

'Milk Can Be Homogenized But Not Children'

A teacher laments the toll of individual Bills and Marys that our assembly-line methods take.

By HANNAH TRIMBLE

I AM a well-greased cog in the machinery of a public school. Along with all the others I have become a Grade A teacher (not Government inspected). But I have subversive leanings. I cannot bear to see a creative child like Bill conform to the mold which I must offer as a group pattern.

Bill could once toss off stories, giving them a slightly cock-eyed angle in an inimitable style. Donna could not have produced more words per man hour of inspiration. Bill loved himself in the doing and was his own press agent.

This is no longer true and it is my fault. Today I realized what was happening. Bill became conscious of an astounding

HANNAH TRIMBLE, teacher of the third grade in Evansville, Ind., and a grandmother, has contributed to various teachers' publications and is known to readers of The Times Magazine for her compilations of notes from her pupils.

fact. Clouds floated. He couldn't. "Tricky, aint it?" he grinned. I was counting Red Cross money into a blue vote purse while I shoved tablet nickels into a red one. "I'm busy," I said briefly, still adding. Bill wrote something on a piece of paper and brought it back to my desk. He had closed by saying, "This is an interesting fact is it not?" His English was a tribute to the well-greased cog, and to English Book III, but where was Bill?

I knew too well. He was coming down with the disease which is endemic in overcrowded schoolrooms. He was becoming introjected. That means that without conscious choice he was soaking up his background as a piece of bread soaks up gravy. He eventually would disappear into it. It meant that he would lose the flavor that made him Bill, or else he would mistrust it and hide it away. It meant that he too would grow up and quote the columnists and would always say, "Fine, thank you," when a friend called out to him, "And how ARE you this morning?"

It did not make me happy to be a party to this crime.

CREATIVE children do not need to be set apart and tenderly nurtured. They do not have the delicacy of a pale moccasin flower in rain-wet woods, and their secret fountains of delight do not always sparkle with moonshine. They are often quite robust and speak as of the gutter. But they are not joiners—they suffer regimentation badly and they need time and overtime to ponder.

ONCE a boy fresh out of the Tennessee Mountains came to the Third Grade. One day he rose from his seat and like a sleep walker wandered to the window, where, with his elbows on the sill, he watched white clouds. It turned out he was thinking of his grandpap's "mewil." This boy had an uncanny skill in reproducing, in exact words, anything that had arrested his attention. He wrote once of moles, spelling with the accent of his mountains. The moles had teeth like "blackbre brushs." Their eyes were like "bug eggs in tree bark." And yet I felt that boy into the hopper with the other forty-four because I was only one person and forty-five are too many.

Free time is the most acute shortage in a public school.

Yesterday I had a letter from my daughter. She said that Tommy, who is burning 8, rushes off (Continued on Page 24)

MAGAZINE, MAY 2, 1948.

5

Two articles by Hannah from *The New York Times*

The SS *American Planter*

Hannah's Brazil Visa

Adolph Volderauer

The Bristol Hotel fireplace with, as Hannah put it,
"... rounded spanking places."

Chapter Fourteen

Alone, Hitting Bottom and Falling Apart

At age sixty-one Hannah traveled with Carrie. At age sixty-four she traveled with Edna and Alice. In 1953 when she was sixty-five, she went alone to South America for several months, writing that she "hit bottom." Solid, upright, Hannah made it hard for me to imagine her hitting bottom. She gave the impression of being put together, maybe in spite of, or despite, the early death of her husband. She wrote not only about hitting bottom on this trip but also about falling to pieces, an expression my mother used. With the mountains of tragedy which the generations of Hubbs women faced, falling to pieces was not "what one should do." Best to stay put together. I never saw my mother in that condition. The only ones who have seen me in that state are girlfriends when I was sandwiched in between divorce and death. I fell apart over my son's teenage "you did what?" trouble. Reading of Hannah falling to pieces was oddly reassuring and lent insight into ways of putting oneself back together again. Whether this trait of staying "put together" and dreading falling apart was learned or inherited, either way, it has been passed along. It takes a lot to fall apart in my family.

Many years into Hannah's letters and essays, I became accustomed to my pattern of transcribing interrupted by a self-imposed lengthy, all-consuming sidetrack to uncover a missing piece of information. No passenger log came up with Hannah's name to explain the beginning of her South America trip, but on her return, there was the evidence: Hannah traveled First Class on the SS Uruguay. She wasn't one to forgo luxury or turn her back on what she felt was the best. I assume, and why not, that she steamed off from New York First Class on a luxurious ship.

What was the lure of South America? Frances's husband may have seeded the thought, having traveled to Brazil in 1947. South America was becoming a popular destination. The region was emerging into the modern era, there was an influx of Europeans after the war, the economy was strengthening yet rural settings were untouched, but it was not without danger. Politics in Brazil were unsettled, Colombia endured violence, and social changes were underway in Peru. What prompted Hannah to head out on her own I attribute to her insatiable curiosity, the possible lure of travel posters, the commercialization of air travel, and once again, the influence of her friends. Even with the connections and introductions made on her behalf, I marveled at a sixty-five-year-old single woman traveling alone for two and a half months through South America. That takes someone with an indomitable spirit. Her story of trying to beat her brothers up the ridge pole is now a symbol of one determined woman's refusal to be deterred. The glaring intensity of her eyes in childhood photographs was as telling as her eyes in the photo on her Brazil Visa. She may have been "afeard" (to use a word of hers), yet "Just try me," emanated from her face.

Hannah sailed from New York in mid-May, destination Brazil. From there, she began her journey: air travel included, disappointment included, unsettled stomach included. The 1950s, the "Golden Age" of flying, had only one travel class, and it was luxurious. That was the upside. The downside was noisy propellers, smoke-filled cabins, and turbulence unlike today's jets' smooth ride. I followed Hannah's tracks through her letters. Letters which also chronicled what may have contributed to her falling apart. Her trip didn't start out well. She flew from Barranquilla to Bogota, and her friends Arthur and Betty were not there to meet her.

. . . the desk at the airport asked for my ticket, they began a waving of hands and a Latin excitement – said, "Imposeeble!" and insisted that my plane number was wrong that instead of 667 it should be 177. I rounded up three other excited officials who said the same thing with the same excitement – so I got on 177, which came along in due time. Result – no one met me in Bogota.

On she went, her letters announcing each challenge for "everyone" back home:

Cali, Colombia: altitude sickness

Lima, Peru: still sick

Cuzco, Peru: no complaints

Santiago, Chile: just about hit bottom

Buenos Aries, Argentina: demise of her Davidow suit due to fligh
  sickness

Montevideo, Uruguay: no words

Sao Paulo, Brazil: still had a cold and nausea from altitude sickness

Rio De Janeiro, Brazil: almost heading home

Nothing is worse than being alone when feeling punk, on top of not speaking the language and wondering if you are on the right plane. Even with all her oomph and fortitude, Hannah let on that she met her match on this trip. Excerpt from a letter to Margaret and Ann, August 7, 1953:

I had just about hit bottom in Chile so I don't know whether to
hope the letter never reaches you, or to decide that any old letter is
better than none at all. If you have time, report on that. The flight
over the Andes to Buenos Aires was another three hours with the
magnificence of the eternal. We flew at 19000 feet above iced peaks,
a brilliant sunset in the west and its afterglow in the east. The cabin
was pressurized at 8000 so this time I remained upright. And by the
way, the suit on which I threw up was my cherished Davidow, like
yours, Ann. They said they couldn't get out the stains and washed

the whole thing without telling me. The result is distinctly negative. Maybe it will fit you better than me, now - - - we will see.

Hitting bottom along with the magnificence of the eternal. Do I sense a bit of the dramatic? Hannah delighted in beauty even if she had thrown up. She sought it and marveled in it. It served as an antidote to the burnt-toast side of life. She reveled in the beauty of nature, the beauty of words well chosen, and not to be overlooked, the beauty of clothes and fashion. She didn't spare her audience from announcing items or shops of significance. Throwing up on her Davidow suit and the "distinctly negative result" had to have added to how low she felt on this trip and the need to do a job on herself. Her cherished Davidow, which, while not couture, was considered a luxury ready-to-wear garment with great attention to detail and silk linings, and as such, a Davidow was not inexpensive. I am certain she looked the part for airline travel posters, modeling the best attire for travel, that is, before throwing up.

One isn't truly alone when you have others in your orbit, and Hannah, the master of that, pulled me in to uncover who of her friends led to whom. She dropped Bert Butler's name letting her readers know she had lunch in Brazil at a country club with a "consul friend of Mr. Butler." I found his name associated with the Canadian consultant in Detroit, leading me to suspect her Detroit cousin Gertrude Hubbs was the connection. Relatives and friends were anchors, and when those anchors were not close at hand, she had an amazing knack of finding and creating others, luring them with her clever comments or playful engaging inquiries, a nice smile or a needy smile. Fears are banished for a time knowing others are orbiting, helping anchor you.

One anchor person on this trip who watched over her, took her places, and came to her aid, she called "my Exprinter man." Her connection to the Exprinter private bank in Uruguay may have been through the Old National Bank of Evansville where Arthur had been on the Board of Directors along with the Iglehearts and the father of her friend Hazel. Bank officers make connections, and Hannah worked those connections.

Connections and collections. The collection of men in her vicinity on this trip in addition to Mr. Exprinter and Arthur, her Colombia host, included a young Swiss man on the plane, a Polish poet on another plane, a sunburned easy-going American, and a redhead from Cincinnati. Further in her letter she moved on to the next kind man. I repeat myself as this is a good time to do so; Hannah needed them—men that is. She wasn't the only one. If I am honest, so do I. Her Cali letter continued:

> Then I got on the plane. I had no seat number so I did my choosing. I picked a young man . . . and even before I fastened my seat belt, he was talking to me . . . a cultivated, highly intelligent, beautiful brown young Swiss . . . he asked me for mine [address] – saying he wanted to write to me. He talked about ideas – his own, about life in general, about the world, about the verities of life, and I listened . . . he looked back with the warmest smile in the world, and waved as he disappeared . . . It is knowing about other people from the inside out like that, which helps me with that awful feeling of fear, whatever it is. Don't know why, but it does. He had a nice warm handshake – said that it was a strange thing that he had talked as he had. I have always thought that this idea about a power that followed each person didn't make sense, but I am beginning to wonder. So many times this week when I needed it most, someone has reached out a hand and straightened me up. Like the girl from Chicago, who said, "May I spend the day with you?" and the Polish poet on the plane, and like the sunburned easy going American with his collar turned back at the neck on the way to Miami, who asked me to play canasta with him and a red head from Cincinnati . . . who bought me ham sandwiches and malted milk . . .
>
> I will never see any one of them again – that is one of the things that helps you. Humans can come very close when they know they will walk across your path and then out. My paper is gone –
> Good-by - - Mother.

Her paper was gone, though I am certain her thoughts continued to churn about the "verities of life," the need for warm smiles, the kindness of others, and the hands that reached out to help. Unlike the intensity of her eyes in her Brazil visa photo, her formal portrait showed she had a smile which enchanted, a kind warm face. Her journey to South America included a journey within, "a job to do on myself," as she put it. As I read that, I knew I had a job to do on myself. That is best done, for the most part, alone and on one's own. My comfort was I had Hannah to turn to now and again for reflection and reinforcement.

In a letter to my mother and her sister on her way to Cali, Hannah admitted to fanciful writing, as if no one had noticed before. She served up an admission:

> This will be facts not fancies. The fact that I'm here at all seems a fancy. THIS, and remind me that I have said so, is the very last long trip I shall ever take. I can find at home all of the same things. If it didn't seem to be written in the books that I go on, I would come home now. But I have a job to do on myself. I have already made a dent in it. That's all of that.

The job on herself, if one was to guess, was sorting out why she was "falling apart" and "hitting bottom." Hannah pointed out the job that had been before me on many a dark hour. I kept myself together most days. Not an easy assignment. Small challenges challenged. One night, though I didn't completely fall apart, I came close when I woke up to a chewing sound and discovered my daughter's cat eating a snake on my bed, a snake brought in through the dog door. I screamed to summon no one. I was it, alone with snake blood on my comforter and a partial snake. Pull yourself together was my mantra. Get a grip. You can do this. Self-talk did wonders. No other option.

I was beyond waiting for rainy days to transcribe Hannah's letters. Work and travel back and forth to Maine consumed me while my commitment to understand Hannah and myself kept growing. I stole time before daylight, sorting out more travel letters, patching together unnumbered pages by matching up sentences, typing up her words, researching names and places, running various theories through my head. To do this job on myself, I was on a mission to discover what put Hannah back together again. That is what she did. She pulled herself together to go back on her words that she would never again take another long trip. Time intervened. Two years later, again on her own, she boarded a freighter for a two-month trip to Europe. Five years out from my divorce I was still on my own putting myself together.

On all trips, again not true to her words in her facts-not-fancies letter, Hannah indeed found things which she couldn't find at home, and she acquired them. I have proof. I have moved many of them wherever I have lived, shipped boxes of them across the country. Keeping and shipping this vast quantity of Hannah items made me realize that she'd nuzzled her way into my life in more than a marginal way. She had a hold on me. I am pressed to remember what I have given away that once was hers. My daughter became the owner of a several dolls from Hannah. My son made claim to her sturdy cuckoo clock on the wall in my Maine house. When I learned my daughter-in-law liked butterflies, I passed along a collection of rare butterflies in an intricate inlaid wooden frame which Hannah brought home from South America. Letting go of external ties to my grandmother is a slow process.

Ties are telling. The ties she forged on her South America trip underscored her need for reassurance and comfort that comes with a sense of belonging. I turned the mirror on myself, a repeat activity. I looked at Hannah, I looked at me, a someone who needs ties that bind and who melts with beauty. Hannah wasn't unique in that. What was unique was she wasn't shy about nosing her way into the details of the lives of strangers. Her description of a lunch supported an emerging theory that she fended off fear by mingling with others who appreciated what she appreciated—beauty. The number of times she wrote, "Who lives with beauty hath no fear," is more evidence.

Dear Everybody

August 7 from Chile

This unbelievable kindness appears and reappears. In Santiago the lovely woman named Crystal de Abelli, called me at intervals to see if I were OK, asked me to tea. In Bueonos Airies was a note and telephone call from the French couple who attracted me, first in Cuzco. The husband had come to the hotel—They invited me to lunch yesterday. They are living in one of these modernly designed apartments, furnished with choice things of great beauty. His business is oil in France and here. He is also a representative of a bank in Paris. She is French but was born in the Argentine. In the first war, he was imprisoned in a German camp . . . escaped with the help of his chauffer,—they swam rivers in darkness and with forged papers, managed to get to Marseilles . . . In the next war he was sent to Syria, where he had dysentery . . . He had two daughters— one, at 24, died of cancer . . . His other daughter came after lunch— was a beautiful, intelligent and charming young thing, studying medicine in a Medical College. The luncheon was perfection in taste and service served with three different wines and winding up with gold knives and forks. The wife is as I told you, the director of buying at Harrods. I wanted to look at leather jackets for the children, so she called the store . . . I had a royal escort. They gave me a ten percent discount on each purchase I made. All of this for a stranger at their gates. They will stay for the weekend but my Exprinter man will come to bring me back this afternoon.

In no time, Hannah extracted life details from her newfound friends and came away with a royal escort. She had to have been more than charming to attract others as she did. One week later:

Sunday the 16th from Brazil,

I am sitting at a white table at the edge of a huge blue pool surrounded by beautiful girls and gorgeous looking men for whom I wouldn't give a dime a dozen. They are drinking pink things. Out on the beach boys are flying paper kites shaped like eagles. The surf is very white and the sea very blue. It looks like a heaven on earth and is not.

Was she envious and needed to remind herself not to be fooled by what she saw? Falling to pieces, hitting bottom and the bad dreams on this trip were proof she knew something lurked about that was not heaven. She traveled on, enveloping herself in beauty, collecting "helpers."

Sao Paulo,

Did I speak of the Polish boy— man I supposed I should say — he's 31 — who spoke to me on the plane from Sao Paulo, helped me off with my things and came to the hotel yesterday morning to see if all was well with me? When I can forget the bad dreams of this month, it will be these acquaintances — of all colors and kinds, who have offered me kindness, that I shall always remember.

Good thing she connected with the Polish man on the plane to San Paulo. Another dose of kind people to shore Hannah up. Her writing also sustained her, sentence upon sentence, too many to share, with the exception of this gem:

Saturday in Lima,

If all this bores you – say so in your next letter and I will lay off. The more I can talk about "things" the more minutes I feel less sick inside.

Further on in her letter she made it a point to share that Mr. Exprinter took her to look at stones. Thank you, Mr. Exprinter. I own the two bracelets she mentioned. I connected them end-to-end to make a necklace, compliments flowed. "Nothing grand, but pretty," to quote Hannah. I say thank you when complimented, giving credit to Hannah.

Went with the Exprinter man to look at stones. The jeweler/stone cutter was Dutch — was the man who cut the aquamarine of 1200 karats that was given to the U S by Brazil in honor of Roosevelt . . . Sorry but no could buy. The lovely things begin at a hundred dollars and soar. Golly but they are beautiful. Handmade settings 18 karat gold. I bought Tommy and George a small box of quartz specimens for them. Then I got a bracelet or two made of small chunks of different quartz, uncut, strung together by silver – nothing grand but pretty. Now I'm thru – up to my quota. I got one purse for me – in Harrods – that's the only thing. Don't seem to want anything anymore.

No more room --- My love – Mother

I'm still nauseated all the time and not hungry. Cold is better.

"Don't seem to want anything anymore." That blanket statement was as far as far can be from the truth. I know that trick of saying to others what you don't want, trying to convince yourself to resist. I do that when faced with an open bag of chips, announcing I only will have a few, and when taking excess clothes to a consignment shop and then looking at the racks while announcing I don't need anything. That strategy usually doesn't work. I eat more chips, buy more clothes. The evidence against this blanket statement of Hannah's to not want anything anymore can be found in a cedar chest of mine, and in a Fieldcrest blanket box which has lived under various beds since the mid 1960s. The cedar chest houses three native outfits for children. Two look to be South American, proving her blanket statement untrue. She did buy items of beauty. On too many Halloweens as a child, I was coerced into wearing a wool handwoven outfit from Peru when I wanted a costume that came in a box complete with cheap plastic mask. Disappointment courtesy of Hannah. One Halloween, I dressed my four-year-old daughter in the native outfit from Greece. It might be time to ask how she felt about that.

Under my guest bed and inside the blanket box, filled to the brim, are the folk dolls Hannah collected. The range of countries either meant Hannah travelled farther than I thought, or she prevailed on friends who traveled to bring dolls back for her. Impossible that the collection was completed on her 1952 South America trip when she claimed she wanted nothing. After this trip, she did want "some-things" after all. She wanted many things. On making blanket statements, she admitted she did what she preached not to do.

> I keep preaching to myself, "Don't make blanket statements about people. Don't have blanket feelings either." I find I do that, unfairly, anyway.

Hannah turned the doll collection over to my mother, and once I had children, my mother turned the collection over to me. The dolls lie one atop another, paper towels spread in between. There are dolls with wooden heads, heads of shriveled fruits, horse hair heads, corncob heads, delicate felted heads. Several dolls, fine in detail, have pinned on their backs the name of the region they represent. There are dolls from Mexico, Hungary, Scandinavia, Germany, Switzerland, Holland, various South American countries, and regions of the United States. One doll appears to be from India. On the lid of one wee box, Hannah scrawled the words, "for the collection." On the back of the other matching box her handwriting consumed the entire two-by-three inch surface with the words: "Canada Gaspe." Inside are an intricately carved aged man and woman with smiles I hope to wear when I am more wrinkled than I am now. On my desk in California stand a finely dressed felted couple, arm in arm. Alert on my dresser are a Dutch man and woman, wooden clogs showing below the man's baggy wool pants and the woman's cotton skirt. An impartial observer would notice my interest in displaying couples. When I was a child and now that I am an adult, the dolls offered what Hannah said her mother offered her: "the stuff dreams are made of." The truth is, I would welcome a right-sized man at my side regardless of any statements I have made that I am done with relationships.

Despite dealing with altitude sickness and loneliness, despite falling to pieces, she pulled herself together after South America and took more trips. The redeeming quality of the people and chunks of beauty won her over. Duly noted by me on my behalf are reminders that strangers at one's gate can appear, offering up kindness and support. A women's support group I attended after my divorce confirmed that being with strangers to talk about feelings was like traveling to a foreign country for me. Reluctant to speak at first, I listened and smiled as others shared their challenges. My career had honed my ability to listen and offer up support, but experience at admitting I might be the one who needed support was limited. Advice from Hannah at the end of her falling-apart trip, the ending sentence in her last letter, was what I needed to read. While the women in my family may not speak feelings out loud, I am grateful for words written down and shared. With many years ahead of me, pushing reticence aside is on my list of inside jobs.

> This unbelievable kindness appears and reappears . . . Those are things that no one forgets. Remember that, darling. Never feel that reticence which covers an impulse for a kindness is better than a mistake on the other side of the ledger.

Chapter Fifteen

Captain Darlington Transports Hannah to Paris

On May 6, 1955, HANNAH, aged sixty-seven, aboard the American freighter SS *American Planter*, was bound for Europe for a three-month stay, accompanied by her typewriter. She made it plain she was sending her letters to a group, the first in her series of "Dear Everybody" letters. Counting who she called out by name, "Everybody" included Frances, Carrie, Adolph, Josefine, Hazel, Jess, Bee, and daughters Ann and Margaret. The evidence for Adolph, the only man to join this group of women, was:

> "Paging Adolph. Don't put your faith in the soap chips I suggested.
> A porpoise could make better bubbles."

How many carbons and onion skin papers could a typewriter handle? I have a vague recollection of adjusting the carriage to accommodate extra pages. Even so, I doubt nine papers would fit. Maybe Hannah selected which friends to include in each letter based on which friends sent her letters. With more than five years as a singleton, I was happy to tag along with Hannah, transporting myself from my day-to-day rhythm of work, girlfriends, tending to my kids, interspersed with a few trips to Maine. I was faring fine on my own though churning in my mind was how I would fare with men who crossed my path. I was savoring my independence while yearning for a connection. The gift for me in her 1955 letters was a glimpse into Hannah's opinions about men, certain men that was, the captain of her freighter, along with Adolph Volderauer.

To launch Hannah on her trip, Frances Leich Hanson, her lifelong Evansville friend and travel mentor, accompanied her to New York. Frances would have left her husband behind in Indiana, and in 1955, I imagine it was not common for a woman to travel without her husband, though when it came to Hannah and her friends, what was uncommon was common. I thought of my group of friends as I read Hannah's comments on men in her first "Dear Everybody" letter and I smiled. In the realm of men, Hannah had more comments in the making.

> Dear Everybody – if you don't mind scrappy and no good reports, here goes. You asked for it.

> The day in New York was not long enough. Frances and I had lunch at the Museum of Modern Art, where there is an exhibit of East Indian jewelry and fabrics. When we went thru the Japanese house which has been built in the court - - do you call it a court, just behind? Carried our shoes in a brown paper bag. Uncluttered and cool - designed to satisfy all the senses. Also designed for the limber of limb - - how, if I sat on a cushion, could I pull up to go on? The bathtub baffled me - - a wooden one sunk in the floor. To scrub out its corners do you lie on your stomach after you're out and reach over the edge? If you are not wanted in the teahouse, they tie a rope around a rock and place the rock on the door step (if there is a step – I have forgotten). Aubrey Menen's* grandmother, in the southern most tip of India was privileged to put her husband's slippers out on the windowsill if she had grown tired of him. Same general idea.

---

* English satirist born in 1912

Putting a husband's slippers out on the windowsill to indicate a wife had grown tired of said husband. That's an idea which intrgued her.

When Hannah wrote about men and slippers, she had no idea what she was going to encounter with Captain Darlington of the SS *American Planter*. Reading her escapades on the Planter convinced me he may have wanted to put Hannah's slippers outside. Her letter continued:

> . . . embarkation would be at two . . . Frances and I arrived, hand in hand . . . we walked in and up to my freighter . . . One woman was round and fat and uncorseted. She had thick hair, dyed very black and frizzed with a permanent — eyebrows a black, penciled line. Her husband, who sat by her side, was more than six feet in his socks. Nervously thin . . . Mrs. Hansen (that was her name, believe it or not) . . . wore a pepper and salt jersey dress . . . around her throat was clasped a rhinestone necklace, from which a cluster of rhinestones hung on a pendant (a dead ringer for me.) Some friend who had been more attentive than mine, had sent her an orange corsage made from roses and tied with a big scarlet bow.
>
> After Frances had recalled to my mind the chapter in Lewis's book in which he analyzed pride, she left me, the meanie.

Hannah was on her own. Frances left her with reminders about pride, which requires a digression. Her friend knew something about Hannah and pride, Hannah with a touch of smugness. Good friends are those unafraid to tell it like it is. A childhood friend once told me I went out with all the "bad boys" in high school. I denied it, then turned inward to face the truth. Hannah's friend pegged her and let her know. Frances sensed Hannah needed to be taken down a notch, having registered a complaint about not receiving a corsage from the one man in her "Everybody" group. Hannah listened, then wrote about it. I listened and thought about my future with men.

The friend in this "Everybody" group letter who had not been attentive like Mrs. Hansen's friend was Adolph. Hannah had the idea that he should have sent her a corsage as a bon voyage gesture. That told me something about Hannah and the man we called "Uncle Adolph." Hannah had expectations of Adolph and made certain her "Everybody" group knew when her expectations were not met. I would never be so bold to announce in a group email any hopes of mine that were dashed.

One year older than Hannah and born in Evansville, Adolph was a lifelong friend of Arthur's and may have known Hannah when growing up. After Arthur died, Adolph watched over Hannah. After Adolph's wife, Elsie died in 1953, Adolph was in pursuit. On this trip to Europe, he appeared several times in remarks that were quite telling about Hannah's view on getting remarried and on men who flaunt their position of power. More on Adolph later. Enter Captain Darlington. At this point in Hannah's letters as her interactions with men emerged, I had a conversation with myself about myself and men. I had given up on Match in Marin having found no matches. Too many were self-absorbed.

With only three other paid passengers to keep her occupied, Mr. and Mrs. Hansen and Ahna, a woman from Germany, Hannah turned her eye to the captain. While the Hansens and Ahna provided material for Hannah's writing, taking on Captain Darlington seemed the extra challenge she needed as the freighter made its way across the Atlantic. A freighter voyage had none of the built-in entertainment of the QE2. Passengers were on their own and needed to be self-sufficient. There was no schedule of events. Port arrival dates were often listed as "on or about." The 1950s and 1960s were the heyday for freighter travel, and writers such as Graham Green, Somerset Maugham and Alex Haley sought them out for the solitude they provided. Hannah was in her element. If I knew astrology, I would say her planets aligned. Her freighter trip offered a world rich with images and opportunities to observe and write, a world unscheduled and unprogrammed. She declared her love of freighters and intolerance for a man full of himself.

> It occurs to me that I've never answered the one thing you'll ask.
> "How do you like your freighter?" I LOVE it. I shall never want to
> ride off in a gilded ship again. I love it most especially, come morn-
> ings, when I walk down by the water line (permit from the captain).

This is the only exercise I get. I walk fore and I walk aft, and let the wind decide which way is possible. Then poppa Hansen turns my blanket underneath my feet and I lie for hours, in a deck chair, and watch the ship slide up and down, against the skyline . . .

A lot goes on in freighters underneath the surface. Too few see much too much. The captain hates the engineer. He hates the captain back. The engineer hasn't spoken to the radio officer in two years — it goes down and down the line. And separately, each one is kinda nice. The engineer seems easy going and integrated . . .

Paging Mrs. Clifford — Did your freighter have glassed in lounges that shine like frog's eyes one on each side of its middle? Only three ships on our line have 'em. We, I say proudly, have. I suspect that one is fore and one is aft . . . Could be stahbud or leeward, or there is a bare chance one is on the port side.

Hannah's first "Dear Everybody" letter was eight pages long single spaced. She could turn a simple task into a three-hundred-word paragraph, bringing friends into her cabin, sharing with "Everybody" her adventure getting in and out of a berth on the freighter. A morsel will do:

The side of my bunk or berth or bed is built above the mattress level. I sit on this, bend my back until it's like a letter C, slide backward. Then my knees are up above the proper level and my feet no longer touch the floor. This is a moment for deep thought. Somewhere, somehow, I must pivot, remaining like a letter C, before I straighten out.

In those first few pages, Hannah was warming up her fingers getting ready to type her comments on Captain Darlington.

Now for the captain. I can't help but wonder if the captain's name really was Darlington. I wouldn't be surprised if sitting on deck, typewriter in her lap, pausing, looking out to sea, Hannah dreamt up a name for the man who she felt was far from a darling as he navigated his cargo and four paid passengers across the Atlantic. I doubt he knew he would have to navigate a passenger like Hannah Trimble from Evansville, Indiana.

> The Hansens and Ahna and I share a table for meals. Protocol is observed. At the table, next door sits the captain, facing the chief engineer. The other tables are dotted with engineers, engineer assistants and their assistants, radio officers and assistant radio officers, etcetera etcetera. Each man comes in at will, speaks to no one, or at least does not speak when the captain is present. He, like the true Bostonian, speaks only to God. To be perfectly frank, I doubt that God has much trek with the captain.

Hannah knew Bostonians. Ann, whose husband did take a surgery job in Boston, lived in the midst of the best of them. No hesitation from Hannah of Indiana to take on a Boston Brahmin or a Captain at breakfast:

> Only the captain was down. He is a sadistic brute, sarcastic and rude. A final touch of the devil, he calls me "Madame" and that coming from him, is quite something. I had asked him, on the evening of the first day, some dumb question . . . he gave me a look, and then said "If you used half of your brain you could see for yourself." Since then I give him an icy stare, if the ship doesn't give a wop with a wiggle between at my moments of passing. This morning at breakfast, for some unknown reason, he felt gentled up and suggested that I learn to play Acey Deucy after dinner that night. When I went down into the kitchen that afternoon to get me some coffee, I told the chief engineer. He and the roomful of others guffawed. I'm intensely curious to know why the captain is such a devil. I'm gathering pointers. He was in a Japanese prison war camp for four years — that could make anyone anything, but I don't think that that's it. I think he has illusions of grandeur. He leaves his door open and since the office is on our ship level where nobody else is permitted to come, we peer in each time that we pass. He never looks up. Says,

when Mrs. Hansen presses him, that he is concentrating and that God knows all boys would be better to have learned as he learned, with a strap applied to his hind side (the words are not mine). Mrs. Hansen then asked (it was one of those hours when she talked about nothing), where he lived and was he southern. He curled his lip for a snarl and said that they had moved from each town as soon as his father's debts caused the sheriff to look for him.

He stood me up on the date for the game.

Hannah would not tolerate someone with allusions of grandeur, let alone being stood up by a man. Her two brothers may have solidified her skills in taking on boys and men. She was one determined woman who fought against other people's feelings of superiority or maybe her own feelings of inferiority. Hannah's memories of her childhood were vivid, some painful for me to read, yet I return to her words once more.

My brother led the assault up the ridgepole of the stable to spit into the chimney. The last to spit was 'poison'. I was always 'poison'. Inferior and lonely even in spitting.

Some sisters would not have followed their brothers up a ridgepole. Hannah did with no mention of her sister, Lulie, who was cut from a different cloth.

Hannah must have had words with her brothers which brought to mind the words of my cousin, George. A few months after my divorce, when visiting him in Sea Ranch, California, he delivered his message on a cliff overlooking the Pacific Ocean, accompanied by a smile and a hug. He shared his view on what he called the infamous Trimble mouth, though he and I decided Hannah showed signs of it before she became a Trimble: "Any man who can't stand a Trimble mouth, doesn't deserve one."

George was referring to the lineup of Trimble women: our grandmother, his mother Ann, his sister Sally, my mother, and in sharing that with me, I knew I was part of the club. I wasn't good at acquiescing to my former husband. When his values conflicted with mine, I let him know, often without speaking a word.

Back to Hannah and the captain with thoughts about the "Trimble mouth."

The next morning (that was today) I was eating prunes quite alone. The captain came in and sat down. He picked up his coffee cup, snapped his fingers for John and said, "We will play Acey Deucy today — at eleven o'clock." "Oh," I said, and spit out a prune stone. Then the Hansens came in and sat down. Momma said good morning sweetly. The captain said nothing. She didn't mind. "He isn't the type of man you speak to at breakfast," she said to me. Later, she spoke again, to butter him up. Still no answer. Poppa looked worried, "He didn't hear you," he said to her kindly. The captain turned on them, "Madame," he shouted, "I was thinking about much more important things. I am not rotting in a mental vacuum as you are." I half rose to knock his block off. But she didn't mind at all. Now you've heard everything! Then he turned his pale blue slits of eyes on me. "At eleven," he said.

There are times I feel sorry for him and wish I knew what makes a human creature tick that way. I still think he has illusions of grandeur — defensively — and I still think he has a lonely job.

My goodness, all of a sudden, I know who it is he keeps recalling to my mind. It's Mr. Hedrick — from Leland Michigan — he was the same sadistic, pleasing character. I was afeard of him until that morning when he made Phoebe cry. Then I turned on him and told him what I thought of him. After that he was just as smooth as cream. He liked it. That's enough on captains. No — one other thing. He asked me if I ever read a book. "Sometimes," I said. He handed me the Saturday Evening Post Anthology. "Return it when you're finished," he said coldly. "I sometimes do," I said.

Who was Mr. Hedrick? *The Chicago Tribune* reported that Mr. Edwin Hedrick married the woman he made cry. He was a Yale graduate and successful attorney who summered in Leland, and no doubt kept company with the "captains of industry." Hannah took on captains . . . of ships . . . of industry. If only I could have been a witness to Hannah taking on Mr. Hedrick — and Captain Darlington. If only I had known about captains of industry before I married one.

I sense a delight in Hannah as she dealt with the captain, egging him on as my mother would say. If I did that, my mother had something to say. Early in my dating years, with reference to a fellow who was more than complaisant, she warned, "Be nice to the poor boy." Was my mother hypersensitive having witnessed her mother telling men what she thought? I don't think I was ever over the top. Hannah may have been. In a letter to my mother in reference to her relationship with Adolph, Hannah wrote: "You think I treat him badly." And, "I have a feeling that you think I am a meanie when it comes to him." Time for reflection. I never was a meanie, never egged on a man as Hannah seemed to have done. What Hannah and I shared was a lower tolerance than most for arrogance. More on Hannah and Adolph later. More on me and men later. Hannah and Captain Darlington preoccupy me now.

C.C. (that means comment on captain). Subject — good luck. Suggested to my mind by porpoises. Mrs. Hanson— momma— has brought with her sundry little idols - - one is Buddha - - which she kisses, so she says, each morning to insure her day. She took them all in to the captain's office, to show them to him. He wouldn't look. He growled, "I have better things to do." Someday I'll kill him for her. But not today. Today I'll kill him for myself. I took the book he lent me - - to the deck and read it in my steamer chair. The sun was in my eyes and thinking he was decks away, I put its cover on my head to shade my sunburned nose. But not for long. He suddenly appeared from God knows where, removed my headdress, and handed me a paper bag to use instead. "You will tear the cover of my book," he said with grim intent. If I hadn't been so guilty I would not have been so mad. Momma Hansen giggled.

C.H. (that means Comment on Hannah). Subject: I wouldn't dare. I can't imagine doing something like that with anything that belonged to Hannah in front of her, such as put one of the choicest of children's books she gave me over my face as cover. I can't imagine. To use one of her words, I was "afeared" of her as a child. It doesn't seem the captain was afraid of her and she not afraid of him.

> I went in and stood before the captain's door. "I want you to talk to me," I said, "about what's happening in Europe." He tore the world apart with contempt. He lashed out at nations and their leaders. He was brutal, clear thinking and contemptuous. When he stood up I said, "Thank you." He said, "you called me bitter." I said, "I did. You are."

The two of them were a match made in heaven. I am coming to realize that I respect a man who can give it to me, tell me to "cut it out." What I could never do, never have done, is speak so bluntly. What possessed her to do that? Hannah's child within was never far away. With a father she didn't hold in high regard for his lack of accomplishments, childhood tales of her successful, hardworking Grandfather Stevenson, and her innate drive to "beat all," is it any surprise that Hannah was hard on others?

> News item C.C. (You remember that means comment on captain). The engineer's assistant, the one with curly black hair - - the fat one who never moves faster than just so fast with his left hand in his pocket - - stopped off in one of the verandas that looks like a frog's eye, and said he had come to get me- that I had promised to wash dishes and make coffee in my hours of idleness. I said sorry but I had begun to enjoy rotting in my mental vacuum. He said, "Don't mind what the captain says. It was before the war, when he was

responsible only to the company. He had sunk his ship to keep it from the Japanese. So, of course the Japanese got even. He told us unbelievable things which I will not repeat."He is a good skipper, - and he has a lonely job," the boy went on. "The rest of it does not affect his work. He can't help that. So, we ignore it."

How can we, tho we'd like to, understand people without the key which is too often denied us. I hope I choke if ever one more time I kill the captain in my thoughts!

Hannah was searching for the key to understanding people. She was persistent, observant, inquisitive. She heeded the captain, if she hadn't killed him fully by the end of the voyage.

News item. We are out of the danger of floating ice and fog. So, the captain should be less crabbed at breakfast. But we're crammed so full of cargo that we lose more time each day. It will be Tuesday before we reach Le Havre.

Hannah was about to land in France. Her days with the captain were coming to an end, as was her eight-page freighter letter to "Everyone."

Last night we began to roll - - ground swells from the Bay of Biscay . . . Everything fell off of everything and broke to smithereens. It will not stop until we land. The captain is making up time - - it will not be Tuesday morning, but Monday night. The gulls are flying overhead - - there were three fishing boats today - - from Portugal. The porpoise flip their tails and play around. All afternoon I have sat and watched the sea. Sometimes it rains a little, sometimes the soot from the smoke stack drifts around us. What's the difference? When the quiet sunset colors come again the water turns blue black.

News item: Our table at dinner is shoved into a corner and lashed to the floor. I can't get out. The engineer said that once a captain's wife

got tired of that, stepped up on the table and down upon a chair. He
suggested that for me.

A salvo sent Hannah's way. Did she take the bait? If she stepped over
the table, she would have smiled at Captain Darling on the way,
thanking him for the ever so nice journey as she held thoughts of
Paris and who and what to take on next. A woman on her own, of her
own, about to march off her freighter sending thoughts to my mother
about another man.

Monday morning - - -

We'll be in the harbor at Le Havre tonight if the tide is high enough.
The ground swell that tossed us around has given up the strug-
gle and is replaced by a deep current moving toward the coast of
France . . . it is smooth this morning.

Thank you, darling, for the letters. You are a dear to do the things
you do. And thank you for the honey of a card for Mother's Day. I
have your pictures in my purse and thank you all again.

What a lot has happened in Europe since I came away. Should be
fun to be there!

Adolph leaves on the 22 of June on the Queen Mary or flies a few
days earlier. Find out which and have a letter there to say good luck.
There aren't too many who will do that. He is most fond of you. I
have a feeling that you think I am a meanie when it comes to him. I
can never marry anyone at all. That's all there is to that. He gets out
of hand. But he could be so nice to have just for a friend. He agrees
but it doesn't stick. I'm sorry. You be sweet to him. You can do it
without involving anyone.

I feel so far away. And you so long ago. Take care of you and yours. I love you all.

Good-by for now - - Mother

There is more to come on Adolph and Hannah, more to come when Hannah was on the loose in Paris, and more to come on my being on the loose in Maine.

Dear Everybody

Chapter Sixteen

On the Loose in Paris

Hannah was reporting from Paris, May 17, 1955. Upon her arrival, she may have forgotten what Frances read to her on the topic of pride.

I have had a permanent, first whack – today. A honey! I look simply MARvelous! And, tho you'll think I make this up, tomorrow there's a party. At the Butlers. I have an invitation, engraved with a crest atop of it. It said to Respond, silvou pl--- oh well, RSVP. I looked over my supply of stolen stationary from various motels, and nothing seemed quite right, so I went over to the Consulate and had a session with Bert Butler. He's just a block or two away. And while we're on my neighbor's businesses. Next door is Cartier's. Please, God, don't let me even look! I've a stack of mail, Mr. Butler said, out at the house. I'll get it all tomorrow. Thank you.

And by the way, he says he's not a consul. There is no Canadian consul in Paris. He was that in Detroit, but here, he is called Commercial something.

Hannah looked MARvelous, had a party invitation with an engraved crest, received letters from her gang, faced the temptation of Cartier and connected with Tony (nick name for Constance) and Tony's husband Bert Butler. Which raises the question how Hannah came to know the Butlers. At this point, my research skills were sharp and my need to know intense. In a "contact us" email to the Detroit Canadian Consulate, I cut and pasted Hannah's words about Bert. One day later, I had a reply. Mr. Butler was appointed the Canadian Detroit Consul and Trade Commissioner in 1951. With that date in hand, back I went to Newspapers.com and found the news that he and Mrs. Butler, aka Tony, attended a Detroit Women's City Club event for Canadian Dominion Day (the holiday commemorating the forming of Canada). Calling Hannah: Did you rub elbows there with Tony? Did your cousin Gertrude Hubbs Hornbrook make the introduction? Hannah also let on that Bert knew my mother and our family with her words that "he sent his love and asked about you all." Love all around. Hannah was smitten with Paris. I was smitten with more than five years of quarterly expeditions to Maine coupled with vicarious adventures with Hannah who conjured up a wealth of sensory snacks along the way. My first Maine adventure with love would come soon, though only after adventuring with Hannah for a few days in Paris.

After she signed off her first Paris letter with "Goodnight and PS," she picked up the next morning further down the same page. She must have been saving paper and knew the limit of how many pages she could stuff in one airmail envelope. If there was ever someone who took in minute details, was sensitive to her surroundings, and simply couldn't stay quiet about what was before her, it was Hannah.

> Now it's morning and I've had my coffee. Also two croissants and orange marmalade, in bed. I coil the bolster up behind the pillows. (It looks like an oversized amoeba.) I'm out from corn meal mush and buckwheat cakes, fried eggs and slabs of butter. When I waked – it was still dark – my pint sized radiator was hissing and spitting bubbles and somewhere down below my level, the hotel's plumbing was making burping noises like the freighter. Reflected in the

armoire's mirror was a hat tree that I hadn't seen last night. It had tentacles, like Edith Carson's undersea monstrosities. They curved outward in a circle at the top, then curved in and down. They had fingernails. I switched on a light and every mirror in the room reflected my face. I'd wallowed off my hairnet.

Time out to comment on an expression crafted by Hannah, twitched out as she typed, such as "wallowed off her hairnet." I looked up wallowed to see how it could be connected to hairnets. Merriam-Webster let me know that yes indeed, that word fits Hannah and how she might feel about freeing her hair: "take unrestrained pleasure: delight." Hannah delighted in coaxing out metaphors from her third graders and penning her own to "Everybody." She required her audience, whether child or adult, to join in her word escapades, teasing out meaning in her expressions. "I'm out from corn meal mush and buckwheat cakes . . ." I take to mean she wasn't eating an Indiana breakfast. She was in Paris after all and wanted to make that clear. Further on in her letter she was collecting observations and launched in on people, food, museums, and no surprise, Adolph.

I love watching people who are inflated by the thought of what they THINK they are and probably are not. One woman came in with her husband – or maybe with her son. She shook hands with the waiters, had two tables moved so they could place her in the spot which she preferred, gave her plate back to be heated and tasted each patisserie before she made her choice. I've decided that I like French foods because they're drowned in butter. My mushrooms had a hunk on top, mixed with parsley and other things and still more other things, and was delicious! I walked miles in the Louvre. Watch it, Adolph - you don't like pictures too much anyway. You start out in the corridor that leads your eye up to the Winged Victory. That is so beautiful, you're drugged. You forget your feet and don't remember that you're rickety. Then there's Botticelli, and you stop before the Mona Lisa. In this corridor (I'm still talking to you, Adolph), are the

Velasquez, one Ribero and one El Greco. Hunt them up but wait for the El Prado in Madrid for the best ones. Skip the St. Sebastions. They all painted him stuck full of arrows. I can live without them.

Attention Adolph. Hannah was talking to you. She knew you were heading to Europe in June and was paving the way for you, like it or not. If my theory was correct that Adolph and Hannah knew each other since childhood, he would be used to her ways. If only he could talk to me from the grave and tell me about their relationship. Pages later, Hannah had another message for him:

> Addressing Mr. Volderauer: I'm sorry to report that the Gardens have no benches, on which you planned to sit to smell the flowers.

Relationships, like people, are fascinating. Hard for me to picture Arthur sitting on a bench smelling flowers, yet here is Hannah picturing someone who could. Answering the question of what attracted me to the man I married is helped in part as I wonder with puzzlement about Hannah, Arthur, and Adolph. A little over five years since my divorce, I was more settled, was getting to know myself, and the time had come to tease out what mattered most to me in a relationship with a man, and this trio gave me context.

Hannah was off to Tony's party. I am not sure what she would have done if Adolph had been her date, though I have a vague idea. He would have had to fend for himself. Hannah would party Paris-style with an overlay of Indiana, and Adolph, if he had been there, would have tolerated how she navigated the party. I sense he was a very compliant companion, leaving Hannah to her ways. Excerpts:

> The room was filled with Canada, all speaking French. Bert sifted out the few who could speak English and introduced them . . .
> Fifteen of them stayed for dinner without invitations. By that time, I knew at least something about each one of them. That was probably because they'd had the drinks – I'd fiddled around with

mine. Among them was a woman who had instantly, on her arrival, become the center of the whole shebang. She was Canada overlaid with Paris. I gathered that she's been a designer of costumes – what's the word ? – "couturiere" or something like that? She was homely, had buck teeth, a deep voice and the most marvelous personality I have ever seen, touched, smelt or listened to. No line – no pretense - - a consciousness of other people's comfort. She is getting me tomorrow an invitation from Dior to see his gowns. I told her I had not the faintest idea of buying any. She said that made it difficult but not impossible. Goody, goody! I can hardly wait.

One man, who has come to Paris to foster trade in furs, gave me a ticket to the fur fair, which is going on… my calendar is filling up. They all talked on and on, in English, out of courtesy to me . . . Then someone started singing - - "When father painted the parlor," it was called . . . The woman with the teeth got up and went to their piano and for two hours she played by ear . . . At twelve o'clock she stopped, turned on a Victrola and danced. There are no taxi offices in Paris - - this I do not understand – patrons, who have no telephones. You walk home --- (ask Carrie) or pick one up by standing in the street and daring him to mow you down. Or, I hated this, somebody in your party takes you home, out of their way, of course.

The woman with the teeth – she took me home – is named Marjorie Dutton. Her card says, "Press attaché, English Speaking Countries." What's a press attaché?

Her comment that others had drinks and that she "fiddled around" with hers reminded me of my mother, who fiddled with drinks because, "one wouldn't want to get woozy." Hannah was fine being drugged by beauty in the museum, but at the party she needed her wits about her to not miss a detail or opportunity. Her wits paid off, given the invitations that came her way. "Goody, goody," Hannah let forth.

Some Hannah messages are too familiar. Example: she hated it when "somebody in the party takes you home, out of their way of course." My ears rang with the mantra I grew up with, "We wouldn't want to trouble you." I have learned that people like to help out; it is no trouble for them, it may give them pleasure, even if it is out of their way. The benefit of collecting Hannah's opinions is I am reminded of worn-out family lines to let go of, and family habits to hold on to. Drug me with beauty, fiddle with drinks, and let others help out.

Hannah was off for more high-stepping adventure, though she lost the paper that would be her entrée into the Dior Salon. How could she? Someone whose mind is in constant motion playing with words and taking in all that is going on may not pay attention to pieces of paper or notice that the threads on her suit button were getting loose. What she did pay attention to, using all caps for emphasis, was her standing that gained her acceptance into the land of the elite. Having never even been close to a designer salon, Hannah's recounting of her day will be the closest I shall ever get. The full Hannah report is worth providing:

> . . . we're going to Dior's. The only thing to recommend us is the note from Mrs. Dunton, and I've lost that from my pocket. A button has come off my black suit and there's no time to hunt up thread to fix it. My hairdo is Evansville again.

> I know now what a press attaché is. Mrs. Dunton is publicity for the whole caboodle of designer people like Faith and Dior. She says Dior is by far the showman of the outfit - - the best they've ever had. She said before the war he starved - - now he has a NAME (spoken with respect, tho the tongue is in the cheek. That's not fair. It really isn't. He's an artist who knows how to sell himself.)

> We went in thru a room which had been sprayed with perfume. Past two slink women who inspected our credentials. Credentials are not transferable. Unless your name is on "THE BOOK" out you

go. The poor thing in front of us had brought a friend. Friend went home alone. She didn't pass. WE did. On account of our names were in "THE BOOK." Just in case, Tony had whipped out a card with Canada elite, with crests and stuffs (she said nothing made Bert quite so mad). What a racket all this is! But IS he smart - - this Dior person, or maybe Mrs. Dunton. They want to sell his wares, so they make it hard to see them. They cash in on the foibles of human nature. There were three rooms of us. WE had front seats. Each model - - not the girl - - the dress - - had a name and number. One girl assumed the pallor - - softly sweet and feminine, of a maiden newly up from childbirth. She wore the floating evening gowns, or garden dresses with wide brimmed hats. She had the most applause. One was dark and dignified. She wore the starkly simply cut creations - - They had on bizarre looking numbers, with pagodas made of raffia or straw, for hats. Their waistlines were so handspan there was no room for stomachs. They whirled and wheeled and disappeared more quickly than it takes to tell it - - so that, unless the eye is quicker than their feet, no one could copy. The tailored suits were VERY ugly. So tight no one of them could sit down. The things for evening were so utterly beautiful that you couldn't stand it - - And the fabrics!! And the color combinations!! I have never in my life seen such lovely things. I wonder where they're worn. Who wears them? When the show was over we floated down the stairs, were squirted fore and aft with perfume as we passed the slinky women, and walked out into the sunshine.

While Hannah was taken in by the high style of Dior and Cartier, none of the items that she passed down to my mother and to me were items of luxury. Her treasures were handcrafted folk art. What she valued were the unique and one-offs, nothing from the masses for the masses. Putting the Dior Salon aside, Hannah's schedule included a flea market:

Tomorrow - - the flea market - - while Bert can drive us. I like stuffs like that. Don't ask me why.

Don't ask why she liked flea markets. Her friends must have had a guess. My guess: a woman who delighted in and collected words that came from the heart of her third-grade children from the tough side of Evansville would delight in unique treasures found in a flea market. As Thornton Wilder reminded us, "We can only be said to be alive in those moments when our hearts are conscious of our treasures." Hannah's heart was more than aware of her treasures.

With two days left in Paris, as Hannah neared the end of this letter, she turned to musings about herself and the impact of not being able to communicate freely.

> Comment. Subject – THE SILVER LINING. I had a thought this afternoon. Maybe I won't talk so much when I come home. Maybe I won't interrupt my betters. On account of I can't talk to anybody here or there or anywhere, until I learn their language. Maybe I'll become a listener. Golly, how I'll hate that.

> Goodnight - - Take care of you. I don't know why I 'm here. Unless I'm crazy. I think I'm homesick. I didn't get my letters. They forgot to bring them. I think one's from Bee and one from Jess. Thank you, darlings.

Hannah was homesick. That can be a lonely state of affairs for a woman on her own in Europe. It's one thing to be on one's own with friends orbiting around, it's another to feel utterly on one's own.

～

Leaving Hannah alone in Europe for a spell, I digress to me alone in Maine. I was smitten with Maine even though after several years of going back and forth, I hadn't been there long enough to make solid friends. When alone, Hannah turned to beauty. I did the same, feasting on what the woods and waters offered up. On one of my trips, two days after arriving on the red-eye, I woke myself up at the East Coast crack of dawn to go on a bird walk. Not many arrive for a bird walk without binoculars, but I did. The result was the wildlife biologist leader of the group had to share his binoculars with me. The unintended result, he and I started seeing each other whenever I was in Maine. He pointed out the beauty Maine had to offer. We hiked mountains and spent weekends in a camp on a remote lake in central Maine, twenty miles down a logging road, wood cookstove included, moose included, outhouse in the woods included, recitations from Thoreau included. We meshed well in the outdoors. He provided adventures with bushwhacking and black fly batting, and I was an eager explorer. I was going with the flow, which led to his moving into my house, convenient for both of us. He needed a place to live after retiring and selling his house. I needed someone to watch over my house when I was in California, which was most of the time. We sorted out a nice relationship, and Mr. Wildlife Biologist brought me back to life. We traveled to Italy and then to France to visit my cousin Sally and her L.A.T. (living apart together) partner. I took in her relationship as much as the countryside, noting the caring affection, wondered about separate houses, wondered if it worked.

One year moved into the next, and two years went by before Mr. Wildlife Biologist asked when I was going to move to Maine. Each year I came up with an excuse. "I can't because of my job." Then it was, "I can't because of my kids." Then it was, "I can't because of my dogs." Practicalities were getting in my way. The truth was slow to show itself. The more time I spent with him, I noticed that small glitches were showing up, and I wasn't ready for glitches. Patterns rooted in childhood such as how to pass the salt along with the pepper, reared up. I hadn't sorted out what I needed at my table. Hannah in the Dior salon brought up the formfitting Prada dress I bought at Valerie's consignment store. It didn't fit with wildlife biology, but I longed to slither into that dress for a special someone. I longed to feel MARvelous and indulge myself in more than the outdoors. I wasn't ready for a live-in relationship. I should have known better. Mr. Wildlife moved out, and we became best of friends.

A few years later, I quit my job, the dogs died, and my kids acclimated to the idea that I was spending more weeks in Maine. It was time to sell my California house. I put the house on the market in 2017. After grousing to my agent that staging a house was ridiculous, I did what she said, and it sold a few days later. I rented a townhouse, unable to fully sever my California connection. I was getting closer to embracing the idea of being a full-time single woman on the loose in Maine, ready to swim in the wealth of its sensory riches.

Chapter Seventeen

Beauty and Sergeants in Vienna

Hannah was still on the loose in Europe, collecting as she went. As with her WWII letters, she didn't include complete dates. I sighed with frustration; I would have to do the calculating. If I was correct, Hannah left Paris for Vienna on Tuesday, May 23. The next day she wasted no time admitting her executive function skills were lacking when communicating to her hosts, Bill and Peggy Nutter.

And horrors! Bill and Peggy met a train. They'd missed my letter. I must have been unconscious when I wrote it. It was quite a day for Peggy. Her houseguests (one is Texas oil and used to having her own way) had gone off thru the Russian Zone to see some famous horses and visit a rhinestone factory. There are what you call check stations. Going in and coming back. They record the time it takes to do it. If you're late for any reason they send the army to look for you. Bill said sometimes people don't return at all. I said, "Where do they go?" Salt mines, probably he said. "Or dead."

Hannah's hosts were warning her and promptly provided a sergeant to keep her in line. Odd that being in my grandmother's presence kept me in line. I dared not stray from unspoken family protocol about behavior. I was learning, to repeat a Hannah phrase, that I held onto several protocols which Hannah had ignored. She whispered to me: take some risks, go outside your comfort zone and look for undiscovered treasures.

> I had found a note at the hotel desk, marked "urgent." I was to come at once for dinner. They sent a sergeant for me. My sergeant was supposed to open doors, to sit up nice and straight and not to speak a word. That didn't last. I learned a lot from him . . . We rode and rode and rode thru narrow streets - - the buildings were dust colored - - the people, coming home from work, were all dust colored too. No hats, no sleek hairdos like Paris. No spots of color in the groups. The women, - - - were certainly not pretty. I'm conditioned by Dior.

A note on the people in Hannah's orbit. My skills uncovering details on her friends were improving, and it would be impossible to count the hours I spent tracking internet leads, connecting the dots that connected Hannah to her people. She collected them through her vast network of Evansville connections. At the time of Hannah's visit, Major General William Nutter was the Commander of the US Army of the occupation in Austria. He was also Chief of Staff of the US Army European Command during the building of the Berlin Wall. Peggy, his wife, the former Marjorie L. Gooch, was born in Evansville and lived there until age nine when her family moved to Texas. Peggy and Hannah, three years apart in age, might have been childhood friends. If so, they had a shared spunk. The *El Paso Times* reported that Peggy was "well-known . . . through her ability as a dancer and dancing instructor." It is easy to picture eight-year-old Hannah dancing hand and hand with Peggy while Hannah played around with words . . . Gooch, goocha choo. Gooches were sprinkled all throughout Evansville. Hannah's brother Thomas married Jess Gooch, who I add to Hannah's vast network of women: Jess, Peggy, Carrie, Tony, Tante, Frances, Josephine, Hazel, Edna, and Alice. Yet, Hannah wasn't without men. First the freighter captain, now a sergeant. She made a point of referring to him as "her" sergeant, a slight display of ownership. A psychologist might want to analyze that. She was a gatherer, a collector extraordinaire of people extraordinaire. Collecting to belong. As the poet Rilke wrote: "Go to the limits of your longing." Hannah did.

Peggy made sure Hannah had an escort for her next day's outing, another man for her collection. Best for someone like Hannah to not wander into the Russian zone and lose a sense of time. That would be something Hannah could do . . . wander and lose herself in more than one way. Bill made sure Hannah understood the risk: some people who entered the Russian zone never returned.

> Another day - - Peggy is sending her car with another boy, to take me to castles. My driver was named Jr. I gave him a pack of cigarettes I'd gotten on the freighter, and he told me all about himself.
>
> . . . Then Jr. drove me thru Vienna Woods, winding up and up. We stopped for lunch at a place hung like a cliff swallow's nest. It looked out toward foothills of the Alps and over the city . . . Then we came back to the city and drove thru the courtyard of the winter palace . . . The crown jewels were locked up. I didn't give a hoot. I DID see a Russian soldier. I had never laid eyes on one before. He looked nice and grim and chunky. Junior pointed out two more. Lolling on a bench . . . There were slim and blonde – good looking boys. Might have been just anybody. Shucks!
>
> There was one more palace. I've forgotten whose it was. Joseph someone. The one who didn't have a manly figure . . . It's an art museum now. With gardens all around it. Page Adolph – it had benches. And a playground. No bigger than a handkerchief. Suddenly there was a cloudburst, so we ran for it. Jr. let me out at the enamel shop.

> After Jr. dropped me I went and yearned over the ceramics. Found
> a print shop - - not yours, Carrie - - on the Kartenstrasse I got three
> lovely prints of Turner.

Crown jewels for which she didn't give a hoot, yet something behind
Hannah's yearnings went deeper than the item, whether ceramics, enamel
or prints. Hannah longed for that which connected her to the heart
and soul of others. In her pages and pages of reporting to "Everyone"
about her encounters, whether at cocktail parties, shopping or on park
benches, Hannah was collecting "stuffs": people, places, and experiences.
She immersed herself in the lives of others. Good company all around.
A way to fend off being alone. A way to look at others in context of
oneself. My endeavor to understand Hannah was helping me understand
myself. I inserted myself into her world, to understand mine.

In the "let's get to know ourselves department," I have been analyzing
her analyzing.

> I've decided that you cannot say, "The Viennese do this - - or that"
> or "Americans are this way" or "The French are so and so." Each
> person is quite separate from each other person. But we tend to
> judge the lot by the one we know. We don't even know that ONE
> too well.

My interpretation is influenced by "the one we know," as Hannah put
it, and that one happens to be me. Her mind and my mind could be
described as over active. I can't help myself any more than Hannah could.

Early in my adulthood, my mother wrote that it was too bad I
analyzed things so much, expected others to be perfect, and that I
should try to be patient with other people. Being married for twenty-
six years cured me of expecting others to be perfect. My over-analyzing
is tempered now and again by pulling weeds, hiking, swimming. I've
analyzed that. My mother claimed she was more of a practical mind
who doesn't want to make a philosophical issue of everything, quoting
her Swarthmore philosophy professor: "Would you rather be a happy
pig or an unhappy philosopher?" She lamented that my father over-

analyzed. He did. He had to have known when advising me to "do something" with Hannah's letters that I needed something to chew on and analyze as I sorted out my life. In my defense, my mother's words about me were written forty years ago. Imperfections are now better accepted both in "the one I know too well" and in others. Examining Hannah's ways, her assets and liabilities, increased my comfort with letting go, almost, of "one should" messages instilled by the one who said she was of a practical mind. There must be something in between being a happy pig and an unhappy philosopher.

And on the subject of "should," the next section of Hannah's Vienna letter was about "should nots," about having judgments, though maybe that word should be replaced with the word "opinions." Judgment can carry a negative or positive connotation. As a child, the statement drilled in to me was, "One should use good judgment." The trick is having good judgment without being judgmental. That may mean staying on one's own side of the street. That trick Hannah didn't always master.

Back to parties in Vienna and one that took place in June after the Marshall Plan changeover in which the British replaced the Americans until the Austrian State Treaty went into effect. I found myself once again sitting back in amazement at my grandmother's skill at finessing these invitations. This was another time I couldn't be alone with what I was learning. I called a friend and said, "I have to read you this!" Hannah was in conversation with Colonel Mallory, with whom she had doings in South America. I searched for how she knew him and his wife Ester—no luck—but I suspect John Leich's foreign service network. Colonel Mallory was from Texas, a physician in the US Army Medical Corps in Brazil from 1952 to 1955, and commanding officer of evacuation hospitals in North Africa, Italy, France, and Germany. After WWII, he lived at Army posts including in South America. Sergeants, Captains, Colonels, and soon a Russian General. A collection theme continued and one category in her collection: interesting men.

After the reception that followed the change over yesterday, where you'd shaken hands with Russians, talked to all sorts of people from all sorts of ideologies, Col Mallory and I were talking. He said,"Just spots of protoplasm, overlaid with what we're taught to do and how we're taught to do it." (Exactly what the book you gave me, Frances said). That was quite some party. The Russians move around with their interpreters. The General in charge here is Molokof (not Molotof). He wears spurs and has a bald spot. From it down to his bull neck, his head was shaved. His wife was with him. Dowdy but unconscious of it. Gold teeth in front. No English. One of Peggy's friends speaks Russian, so she made conversation for us.

Comment on Hannah: Molokof is spelled Molotov. Spelling sometimes eluded her, as she admitted earlier in this letter: "I saw a book in a shop window, called 'How to learn to spell in six minutes a day.' I don't have six minutes." So much to write and so little time for spelling. Hannah's philosophy was that getting ideas down on paper was more important than being stalled over spelling, and spell check was not an option.

Hannah couldn't finish a letter without an observation about people and what made them "tick," though that might be ever so clear by now. The following supplies more evidence that gathering up warm hearts was part of fending off insecure feelings about being alone.

Here's another instance. A boy on the freighter, as part of training in the Merchant Marine, was working on the ship as a cadet to learn to be an officer. He loved Germany. Everything about it. Why? Because one man, on the docks in Hamburg, had smiled at him. Then he took the boy out, bought his dinner and took him to a roller skating rink. He never will forget that. I think of South America in that same way. Because of kindness beyond the call of duty, that was offered me. But break down my feeling: the kindness I remember wasn't South America. One woman was Italian, one was Spanish. Two were French. One man was Portuguese. And so on. But when I think of them I think - - South America. You just can't make blanket judgments.

I have a second sergeant - - a more hard bitten one . . . He thinks the Russians will "pull a fast one." . . . I haven't any business to talk to sergeants. Of course I do, the minute we're left alone.

I am now collecting Hannah thoughts on both women and men, whether Captain Darlington, Adolph, or her sergeant, and coming up in the next section, a male secretary, her waiter, and the young women she met at Peggy's house, Susie and Charlotte.

I wish I had an aide, like Bill's. They're the masculine for social secretaries. They introduce you and bring you drinks and are broken hearted when you take tomato juice. They think for you, fetch and carry and pick up what you drop . . .

/re/ atmosphere once more. Grinsing. Where everybody is happy and you sing and drink together. Peggy doesn't want the girls to go there with their dates. (Remember, Jess, when you wouldn't let me have a buggy date with Strother Banks?) Same thing, magnified. Peggy says the men crawl over tables and chew at girls.

Susie's back again. And Charlotte. They are both slim and the last word in "smartness." Susie's floating round all summer . . . Peggy says that Susie's father divorced her mother to marry an opera singer. Later on, he died. Susie went to pieces. Has been taken down to see what makes her tick by psychiatrists. Can't get herself straightened out. You'd never guess that from the surface. She seems poised and quiet. Too much money. What she needs is a need to work (Who am I to know answers.) She asked me to lunch with her tomorrow.

We talked for ages . . . Girls today are so darned interesting - - Susie has a master's in English. Charlotte has studied voice and painting– she has a job in the Walter Reid Hospital . . . She makes scientific drawings of surgery and stuffs. They both are decorative - - know their style and dress it - - appear poised and confident. If they are, I miss my guess. They're not a bit more confident than we were at their age. Underneath defenses. They still have emotions to be dealt with.

Who doesn't still have emotions to be dealt with? When I think I have addressed some, others emerge when unexpected, or the ones I thought I had handled, reminded me that was not the case.

Back to Hannah. More than a few paragraphs later, after she meandered through the topic of concerts, streetcars, castles, and flowers, she interrupted her broadcast to return to analyzing people, herself included. Nothing opaque about Hannah.

> Interrupted broadcast. For psychiatric probing. It occurs to me that
> it may occur to you that I ask only men for help. Come to think
> of it, I guess I do. I'm not quite sure why. Men don't think you're
> dumb. They think you're a helpless female. They respond more
> quickly. Women look right thru you. Not always - - but sometimes.
> I've tried 'em. Every time I make a sure fire statement like that one,
> I know it is true. IN Paris, a shabby woman walked two blocks with
> me to show me where to turn a corner. But a smartly set up woman
> doesn't do that.

Hannah's first letter from Vienna to "Everybody," all seven pages of it, was coming to an end. She was hobbling and not close to dying. She was still taking in all that she could see and sending off what she dubbed "riff raff." One of my favorite passages showed her personality in spades:

> I could hardly hobble home to lay me down to die. Had dinner
> for the first time at the Bristol. Under crystal chandeliers, in a rosy
> haze from pink silk candle shades. Carrie, listen! Do you recall the
> fireplace? OK. Do you remember the pillars that flank it at the sides?
> Flesh colored plaster - - fat, with wavy upward curving lines, just like
> rounded stomachs and more rounded spanking places - - and with

bosoms here and there. I couldn't bear to look at it and I couldn't look the other way. I've seen too many statues, they possess me. Or do I mean obsess me? I kicked off my slippers - - I'd removed my Archlocks in honor of the evening. Lost one under the table. So, I thought I'd better go to bed. Tomorrow is another day.

When you're tired of all this riff raff, say so.

Love - -Mrs. Trimble

How could anyone privileged to be in Hannah's "Everybody" group tell her they were tired of her riff raff?

Not long after her first Vienna letter, Hannah was back writing to her contemporaries, making up for lost time. At age sixty-seven, she was having fun, bringing smiles for "Everyone":

Dear Everybody,

Good gracious, I haven't written for two days! I'll be lost in the past. Tonight, for no reason at all, I was thinking about Lugano, so I ordered venison for dinner. Remember Carrie, that was where the waiter brought a needle point footstool, because the chairs were so high you couldn't touch the floor? It was there we ate concoctions for dessert. A concoction (quote Miss Heim) is "a sweet, compounded of various ingredients." I had one here last night. It turned out to be nothing but a kokonuss cream cake.

Comment: I didn't like the venison too much. I thought of Bambi. For the present I have given up the under sidewalk kellers. I'm eating at the Bristol, where I can wear the new junk jewelry I'm accumulating. And eat butter and green salads. There is music – the Blue Danube and the Merry Widow - - the sort designed to aid digestion of "refreshing" foods. That's Hazel's word.

I can attest that accumulating what she called "junk jewelry" meant more than a few pieces. I am the owner of much of her junk. In tribute, when I wear one of her pieces, others are intrigued and call them unique. They are hardly junk. A woman with a wrinkled life-filled face sitting next to me during a monthly luncheon lecture leaned over to ask for a better look at my necklace, once Hannah's, made up of pecan, walnut, hazel, and Brazil nuts, each with a wire through the center, each crunched together and secured to the neck chain. I told her about my grandmother and the junk jewelry collection. The woman's next question surprised me. She asked if at each of the luncheons I could wear a different one of my grandmother's necklaces for her to see. I obliged.

Hannah was working on her German skills. As usual, along with her lighthearted comments she added introspection, worthy of thought, another theme that was trending.

> In some ways it is better not to know a language that's spoken all about you. You have a sort of privacy of thought. Your attentions are not divided. When you don't have to listen to what a person says to you, or think up a reply, you are perhaps more conscious of a person as a person. (That's as clear as mud, but I know what I mean.) Like turning off a hearing aid. Thank goodness you can turn it on again. I've not been lonely for a minute in Vienna. The atmosphere is kind and friendly.

I lingered on one word, "lonely," and began an interior monologue about the relevance of loneliness to collecting. Hannah made a point to say she was not lonely, yet by writing about it, she had to have thought that would be a possibility. During her South American trip, she fended off loneliness, took solace in the kind Exprinter Bank man who told her about his loneliness. She vowed at that time never to take another long trip, yet here she was in Europe, partway through another long trip alone, with claims she was not lonely. Without altitude sickness and having the "Everybody" group and Tony in Paris and Peggy in Vienna along with Sergeants, Colonels and a long list of others, she fended off loneliness.

The maid has just brought your letter, Carrie, and a bunch of
peonies from Peggy's mother! That postcard, Carrie, is a honey! And
feel very grateful for my friends. Your news is terrible!! I can't be a
secretary.* Can't I change my name or something? Last night I had
both a card and letter from you, Dorothy. Full of news for which
I thank you. One from Ann and two from Margaret. All three of
the letters that you thought might not reach me, have come in on
schedule, Adolph. I'll take all of them with me, Sunday, when I go.
There is one from Hazel and from Bee, a fat one from Alice Fraser, -
- Edna Page, from Paris, on the way to Minneapolis - - Have you all
my new address, say I greedily?

I've said goodbye to Sergeant Pierce. I'm on the loose without a
sergeant.

Hannah's list of who's who in the letter-writing department is like
a list of who donated to a deserving cause. Her cause was to not feel
forgotten. Might she have put out this list of names to trigger others
to give her letters? Hannah needed letters, a stack to be sure, to not be
lonely. Calling out friends by name gets their attention. Case in point,
Frances came up multiple times in the letters referencing the book about
pride Frances had mentioned, a topic that reached deep within Hannah
and fed her need to figure out the unfigure-outable, the unknowable
parts of who she was. Frances's book came up when Hannah was sorting
out the reaction of a Viennese woman sitting next to her at a Japanese
ballet. The woman was not enchanted. Hannah was. Looking at others,
those with courage can look back at themselves without defense, a lesson
I am learning. The ballet meshed with Hannah: sensual, atypical and
imaginative with fairies, dreams, gardens, and a lover who couldn't be
grasped. Lovers out of reach. Yes, I noted.

And that Japanese ballet. No other people could have done it. A
thousand times this summer I think of Frances' book - - "We are

---

*Hannah was nominated by the Clio Club to be Secretary.

the sum of what we've done and how we've done it." They danced
against a black backdrop. The costumes were sensual perfection.
Their dancing wove a fairy story - - the first one was a dream - - an
artist, painting in his garden, fell asleep - - the dream quality was
perfect - - his struggle to escape - - the sting of insects - - the maiden
that he couldn't grasp - - the witch who controlled his movements - -
- It was more interpretive than ballet....Precision movements. Slow,
then frenzied. No other people could have done it that way.

The woman next to me - - a Viennese - - didn't like it at all. She said
it was primitive - - it was. She said there was no music - - There were
five instruments - - one you plucked the strings - - one was like a
flute - - The players sat up on the stage with the dancers. She likes,
instead, the Viennese ballet - - Some ones of us like ham and eggs
for breakfast - - some like croissants and coffee. An Austrian can
never be a Turk. Why is that?

As I read Hannah's philosophic musings, I pictured my mother looking
straight at her mother stating, "Oh Mother!" with the same tone of
exasperation I often heard her use with her sister when she said, "Oh
Ann!" While Ann may have been captivated by Hannah's philosophic
wanderings and her delight in sensual details and what verged on the
avant-garde, my mother, the practical realist, had little patience for
such things. What would Hannah have said back to her daughter? The
two words were in front of me in her next paragraph, words from my
childhood associated with Hannah: fiddle-faddle.

Hannah's fiddle-faddle was going to American Express for traveler
checks. After another man tended to her, this time a Mr. Schuller,
whoever he was, she mused about whether she was up to her next
challenge, managing on her own. Early on I found it hard to imagine
she needed tending, though people who come across as capable can
put on a good front. People whose minds meander, who lose buttons,
who lose entry papers to the Dior Salon, could welcome someone
organizing for them.

Like Peggy, I have JOBS. Only mine are really fiddle faddle.

I had to go a second time out to the Bahnhof - - to get my ticket for
Nurnburg. Sat in a padded armchair while Mr. Schuller bought it,
reserved my seat next to a window, insured my bags and so forth.
This is the life, my darlings. But tomorrow is another day. I wonder if I'll have what it takes to manage things alone. The stations at
the end of a long shopping street for common people. Not like the
Kartnerstrasse. Women there wear the most Godawful clothes. But
men who step out with them look happy. Not proud and sleek, like
escorts on the Kartnerstrasse. Happy. They laugh together. They
look worn together but as relaxed as Aetna after an eruption. Such
women don't play up to men. The young hold hands, or throw an
arm across a shoulder - - not with a studied gesture, as per Paris.
Teenagers have that brook and river look. Softlike and rosy.

A question to consider: did Hannah play up to men? That game
never has been mine. I may send the message I can do fine on my
own. Deceptive. In reviewing my collection of Hannah's men, she may
have sat at that "playing up to men" game table. If not, she certainly
found a way to get them to come to her aid, to offset her alone feeling.
Insecurity noodled within her, she was not as independent as she let
on. She isn't alone in that. Once on her own, she again fell prey to one
of her weaknesses, one that she managed well on her own—collecting,
buying, and making commentary.

On the way back - - - I passed another gallery of prints and pictures . . . I bought one very small woodcut because it made me think
of me. An old farm horse had been unhitched out in a field, and
stood with drooping muscles, against an evening sky. Then, later
on, - - - I spent two hours there - - - I bought another, just because
the little man who owned the shop adored it. He told me, in the
few words we had in common, that it was the highest art. He'd get
all hazed up when he looked at it . . . When I finally left I got no

farther than the window. Wait until I show you that one! A fourteen
century Madonna. She looked exactly like the woman who shared
my table at Demel's yesterday. A red cheeked butterball. Full of
schlag, She weighed three hundred, if she weighed a pound. She is a
picture of Vienna. I see her every day.

I might as well tell you and get it over with. I've bought you a
dirndl, Ann . . . And while I have the line to you, - - I called the
friend who is a friend to some friend of yours - - she will have lunch
with me on Saturday.

The department of complete confusion speaking. Why is it that
uncorseted roly poly Viennese carry slim, elegant umbrellas, in a
case of silk? While in Lisbon the people on the streets are slim and
elegant, and their umbrellas, big, black cotton ones, with wooden
handles, crooked around their arms.

Hannah's riddle about umbrellas aside, one line in the above provided
more evidence to clarify how a woman from southern Indiana came to
know so many people in Europe. Hannah wasn't hesitant to call a friend
of a friend of a friend of her daughter's. Many people would be hesitant
to reach out to such a loose connection; not Hannah. She was a master
of networking. In her essay "That Inner Me," she wrote she was very
shy as a child. Not just shy, but very shy. That doesn't seem to be the
case later in her life. She knew what she wanted and went after it. If she
wanted to walk to chance upon shops, she did. If riding streetcars to
collect parks called out to her, she answered.

Besides parks, junk jewelry, enameled items, prints, ceramics, books,
and gardens, while she never admitted it, she collected people.

I ride the streetcars to collect my parks. Parks, like palaces are all
alike. In each one there is that sleeping woman, who throws her
feet outside into the open - - the same mothers pushing babies with
self-conscious pride - - the children - - these were throwing red

balloons into the fountain which took the place of Mozart's statue. And there were the lookerson. This park is full of ancient trees, that spread shadows on the paths. Someone told me they were maples, but they were hung with gumballs.

Trees hanging with gumballs? Was she channeling one of her third graders to come up with that? When you teach children, you can't help but teach yourself, that is, if your mind is receptive. Before she ended her Vienna letter, there was another sentence to add to my collection of Hannah reflecting on Hannah, and to my bewilderment at one of her actions.

I learn only by the trial and error method. Briefly, never mail a package in Vienna. Nobody in the office here, speaks English. The forms are all made out in German. Someone always bails (or is it bales) me out. This time a sweet young voice said firmly, "I shall help you." She was stuck with me for twenty minutes. You'd think she really liked it. While we waited in a line she lighted up about my necklace (the way they all do here when they are pleased with something). The necklace was that black and silver Siamese one. So I yanked off my earrings and gave them to her. She put them on and we went together to the Albertina Art Museum, which I hadn't tackled because you have to climb a million steps to reach the galleries.

Help and compliments aside, what perplexes me is how Hannah could yank off her earrings and give them to a stranger, and then head off to a museum with her. Accept the compliment and give a smile in return, yes. Take off her earrings and give them away? I suppose if she considered her jewelry to be junk, she could yank them off and take pleasure in giving them to someone as a gesture of thanks. Still, I can't fathom doing that.

Dear Everybody

Chapter Eighteen

Collecting and Gathering

Two years earlier, while throwing up on a plane in South America, Hannah was drawn to the magnificence of the eternal outside her window. Outside the train window on the way to Germany while suffering a head cold, she succumbed again.

> My train left the Vienna Bahnhof at some ungodly hour before
> breakfast. I had caught a cold . . . when I wasn't sneezing or asleep,
> I was conscious of beauty all about me - - meadows sprinkled with
> wee flowers, like the Alps – forests – with grey mountains all around
> - - Women working in the fields - - raking grass up into heaps. Some
> they patted into shapes like loaves of bread. Some - - the messy ones,
> looked like those moon-faced, long haired sheep dogs that you see in
> Scotland. I mean the hay stacks - - not the women.

In 2018 I was tagging along with Hannah as she moved on to Germany, and at the same time I was packing up to move to Maine. It took me ten years to decide where I truly belonged. Ten years from buying the Maine house to giving up Marin. I was a slow learner. No rushing the process.

No rushing my tagging along with Hannah. She was teaching me to go to the heart of desire, knowing life would throw unpleasantries along the way. One nugget in my collection of Hannah wisdom confirmed what she was doing for me:

> Little words spoken in odd moments play their part. I could not
> foresee these moments, but come upon them around many corners.
> I twitched them out and used them. They are fun. They leaven the
> whole lump, which goodness knows, becomes pretty lumpy at times.

Hannah spoke truth. Gathering up beauty provided an emotional bank account for tough times. If the Hubbs family tragedies started the chain of women in my family who found solace in beauty and collected whatever warmed their hearts, I am the beneficiary of that legacy.

Hannah's spirit was nurtured by infatuation. The beauty of poetry seduced her. A paragraph in her first letter from Germany was a reminder:

> A long time ago Aunt Hannah had a book that was my favorite
> dish. "Curfew Shall Not Ring Tonight" mit pictures. "Far, far out
> she swung" just like a dust rag, shaken from an upstairs window.
> She was barefoot and wore floating garments....Well, this morning,
> when I was not asleep or sneezing, I saw those bell towers every-
> where I looked.

Excerpts, tragic and romantic, from the poem that spoke to Hannah:

> SLOWLY England's sun was setting o'er the hilltops far away,
> Filling all the land with beauty at the close of one sad day,
> And the last rays kissed the forehead of a man and maiden fair,—
> He with footsteps slow and weary, she with sunny floating hair;
> He with bowed head, sad and thoughtful,
> she with lips all cold and white,
> Bessie comes with flying footsteps, eyes aglow with
> love-light sweet;
> Kneeling on the turf beside him, lays his pardon at his feet.

In his brave, strong arms he clasped her, kissed the face
upturned and white,
Whispered, "Darling, you have saved me,—
Curfew will not ring tonight!"*

Darling, you have saved me. Brave strong arms. Enticing.

Hannah succumbed to ethereal images, and when beauty was in short supply, as in Nuremberg, she let it be known with words that weren't in short supply. The war's aftermath in Germany was stark and grim, challenging Hannah's appetite for warmth and smiles.

I miss Vienna. I miss the ruffles of rose colored glass beneath my ceiling light. I miss my rose brocaded walls. And I miss the worn path down the middle of my carpet at the Bristol. My background in the Grand Hotel is super modern. My fixtures are brass abstractions. Even the water faucets are more functional than most. The hotel is not manned by human beings. They are automatons. The young waiters in the dining room deliver one poached egg, three abreast. All they need's a touch of lipstick and a circle of red paint on both their cheeks, to be chocolate soldiers. I'm intimidated by the doorman. He looks like the kind of bruiser who throws people out of bars if they don't behave themselves. When he bows and says, "Good morning", he is out of character. The concierge is furtive. The elevator operator has lost an arm. He will take no lip from anyone.

I have a hangover from Vienna. I can't move smoothly from one background to another. To do it, I have to slough off something imitative, and add a new protective coloring. I've been asking for Grimm's fairy tales. This is grim, all right, but it sure doesn't have the feelings of a fairy tale. From my window I can see a row of bombed out buildings. The silhouette of Nurnberg . . . is solidly rectangular. The Grand Hotel is antiseptic. It doesn't shine. It glistens. I just

* "Curfew Must Not Ring Tonight," Rose Hartwick Thorpe, 1867

don't like the atmosphere. There are attitudes around me that I react against....

. . . No one ever laughs. Everyone is in a hurry - - late for an appointment. Crowds have personalities. They have tempos. Their movement is defined by some contagion of emotion that pushes them all toward the same objective. They move with uniformity. That is, in Nurnberg. In Vienna men and women blow in all directions, in a hurry. Here they move lock step in one direction. And yet these crowds are all made up of people as different from one another as you're different from me. I just don't get it. I understand exactly nothing about everything that makes us tick.

I keep preaching to myself, "Don't make blanket statements about people. Don't have blanket feelings either I find I do that, unfairly, anyway. I just don't like Nurnberg. I like certain people in it. That's a different thing. I liked our shabby guide who walked a block out of his way to show me where to ask for bobby pins. I liked my waitress in the keller thing at the Kaiserhof. Every time she passed me she stopped to smile a broad, warm smile, and said "Yaw, yaw, yaw, ees goot, huh?" I like a woman in a grocery where I bought some oranges. She spoke to me before I looked at her. "Your hair is beautiful," she said and helped me with my change. You have no idea how much that cheered me up. After all, Americans are human beings too. I liked a woman who shared my train seat when I went to the Rothenburg which was simply marvelous. It has a glackenspiel to end all glackenspiels. (I know I spelled that wrong). At twelve o'clock the figure of the burgomaster stands in an open window . . . I'm getting off the track again. I liked the woman on the train. She touched my silver necklace - - the one from Mexico and said "Fair shern." I touched her skirt and said, "Beautiful," she said, "Pairlawn," smiling. I touched my stockings. "Pairlawn, too," I said. I am repeating this idiotic conversation to show you the stuff friendships are made of. She showed me all the little cities that we

passed - -- - took out a tiny bottle of perfume - - made me share
it - - gave me a mint - - We got off together in Rothenburg....If we
weren't friends what were we?

One more "I liked" and I will stop. I liked the boy who did my hair.
He was an artist, relaxed and laughing - - He felt a sort of rhythm of
excitement thru his fingers.

I included all of Hannah's "idiotic conversation" as it adds color to
her portrait. Warm caring connections, feeling valued, and beautiful,
hair included. I subscribe to each.

Leaving grim Nuremberg behind, the role of beautiful hair in the
lineup of women in my family can't be ignored. Hannah knew its allure.
"I have had a permanent, first whack – today. A honey! I look simply
MARvelous!" I wouldn't be surprised if she were alive today to learn she
wrote an article entitled "The Seduction of Hair." She wrote about her
hair several times from Europe and in her war letters about Margaret.
A few reminders:

Monday morning - - the 16th and still dark
    Her hair is still done your way and is brushed dutifully every night.

Undated letter
    She has a new permanent done by a Mr. Isaacs, formerly of New
York and Paris, which cost her many hours of domestic servant
interviewing . . . it had to be none but the best because you might
see it.

Thursday the 6th of January
    Margaret attacks her hair fiercely each night with a hair brush
and emerges shining as never before. I have even contributed another
brush, since the life of this one cannot be long. She is firm in her
determinations born of love. She will, she says, wear her hair exactly
one way until you come home, because you like it that way - -

Using a scale measuring the role hair plays in a woman's life, my mother would score on the high end, Hannah would not be far behind and her mother Fanny Rose, who almost was hidden away because of her hair, might edge in between Hannah and my mother. I place myself near Hannah.

Before moving to Maine, I weeded out photos stored in my linen closet, spreading the ones from the folder I labeled "Mother's family," out side by side. A pattern became clear. Sarah Ann Hubbs's long dark brown hair was pulled back, parted in the middle. Her daughter Fanny Rose's long dark hair was pulled back, parted in the middle. Her daughter Hannah's long dark hair was pulled back, parted in the middle. Skip my mother. In every photo from a young woman on, she pulled her hair off her forehead straight back, no part. In my college photo, my long dark hair was not pulled back, but, yes, it was parted in the middle. I framed our photos in a line up, a reassurance that I belonged, generation after generation of shared hair, a reminder of the ties that bind.

Hannah knew a haircut was more than a haircut. Rick has styled my hair for over twenty years, and we share our ups and downs, joys, and sorrows. A man who knows women, hair, and care. Hannah and my mother understood. With my mother's move to Maine, she lamented the loss of her hair appointments with Robert who, for over thirty years, gave her permanents and washed her hair weekly. She would now have to wash her own hair, which I note, looked like Grace Kelly's, soft flowing waves framing her face. After my mother's stroke when she was almost ninety, she insisted that the beauty parlor in the assisted living center had been moved and she couldn't find it. Confusion became agitation verging on panic. I told her I would find the salon. As she was dying, I brushed her hair and reassured her that her hair looked fine. Holding on to scraps of beauty until the end.

On one of my visits to Rick's salon the girl washing my hair commented that she had never washed undyed hair. In her words, "It feels awesome." Not lost on me is the irony that the salon's white, silver, and black décor matches my hair. Silver strips of aluminum foil adorn most heads, the furniture is black, the staff wear black in varying degrees of edginess and body clinging, a black cover drapes over the black gown which you put on in the changing stations, a stopping place on the journey to beauty, the words "Selfie Room" on the doors.

Among the many reasons to be full-time in Maine, I wouldn't hear "awesome" so much, and I wouldn't be surrounded by women in salon chairs denying their age, looking over at my untreated hair exposing mine. And yet another reason, over the course of twenty years, very few men in Marin have said I have great hair. One called me "White Fox." That was unsettling. I took pride in being among the one percent of Marin women with natural hair color. After my divorce, a friend told me I should dye my hair. Her proclamation: "Men don't like white hair." I was shocked. I had never dyed my hair, could never dye my hair even if it meant not meeting the standard for what men in Marin found attractive. I said nothing to my friend whenever her telltale grey stripe started to show, revealing her real aging self. Her jig would be up. If Marin women were known for farm-to-table organics, they certainly looked the other way when chemicals saturated their heads. My white hair is at home in Maine. I justify my Marin hair styling extravagance as an offset to having no manicures, pedicures, hair coloring, and make-up, except "white out" for the tired look under my eyes. I do use lipstick now and again. If lipsticks had expiration dates, mine would all be past due. Like my mother and Hannah, a part of my identity is tied up in my hair. I am in the collection of women tied up in needing to feel desirable, to feel parts of ourselves hold beauty.

∽

Back to Hannah in Nuremberg and my collection of Hannah's comments on Hannah as I continue to comment on me to myself.

> You can't add people up and judge them. You can't add unlike
> factors. But in spite of that, you get a mass impression. I don't like
> Nurnberg. I feel frustrated because I cannot listen to what they say.

They must have reason for their resentments against those of us who didn't harm them.

Everywhere you look the future is emerging from the past. Everywhere I looked the past was folding into the present. Hannah planted landmarks as I mapped out who she was and the parts of her which landed in me. In a letter about American soldiers, she started off with, "There are so many unrelated things I want to talk about. Talk too much already . . ." and then proceeded to offer up a lengthy befuddlement about the wartime morals of girls and our soldiers running after them. Her ending thought: "How can anyone live so long and know so little as I have lived and haven't known." Which harkens to my comment of late about why at my age I continue to be surprised that I am surprised about the actions of some people. I'll leave off where Hannah leaves off:

> Goodby again. I'll write letters tomorrow for each one that I have. I keep them and read them over.

> Much love - - - you know that, Hannah.

I was collecting letters, returning to them over and over. It didn't take Hannah long to leave the stark reality of post-war Germany behind and return to comments about her purchases. She claimed, in part, to hold Ann responsible for all she was buying, which seemed unfair given her previous claim of becoming a jellied mass of non-resistance when facing a store. She may have needed to look at herself in the mirror, a practice she confessed to avoiding when not wanting to face reality. If I counted up the number of times Hannah brought up the subject of handcrafts, I would need many hands.

> . . . partly because of Ann's handcraft yearnings. I shall probably swim home . . . I've bought us each a music box with those dainty woodcut outs of Grimm's fairy tales. Some I didn't get before. For myself, I bought a rubber duck. Its head's tied up in a scarf and

her eyes would make a melancholic laugh. I keep it by my bed at
night. When I switch on the light to see what time it is, it keeps
me company.

That's another contradiction in these German people. These sealed
up, unsmiling men are artists with imagination. They design their
toys with subtle humor - - they don't go in for slapstick, like car-
toons in our movies. The stores are full of mass production - - cheap
merchandise of every sort – but here and there you find the handcraft shops. Full of beautiful designing. I almost lose my mind - -
because I want to take things home.

My home is full of Hannah's handcrafted "beautiful designings." Items
that she never mentioned buying, but I have in excess, are postcards by
the German artist, Sulamith Wulfing. One day as a diversion, I spread
out the four-inch stack of Wulfing cards on the floor. There are thirteen
of one of the images, nine of another not counting the three I sent to
friends. Several more images are multiples of three. Ann mailed Wulfing
postcards now and again, which showed my mother wasn't the only one
given a stack. Each card required a pause to take in the romantic ethereal
images of suitors and women, children and nature. Quoting Wulfing:
"To people attuned to my compositions, they may well be mirrors of
their own experience." Once exposed, these images are infectious for the
vulnerable. My mother and aunt are evidence, and I was not immune to
being swept into Wulfgang's spell at an early age. Hannah did lose her
mind with these postcards. Did she say to the clerk, "I'll have twenty of
these please, and ten of those, and while you are at it, please throw in
any remaining single ones?"
  More evidence of her need to "have":

When I went to bed, I felt lonesome without my hat tree with the
fingernails, but I have a recessed, marble lavatory, and an upper light
that has a cartwheel of ruffled, cherry colored glass below it. I have
equipment for shining shoes . . . have brocaded armchairs to match

my ruffled fixture, and brocaded, cherry colored hangings with red
tassels . . . I have an entrance with a hat rack . . . in the hallway, is
my little tootlejohnny. I consider this last word in consideration . . .
I'd love to write a "thing" about toilets I have met. In Paris you
leaned back upon a button, with idle grace. Here, you press down
on a gadget and a rush of water from some mountain waterfall
descends. A noisy torrent. I have an ivory telephone. Oh shucks, no.
It must be a cow horn. Anyway, it isn't plastic. It stands erect, just
like my sergeant. I have put a print I got in Paris on my dressing
table . . . I love my bed. It has turned its back on both the windows
(the sun rises at 3 o'clock . . . The first morning I rose with it.) I have
a huge down pillow - - not foam rubber. Not used up smashed feath-
ers - - DOWN. And a down puff. If I decide to live on in Vienna,
these will be my reasons.

"I have . . . I have . . . I have," over and over. Having fills up emptiness.
    Hannah crowed about her "stuffs" and the sensory delights that
seduced and comforted her. While I am not inclined to write about
Tootlejohnnies, I could write about DOWN. I can't live without it.
Puffs of pleasure embracing me at night and greeting me in the morning.
On the subject of getting carried away and "haves," before Hannah left
Nuremberg and moved on to Munich it didn't take much for her to
claim to only have "one more comment" on the beds she met:

The sweeping up the crumbs department: Subject, beds. Did I, or
not, report to you that in the Grand Hotel, I had a feather bed?
Getting in requires reflection. Is it on or under? I got under, with
a clipper jacket buttoned up. That left a second puff, a huge square
one. What do they do with that? I dropped in on my stomach like
whipped cream on meringue.

Hannah had a childlike sense of wonder and words. How else could
she drop "like whipped cream on meringue." Any doubts about why
I succumb to sensory sensations are dismissed. Like a leaf, traits land
where fate takes them. I'm not pushing that gift from Hannah away.

~

Hannah's letters from her 1955 Europe trip confirmed what hit me while packing to move full-time to Maine. She was a collector extraordinaire, and I was the owner extraordinaire of a houseful of what she collected. I was surrounded by things from Hannah. Her items had accompanied me on each of my moves—Boston, Pittsburgh, Marin, and now Maine. Regardless of where I lived, representatives of my family came along, my roots carefully packed up and transplanted, making a house my home, comfortable and familiar.

The price to move across the country wouldn't be cheap, so I was going through what I owned, asking myself whether I valued each enough to pay for its journey. My move to Maine was about value, a deliberation that went on for almost ten years after my divorce. I found my bearings through Hannah. If her twig was bent for Indiana, mine wasn't bent for California, and I was packing up for the landscape that felt like home with Hannah right beside me. I had fallen under her influence and discovered where my heart belonged. Her musings about what made people tick and how we are the sum of what we do and how we do it, made clear my tick wasn't working in California. Despite the people there whom I loved, my children foremost, and my group of women friends, Maine called me.

Besides acknowledging that I owned a lot of Hannah's stuff, three other realizations hit me as I packed. One: heart items were prevalent. Two: she purchased many items in multiples. Three: Hannah gave to many. In addition to what she kept for herself, her distribution group included my mother and Ann, her five grandchildren, other relatives such as her sister-in-law Jess and various of her Dear Everybody friends. No wonder she referred to her purchases as her loot. As I inventoried what I packed, there were items Hannah gave me as a child, items passed down from Hannah to my mother which, as my mother aged, she distributed to me, and items that my mother had kept that my sister and I divided up after her death. Something from Hannah graces every room in my home. Apologies to Hannah for items left off this list.

- Five European children's Waldorf-style prints and a box full of folk dolls under a guest room bed,
- At least a half dozen silver arts-and-crafts jewelry pieces hidden in boxes in various places, supplemented by a rose quartz heart and an amethyst set in gold,
- Four handcrafted felt-backed beaded heart pendants and four beaded leather backed necklaces,
- Six Austrian Steinbock enameled bowls and trays with images of Victorian ladies and gentlemen; two are on my wainscotting tub surround, four others dispersed on dressers,
- Seven dish sets: Arabia, Nils, Quimper, Meaken, Royal Doulton, Gustaveberg, all housed in the dining room cabinets intermixed with a hand-hammered brass and pewter coffee set,
- Six hand-painted wood fairy tale figures, two of which live on the upstairs bathroom wainscotting ledge, the others stashed in a drawer,
- Austrian silk scarves, two with braided silk fringe and two without and two handmade belts, clasped together with hearts,
- Four small gold-gilded, hand carved wooden angels playing instruments on my mantle, singing for two wooden gnome men on the bookshelf across the room, one in a boat with oars, the other laughing by his side,
- Children's folk outfits plus hats and aprons from Greece, Peru, Sweden, Lapland and another, possibly Guatemalan; two hang on the stairway wall and one draped on a banister,
- A pottery man holding flowers for an accompanying woman, both standing on my dining room cabinet framed by Swedish hand-hammered sconces with hearts at the center, and
- A heart-shaped Mexican wrought iron candelabra atop my refrigerator watched over by the wooden hand carved rooster on the shelf over the stove.

The above doesn't include all the single items Hannah bought made by people who, she wrote more than once, had sunshine in their hearts, or smiles from the heart.

Hearts shaped Hannah's life. Her husband, George Arthur, died of a heart attack. The heart of her infant grandson, George Arthur, failed his premature body. Her other grandson, George, was born with a heart defect, one of the first children in the country to have open heart surgery and survive; his life shaped by his heart. Hannah had to notice the connection between hearts and those named George. I would have begged, please don't name anyone else George. The suicides, alcoholism, and disappearances in Hannah's Hubbs family were also heartbreaking. Hannah, her mother, and grandmother lived with loss and a mountain of grief that is hard to comprehend. These women soldiered on with courage, the root of which is "cor" or heart. Courage is needed to tell what is in one's heart, not hide it away.

Despite my goal to weed things out, I wasn't successful doing that with anything from Hannah. I lingered over her items as I packed each one. Even with moans of how much work it was packing all the china, I couldn't part with one plate, one bowl from any pattern. A friend who was helping asked, "How many dishes does one person need?" This wasn't about rational thinking. I was in good company with Hannah in having habits that seemed irrational to others. My collection of Hannah's collections was a comfort and a connection. She passed along more than an average appreciation for the heartfelt. A few Hannah-isms in my collection of her collecting:

  • Window shopping. On the way, I bought two books of French songs
  for the children . . . I think they're beautiful. They should be! [Paris]
  • Being weakened by will power, I went in to Cartier's. I'd promised
  me I wouldn't. [Paris]
  • Here and there you find the handcraft shops. Full of beautiful
  designing. I almost lose my mind - - because I want to take things
  home. [Nuremburg]
  • There is a potter whose atelier is here in Paris, that I dote on.
  He makes the most wonderful cockeyed figurines. No one else in
  any other corner of the world could do it the way he does. And I
  couldn't buy them because they'd smash to bits. Why do I have to
  like such things! Oh shucks. [Paris]

• There is a shop around the corner . . . I took one look and have
become a jellied mass of non-resistance . . . Jewelry . . . And she had
tiny hand-carved angels, with violins. Gilded. [Vienna]
• . . . there's a street called Graben... There are china and ceramics
there. I won't. I promise. [Vienna]
• I've found your print shop, Carrie. Print shops are a disease. I
think I've passed the crisis. [Vienna]

Passed the crisis of her disease? My experience is, it is a chronic illness
with periodic crises. Hannah's view that collecting was a disease might
have meant she thought it was not her doing, that it was done to her. I
take responsibility for my habit, and I don't appear to be past my crisis.

In the realm of the irresistible, words were included. Hannah gathered
them and played with them. Some of her words were surprising given
my image of her as a stickler about what was proper, an image I keep
adjusting. We were careful what we said around her. None of us used a
warm, endearing or playful name for her like Nani or G-mum or Granny.
She was Grandmother. If she had used the words "loot" and "stuffs" not
to mention "gotta" with me, I would have covered my mouth to hide
my response.

This loot - - there isn't much of it - - - and they say it takes about
three to four weeks. I hope you will be there when I come home so
that you two can divide stuffs. And I like to look you in the eye to
be sure you like it. [Austria, 1955]

As for her using the word "loot," did she mean to imply pillaging treasures
from whatever country she was in? Stealth comes to mind when I think
of looters.

Hannah did have a knack for sleuthing out treasures. She wrote that
the loot she bought for Margaret and Ann wasn't much "stuff." That is
hard to believe given how much she bought. And, on the word "stuff,"
my mother hated it when I used that word. Maybe Hannah used that
word to give her daughter a poke, to make her eyes roll. Maybe I did the
same to my mother. Maybe, like Hannah, my outer self doesn't match

what is churning within. Maybe her interest in "being integrated" was something for me to consider about myself. Maybe my father knew that her letters would guide me. He had to have known that Hannah's exterior didn't match her interior. Underneath the proper formal woman was a woman overcome and seduced by the sensual, a woman who had fun collecting "stuffs" and giving them away. Fun with words and sharing them. When thumbing through her scrapbook, a piece of lined paper entitled "I like the sound of it," fell out. Hannah, word connoisseur, had typed words she liked: "a tottering ghost," "a flushed moon," "flakes of drifting fear," "just a mite on the side of alone."

To use one of Hannah's phrases which I have collected, "I interrupt this broadcast." Yes, I interrupt this broadcast to go out and pull weeds. I did that to break up my packing and settle my mind. I was searching for the right word to explain Hannah's buying habits and couldn't find what I needed. I knew I would find California weeds and might find the word when pulling weeds out. Kneeling on my well-irrigated grass reaching in to my well-irrigated sunny garden of roses, I started my inner weeding mantra: "There's one," followed by "There's one." Repeat over and over until the area was cleared. I found many weeds, and reporting back on words. I found several. Compulsion came to mind along with acting on impulse, within both is a word associated with the heart, pulse. Something coursed through Hannah, driving her to collect in excess items made from the heart: many were hearts, a possible offset to her broken heart and the hearts of those she loved that were defective. My cousin born with a flawed heart lived a fragile yet full life. I am sure Hannah influenced the heartfelt way he lived. He beat the odds, surviving decades with congenital heart disease. He became a pathologist and was on the board of the National Congenital Heart Association, counseling others on how to live with a heart condition. Over her life, Hannah gave all of us more than "stuffs." She gave us intangibles.

On giving in to desire and impulses, I can't picture my mother, always so in control, doing that. Each evening at 5:00 pm, no earlier, she had one small drink of Dubonnet accompanied by a small bowl of crackers. No refills. Margaret kept a clear head. Hannah followed her heart. My mother's voice tells me to push my impulses down. Her voice often loses out. I refill my snack bowl, pour a second glass of wine, but only half-full. Thanks to Hannah's self-proclaimed collecting "disease," I have beautiful loot to treasure. Her well-curated handcrafts put me at ease. There is no dis-ease. I can't walk through a room without being taken by one item or another. Their spirit seduces me. I was inculcated by Hannah and also by my aunt who had the same impulse to collect.

> I like pretty things also . . . but mostly, as did my mother in addition
> to her interest in many things, preferred the native crafts as indica-
> tive of the people concerned. Do not degrade primitive arts . . . they
> were the beginning.

Value things from the heart, value people who give from their heart. Now out from my marriage where my heart was lonely, my warm-hearted inheritance was shoring me up. I was rediscovering the courage to be true to myself, opening up my heart to embrace what I value.

Things from the Heart

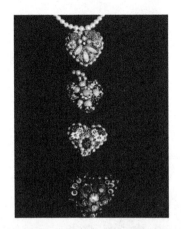 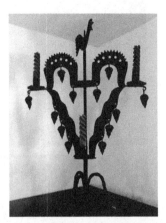

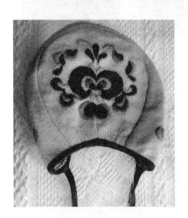 

Chapter Nineteen

How Could She Be Lonely in Germany?

After Nuremberg, sixty-seven-year-old Hannah took a day trip to Munich still wondering what makes people tick. She couldn't help herself. Her mind was ever churning and needed an outlet. Sentences poured out of her, many of which I've omitted, too many of which I have included. I was sitting at my dining room table for the last time before moving out of my Marin house, weeding through her words. The mahogany table, chairs, and sideboard wouldn't fit in my Maine house and were of interest to no one in Marin. A fellow who helps people move offered to "take them away." My mother, whose furniture it once was, would have said, "What a shame." With a smidgen of guilt, I said, "Take them." I skimmed over sections of Hannah's letter laden with tales of her Germany meanderings and focused on gems, such as wanting to knock the blocks off husbands for not helping their wives with their children. I paused, wondering if she knocked Arthur's block off when he didn't help, or did she only come to that conclusion once a grandmother? It is easy to look back and dole out admonitions.

Dear Everybody

My impressions become more and more confused . . .

Here, as in Nurnberg I am confused by contradictions. Taxi drivers keep a tiny bunch of flowers in a vase beneath their windshields. Men sit with women in buses as rigid and as silent as the faces carved in wood at Oberammergau. Those young mothers who bring their red cheeked blue eyed babies into restaurants - - those wooden table restaurants - - - - - all have that mother look - - a soft tenderness. They smile at you. While they change the baby and feed her, and put her down with a pillow on her tummy, like a feather bed, the fathers eat their dinner. They sit beside their wives and never even turn their heads. I'd knock their blocks off. But that young mother would not look the way she does if she were not contended with said husband. I don't get it!!!

There is a sensitivity to beauty here in Munich - - else why all the galleries . . . I spent hours yesterday in art museums, with a young Swiss girl. I met her on the street . . . We walked together in a park, shadowed by ancient trees, and planned with gardens. It was empty. Not one single child was playing there. No baby buggies, like Vienna. None of the old who come to feel less solitary. But the finch was in the trees.

In Garmache our waiter said "Good appetite!" and something that meant God keep you, when he served our mountain trout. Someone asked him, "Where do your girls get the lovely color in their cheeks?" He answered. "Pumpernickel - - milk - - and sunshine. Most of all, the sunshine in the heart." Heavens, you must be sick and tired of my wonderings. But - - if more of us could come to know more people - - as human beings, not as headlines in some paper, maybe we could understand more besser. Or maybe you just can't have blanket feelings about anything.

I have to go - -- this time to Salzburg. Good by - - tell me when you're bored. Or just – don't read this.

Thank you seven people who had letters waiting for me here in Salzburg. If you had the slightest idea how much they mean to me.

Collection themes are lining up: hearts with sunshine, letters as valuable as gold, strangers converting to friends, odd companions, including a duck, to avoid the lonely feeling.

~

One summer when I was visiting my parents in Maine, my mother asked me to drive her to see a friend. Neither of them could drive anymore. Both were in their eighties. Both had tasteful permanents and were among the women who age with grace. My mother's friend offered us lemonade and Pepperidge Farm cookies as we sat looking out her picture window with a full-on view of Penobscot Bay. The occasion almost called for white gloves and cloth napkins. Polite conversation was in order. My mother asked how her friend's children were doing, adult children that was. I listened with an attentive smile until inner rage set in upon hearing that her son was on his third wife, had left the other two to fend for themselves with young children. She chronicled the horrific behavior of her son as if she was merely describing the contents of her living room. I was stunned. I couldn't fathom the nonchalant look on her face. I was raging within at the tale she was telling. My mother's face was un-stunned in partnership. She nodded and stated a few "Oh dear" and "Oh my" responses. I was confused. How were these women responding as they were? With age had they accepted that in life which I had not? There was a contradiction similar to what Hannah saw in Munich. I gazed at the deep blue of the ocean, green islands dotted throughout, clear Maine sky with soft unthreatening clouds, and took in the beauty, wondering if, at their age, I would look as serene as these two when confronted with life's disappointments. At forty, I held on to my views about how life should be. Now in my sixties, I am more accepting of deviations, vow to age with as much grace as my mother and her friend, drink lemonade, eat cookies, take in the beauty the world offers up and temper down my expectations.

My career focused on observing human behavior, sorting out of the whys and wherefores. Being open minded was vital. Hannah's keen observation skills were paired with blanket feelings which she attempted to mute. Not easy pushing back judgments and preconceived ideas.

Dear Everybody,

I'm in Salzburg. This morning I couldn't stand my hair another minute . . . The desk sent me out to Emmy, who cut me so I'll never have to touch it . . . Emmy was a sweetie - - young and pretty and adept. She says she likes Americans - - at least, the women. She says the children "speak by me too much." She says the mothers tell them to sit down. The children say, "I don't want to." She says that "mothers speak by children more than children speak by mothers." And while we're on that subject, another week's gone by and still I haven't seen a European child who misbehaves in public.

Her expectations about behavior in children were high and unwavering. Her demeanor commanded it. No words need be spoken.

The impression she must have given during her travels was one of openness and eagerness to engage, while the impression she gave her grandchildren was to meet her expectations. She was not someone to disappoint. One time and only one time, my sister went to visit Hannah. When asked if she liked bacon, my sister said, yes. Hannah proceeded to cook the entire package and was upset when every slice wasn't eaten. The staying power of my sister's childhood bacon memory reflected the intense emotions Hannah engendered. Cousins had a similar memory. During one of her visits, Hannah refused to allow them to return to school after lunch until they ate all their creamed mushrooms. With their mother away, the house cleaner intervened.

I paused often, gathering up Hannah anecdotes from my sister and cousins to aid in cobbling together a picture of her. I was in no hurry. My move to Maine was in two parts, out of the house and into a temporary Marin townhouse. Respite was needed as I sorted out what to move where and when. Always at hand were my Hannah binders. Traveling with her through the pages and pages of single-spaced type required pauses. I was pacing myself. In Hannah's second month away from home, on her own, with one month to go, her stamina was impressive. Her stay at the Weismayr Hotel and Spa in Badgastein, where she was in full throttle wallowing in comfort and collecting opinions, helped. Lonely, how could she be, with a masseuse?

> Gosh, how quickly plans can change. I bent to pick up some-thing . . . I had it coming. If I'd just act my age. This may mean I'd better stay in Badgastein one moment longer than I'd planned to, to take the baths with trimmings.

> That is what I'm doing. One bath is for free, so I tried it. After that you've got to see the doctor or they won't permit it. This water is radioactive . . . It makes you feel extremely funny. You have to go to bed and rest. When you get up you feel simply marvelous. The doctor person was young and thorough. I'm quite encouraged. He has sent a guy to do massage . . . He almost killed me but I feel like another person. Send mail to the same addresses I have given you. I will ask them to hold or forward letters.

> Is it OK if I interrupt myself? I met two California girls in Salzburg. They were on their way to Peggy's although she doesn't know it . . . They came to Europe, bought a little German car - - are doing all the countryside. Asked me to come along that day. Couldn't do it.

I continue to be amazed at how easily Hannah met people who were connected to other people she knew, which reveals how little I knew about her when she was alive. Never did she talk about the people in her life. When I was old enough for letters that could have been full of news about either of us, there were none. Custom back then may have dictated that life details weren't shared with grandchildren. Maybe that was her protocol. We could have been called a "mums the word" family. That aside, back to the topic of how easily Hannah pulled others into her orbit. Hannah's inquisitiveness, her need to connect, was on the high side of average, though average is a word that is hard to apply to Hannah. I am learning that being out and about on one's own as a singleton can make it easier to meet people, if there is an interest and overtures are made. I'm trying it.

The last "Dear Everybody" letter or, at least, the last to survive, enticed me to sit back and linger over spas and massages. Her details transport, hence edits are few.

Dear Everybody,

No more travelogues. I've settled down at Badgastein at the Weismayr. Every morning at six o'clock I poke an elevator button . . . and descend and take a bath . . . The attendant conducts me to my cubicle, says "Veedersane" and shuts the door. The rest I do by ear. I take off my glasses, grab a sort of banister and walk down three marble steps. I sit, a little gingerly, below sea level, on a marble bench. All that's left of me's a head, like John the Baptist's, on a tray. In fifteen minutes, I wrap up in a towel that covers me just like a tent . . .

In twenty I am back in bed . . . At six thirty comes breakfast - - kaffee complete, with honey. The waiter holds my tray above my head, and his, balanced on four fingers and a thumb. While he makes a valley in my feather puff and puts the tray down on my stomach, he tells me that it's raining. I sit up. He pours my coffee. (Almost too much effort to drink it down). I feel a false exhilaration, drop the Herald Tribune and go to sleep. At eight comes my masseur . . . He is a pianist, a baritone and plays the violin. He has competed in Olympics, twice vounded in the wars . . . He drives a sporty German car . . . He is my source of gossips of the Weismayr. I said, - - a little muffled as to voice – my nose was smashed against the mattress, "How do you know this stuff?" He said, "the maids, my lady." Then he changed the subject. Playz they jin againz thay bust," he told me. I ask you - - if you place your chin against your bust, WHAT do you do with your nose? It's already smashed against the blanket.

How Could She be Lonely in Germany?

Badgastein, you have guessed by now, is a health spa. All health spas are alike except in the degree to which they're gilded. This one is gold leaf gilded. Everyone says things that everybody else has said in every other health spa from Baden Baden to White Sulphur. The inmates speak in tongues, like Holy Rollers. They use a practiced pattern – a pattern they design to fool others into overestimating what they're not. No one ever does. Each person calculates and measures before he smiles. They walk with canes and dress for dinners, darn it. I change my necklace to conform each night.

If I hadn't spent that summer being "hostess" at Buck Hill, I wouldn't be so conscious of the completely artificial surface of such places. Managements cash in on every human frailty. Vanity pays dividends for someone else. Of course, Buck Hill is not a health spa. Guests who walk with canes are not supposed to have the same objectives as the young who walk with dates.

I have never seen such cut throat manners at bridge tables. Now and then someone says, "yaw yaw yaw" when his partner bids a grand slam, but mostly they spare no punches. Last night I saw a woman throw down her cards and say she wouldn't play with such illiterates (or the equivalent of that, in German). Me, I turn pale at the thought - - I play Samba with a woman who lives up in Caracas. She has dimples and a purring voice. I'm not afeard of HER.

P.S. I meet all these "best people" in the elevator every morning when I go to take my marble bath. I must say they all look fat and funny in their nightgowns. Including me, - - but Russel Lynes would list me only lower middle class.

Russel Lynes, an editor of *Harper's Magazine* and commentator on social affairs, published many essays, one of which was "Guests," an analysis of boring people. One quote of his was right up Hannah's alley: "Camouflage is a game we all like to play, but our secrets are as surely revealed by what we want to seem to be as by what we want to conceal." Hannah thought Lynes would have ranked her as lower middle class, though she wasn't fooled by those "overestimating what they are not." Do I sense insecurities at the bridge table? Best to stick with people who "purr." Hannah was wise to the ways of people, and with that, changed her necklace to conform, one from her junk jewelry collection to be sure, and once again crowed about her whereabouts.

Having a masseur was unlike what anyone in my family would do. My first massage was in my mid-forties when my former spouse was considering a job in San Francisco and the company housed us at an inn at Big Sur. Our room sported a deck that appeared to hang out over the ocean. Ceiling-to-floor windows counterbalanced the redwood paneling behind the down-comforted bed of the kind Hannah fell into. Indigenous flute music and lavender scent wafted throughout and two thick terrycloth bathrobes hung on a wall, ready and waiting for the complimentary couple's massage. All an extravagance. I agreed to the massage, took in the decadence. Since then, I have massages on occasion, letting go of guilt for the self-indulgence. When my mother was in her eighties, as I struggled with an idea for her birthday gift, with reluctance and hope, I gave her a massage gift certificate. She didn't resist. She gave the impression it was her first massage. When I asked how it was, her reply was a short, "Just fine." I doubt she ever had another. Hannah had several.

Despite waxing on about "the artificial surface of such places," spas that is, Hannah stayed on.

> This seems to be turning into something that I read the other day . . . The man called it an interior monologue. I'm sorry, but what else can I do? In a health spa? The less you do the less you do. And the duller letters you will write. Repeating nothings. Repeating nothings is exactly what I do each day.

> Today, after I said, "Good Morning, how are you?" I started out alone. Got on a bus and got off by ear, somewhere, where a village opened up into a valley, beautiful beyond your dreams of beauty. I

climbed some rocky steps up to a whitewashed church. Stood in a
little graveyard, planted in forget-me-nots and garden pinks - - the
spicy kind that mother always had in her backyard. Then I came
down thru a lane between unpainted picket fences. On one side
was a gathering of those silly looking hayricks . . . I turned in at a
gasthaus and lay down on a steamer chair. Ordered coffee and ate a
torte. It was covered with wild strawberries, picked, up in the mountains. For two hours I lay there in the sunshine, looking at the hills
and listening to the falling waters. I like little quiet places.

When I reached the Weismayr it was time for dinner. Everybody
said, "Good gracious, weren't you lonely?" Why should I be lonely? I
changed my necklace and started in on dinner.

Before moving on to Hannah's dinner, the village scene she painted
"beyond your dreams of beauty" captivated and enchanted. A repeat
performance gaining my applause. Once at dinner, she pushed away
queries about loneliness. Why should she be lonely she asked her "Dear
Everybody" group. Did she really wonder about that? And, once again
she let everybody know, she changed her necklace.

The fear of loneliness can rise up when seeing someone alone. Thoughts
well up that the situation could be ours. A divorced friend when out
to dinner alone worries, as I have done on occasion, that others might
think she is alone because something is wrong with her. Insecurities
surface when the maître d' says, a little too loud, "Only one?" When
seated, one scans for other singletons; often there aren't any. To avoid
looking lonely, one brings a book for a dinner companion. We decided
the strategy is to create a story for ourselves that the couples we see are
miserable, that they are putting on a good face, and how lucky we are to
not be in an untenable relationship. Telling that story works most of the
time. What worked for Hannah was editorializing about the goings-on.
Why should she be lonely?

The dining room is fun. Once every day the hotel manager appears.
He walks thru the dining room, bowing with deferential calm. Now

and then he stops to kiss a hand. I've never rated that. I'm always a little tense at meals because my waiter has such hair-raising habits. He removes a plate and sets it on his left hand. (He scorns a tray.) Then he removes four others and piles them in a tidy heap just below his elbow. I wish he'd go ahead and drop them. And have it over with.

Everyone uses knives for filling forks. Everyone but me. I'm afeard to try it. The twig wasn't bent that way in Indiana.

On one hand, Hannah was a savvy international traveler, on the other, a deeply rooted Midwesterner with insecurities. My bias makes it hard to fathom how a woman from southern Indiana in the 1900s got to Pasadena, traveled to South America and beyond, mingled with generals and consulates in Europe, and had such far-flung worldly connections. While Hannah's twig may have been bent in Indiana, that twig also made it possible for her to reach out, seek adventure, find the beauty to sustain herself. Biases, those blanket feelings Hannah referred to, should have warning flags that one might lose one's way, misjudge. For too long I misunderstood Hannah. For too long I have been without her wisdom, her humor.

P S I've just come back from opening my window - - the little orchestra's begun to play Blue Danube. I hung out to watch the passersby. Did you read in the last Colliers - - or maybe not the last - - Dior's comment on the aging? He said, (I quote - - don't blame ME) "I rarely design anything but wedding gowns for young girls. A woman does not really need chic until the animal has lost some of its spring and the mind has begun to prowl." Unquote.

The Dior comment fits with the number of times Hannah changed her necklace to belong, gain attention. Wisdom from my friends on style and aging is to accessorize—scarves and jewelry—though none of us mention the word chic. Maybe we never wore chic. Speaking of minds beginning to prowl or wander, I can't make out how Hannah's mind wandered from hearing the Blue Danube out her window to Dior and aging, unless she noticed a passerby who was young and chic.

Dear Everybody

Chapter Twenty

Intangibles

Ten years had gone by since I started in on Hannah's letters, and I was hardly feeling young. I was stringing out the project, learning more and more with no intentions to not have Hannah as company. After selling my house and with each month in my Marin rental, I was more than ready to call Maine home. My mind began to prowl thinking of the interesting men in Maine who might open doors to Maine's outdoor delights, men who valued what I valued: beauty, creativity, smiles from the heart, things of the spirit, the intangibles which Hannah knew.

Hannah's mind was prowling at the Badgastein spa, her typewriter keys clicking to release all the ideas which floated within.

I'm supposed to go to sleep after this back business. Instead, I read a book that Frances gave me . . . an essay by the Curator of the Huntington Museum. He had his say - - a very good say - - about creative art. He thinks civilization will have to be saved, not by material things, but by things of the spirit. I don't remember the rest of the essay too well because I began thinking about women who wear dirndls. They have what the curator is thinking about. Things of the spirit.

A dirndl stamps a social level. It's bread pudding with a dab of apple jelly. There's a warmth and spontaneity about a dirndl woman. She is quickly sympathetic. Meet her on the mountain or pass her on the Promenade, if you smile at her, she smiles back with no self-consciousness. She is more completely free to be herself than the hors d'oeuvres women at the Weismayr.

In the faces of these women, that intangible the writer calls a "spirit," is so near the surface that it is unmistakable. For instance, that person from Vienna. I met her yesterday in a swinging basket thing - - they use them on the ski lifts. You know ME - - I curdle if I look down or up from any place that doesn't touch the sidewalk. I had shut my eyes and said, "This scares the living daylights out of me." She knew about twelve words of English. It was enough. She laughed me out of being frightened. "Sair shern" she'd say. She made me look down from the window. "Sair shern." She must have weighed three hundred pounds. I thought her face was very beautiful. She felt honest warm concern for me although I was a stranger. "Things of the spirit," quote the curator.

When we reached the mountain top I disappeared into the Gasthaus, ordered coffee, and looked out thru the windows to the snow. Before my cup was emptied, back came the woman . . . "Koom," she said. "I luke for you. I koom to get you." She MADE me come. She held my hand and together we climbed over paths that alone, I would not dare tackle. She had picked a bunch of "butterblumen" with one white hepatica, to give to me. "Sair shern." She pointed out the towns down in the valleys. She named the peaks. She put me into that swinging horror with her. When I left her, she handed me a card on which she had written something. I can't read it. "Ein lieber mensh sind Sie" or something like that. Isn't lieber something like love??? It's a kind word, anyway. When I get back to

Boston . . . I go right past the Huntington. I'd sure like to see the curator. I want him to write another "piece" about creative arts - - against a background of the dirndl.

P S. What is creative art, anyway? I'd like to know. It can be anything that isn't copied, can't it? I used to tell Third Grade Fulton, "look down a well. Holler into it. What comes back? Your voice. Not William's. Not Bill's. YOUR voice. Write down what it says on paper." It's the same if you use a paint brush - - or a needle. No two dirndls are alike. They're as individual as the women who made them. I've seen old twisted women with sun-bright yellow scarves and red aprons. If they feel chartreuse, they wear it, with blue violet. If they are shy or quiet people I notice that their dirndls are often powder blue. If that's not creative art, what is it?

P P S. Frances's book again. Speaking. Quote Walt Whitman. "There is something in me. I do not know what it is. But I know that it is me." Somehow this gets covered up by polished social patterns. Me, I like the dirndl women. That's why I ride in buses.

Creativity and her third graders were never far away. In 1961 when Hannah was seventy-three, "In All Innocence" was published in the *Literary Cavalcade.* She put forth her truth about children: "They supplied what every teacher's heart needs – constant replenishment from the well of childhood." To quote Hannah quoting Walt Whitman, there was something in her that she knew not what it was. Yet, she knew how important creative endeavors were, and that she needed regular replenishing whether from children, or the people and sights around her.

The last letter from Hannah's three-month trip was another that told me more about my grandmother than I expected. The first was the one to my father about taking care of his "urges." Excerpts on a topic of interest: remarrying.

This is July 10th - - Sunday, cold and rainy - - the day before I leave Badgastein, for Innsbruck, where I will stay until the 15th, when I will leave for Lucerne, where I shall stay until the 21st, when I shall leave at what unpredictable hour in which I can get a flight for home, from Paris. THAT honey, will - Be all

Dear Mrs. Smith,

NO ** I did NOT get a letter about Helen. What on earth has happened? Repeat. No, I have not RUN INTO Uncle Adolph. But, since he was in such a stew about my not coming to Paris and about my returning the check he sent me for it, I am going to Lucerne . . . I have a reservation in the hotel where they are staying, after Innsbruck. You think I treat him badly - - - its because when I open the door a crack, he puts his foot thru the opening. If I speak the least bit fondly as I would to any one, he remembers what I said and considers it a step into the direction that he has plotted out. I CANNOT marry anyone. And won't. So help me, Peter. I shall travel free the road to anywhere. It might make it easier for you girls. That's the ONLY reason that I hesitate. (NOT FOR LONG). So far, I haven't clogged your footsteps - - what you bet my luck will hold? Anyway, I'll take that chance.

. . . One thing that has sort of bothered me. I'd hate to be delinquent in paying dues at the City Club. Am I posted?

I have a few things for you all- - hope while I'm in the east I can present them . . . Not having my car will be a nuisance. Its in Adolph's garage.

You sounded pushed, hot and headachy in that last letter - - wish you could be here to take these baths - - THAT'D fix you! You don't relax because you chose to. You can't do otherwise.

Love - - - Mother   And another love for both girls.

Hannah was in a huff about Adolph and "heavens," as my mother might say, could Hannah be posted at the City Club? The shame would be too much. Marrying was too much. My mother relaxing? That would be too much. Not having a car, what a nuisance. Boxes of things, that could never be too much. This letter revealed so much.

By 1955 Hannah had been widowed for twenty-six years. She reconciled and grappled with loneliness while insisting on independence and not remarrying. I have not reconciled. I can't say I do not want to remarry. My heart has lonely moments even after increasing my time in Maine, the place that pulls on my heart. The competing themes of intimacy and independence go hand in hand, pull against each other, a balancing act, each carrying more weight during certain times than in others. In Hannah's "Dear Everybody" letters she wrote more than a few times, "I am not lonely." A suspicious claim. Why bring it up if she wasn't feeling it? A few of her references for full impact:

> • Some of you sort of worry because you think I must be scared, alone here. I never am alone until I go to bed. I sleep in Salzburg, by day I live in buses. You couldn't possibly be lonely in a bus.
>
> • You needn't worry. I am not lonely.
>
> • When I reached the Weismayr it was time for dinner. Everybody said, "Good gracious, weren't you lonely?" Why should I be lonely?
>
> • I've not been lonely for a minute in Vienna. The atmosphere is kind and friendly.
>
> • When I went to bed, I felt lonesome without my hat tree with the fingernails.
>
> • Adolph wanted me to come to Paris… When he couldn't get a passage on a ship, his plane would put him into Paris - - alone for few days. After pressure - - the you know how kind - - I said, "Sure - - OK . . . Then I checked costs and mileage and found that such an enterprise would cost about a hundred and fifty dollars - - so I said, "No can do." In the mail I got a check for two hundred from him. Said it was buying happiness for three days. What do you do with such a creature? I sent back the check - - of course . . . - - I can make wavings to them . . . So - - I guess I will stay until I'm homesick. You never can tell about that. It grabs you from the bushes.

Loneliness grabbing you from the bushes. I don't have bushes at my California rental, though loneliness grabs me from around corners. I was lonely in my marriage. Now that I am divorced, loneliness finds me now and again. It comes and goes. I need doses of solitude, value alone time. There is much to learn about oneself when loneliness appears. Hannah confronted that in the conversation she had with herself in her essay "The Inner Me." Excerpts:

What is loneliness? A consciousness of solitude? Does it depend upon the receiving apparatus? I do know a solitude that is a poignant beauty to remember. Perhaps loneliness is a sickness of the mind, the spirit or the soul. It does go with me into solitude. Even among loving friends. It overwhelms me in a garden in the springtime.... all apple blossoms and purple iris and white trillium. It waits for me in sapphire waves dancing in a sea of sparkling sunshine. It lies hidden in the peacock iridescence of tropical surf. Ripples with cirrus clouds into a laughing brook. Only banished by the golden intimacy of a burning ecstasy. Can be unpredictable like cold gray mists piling up in mountain chasm, or nebulous, or incubating like influenza. Even a sudden claustrophobia verging upon panic. A stagnant, dark fear, an unwholesome sediment that builds and if not dredged out, becomes self-pity. Self-pity is defeat. Look down on self-pity.

A good cry at a movie has top priorities. Swap my emotions for synthetic ones. I weep for what never happened to me. I am purged and step briskly into the sunshine, a woman of affairs once more intent upon buying butter. I also charge red hats, chinchilla furs or Altman sweaters to ease the hurt . . . Sometimes I wake to face a loneliness that smothers. Recurrent dreams. I cannot be hurt or I am a sissy. My feet drag and sink. No footprints left. Nighttime. Those privileged hours when the moon walks from left to right on old colonial windows, awakens that someone who lives down deep within. That 'within me.' I do not know what it is, but I know it is there.

I remember one day . . . at an auction, my father bought for me a dozen pair of round-toed, buttoned shoes. My friends wore Trilbies. Trilby shoes laced up in front. What a devastating solitude. I was lonely.

But I was lucky. A game of hopscotch quickly dissipated any chill from drifting clouds when a little girl. Adolescent loneliness came and went protected by pride. Now that I am what the young call old, I am less lonely. When I am really old I will expect the waves of torment to have tossed and broken.

Last night in bed I had a session with me about last summer when I went alone to Europe. I began, "when no one went to Europe alone at my age, specially a lady." The friend who lived down under in me groaned. "Remember? You thought I should not go because I spoke no language. It would be as if without a hearing aid." I hurried on to keep center stage. "That was not true. I was never lonely. I made friends more easily than at home. I want to know how come?"

. . . I went on talking to myself. I found in some queer way I more quickly recognize a person as he really is. No struggles through pretense and camouflage that every woman knows and uses. I did not need an intellectual approach.

When I left the cities and rode buses into mountain valleys I passed toasted wheat fields leading up to grass lands. Women worked there, tossing hay to dry on frames, which looked like ragged ghosts on Halloween . . .

"But there was more than that." "The mountain woman is bread pudding with a dab of apple jelly," I said stubbornly. "There is a warmth and spontaneity about her. She is quickly sympathetic. Meet her on a mountain pass or on a hotel promenade, or eat her sausage in a market. If you smile at her, she smiles back. No self consciousness."

The one who lived down under stirred, but waited. "These mountain women, they have sunshine in their hearts," I said jealously.

My friend had had enough . . . "Of course they do, they don't moon around believing they are little islands in the sea. They do not accept eternal loneliness of the human soul as undeniable." "You just won't face the fact," she answered, "that they, you and I and everybody are the sum of what we do and how we do it."

I turned on my side and drew my knees up to my chin to think this over. "What you're telling me, of course, is that loneliness, like sunburn, and all my other doldrums, is self-inflicted?"

"Of course," my conscience answered.

In "An Old Woman Refuses to be Aged," *New York Times Magazine*, written when in her sixties, she again claimed she wasn't lonely. In "Intangibles" she had more to say on the subject:

Everyone overlooks the fact that loneliness has little to do with numbers. Loneliness is like homesickness. "It has its seat and center in the breast."

Lots of writing about loneliness. My heart goes out to her. Hannah's heart was hunting for whatever could fill it up. Despite her "Dear Everybody" group, her children, her extended family, her gathering up beauty, loneliness followed Hannah. She could have remarried. Adolph courted her. I repeat her message that is hard to forget:

I CANNOT marry anyone. And won't. So help me, Peter. I shall travel free the road to anywhere.

My story on why Hannah would not marry is under consideration. My story about her collecting stuffs and traveling free the road to anywhere has something to do with fighting loneliness. Her gifts to others reinforced connections, made her feel accepted, not alone. The child who felt like poison around her brothers, who stood alone in the coat room at school for something she didn't do, who had to wear clothes that isolated her, was the adult who reached out to others, made efforts to engage, to connect.

If it is true that collecting is searching for one's heart's desire, a lifelong quest that is never complete, there is plenty of evidence that held true for Hannah. Her collections were diverse.

> *New York Times*, "Cherchez le Spring: A Tourist Tracks it from Norway to Morocco."
>
> Collecting gardens is a fever, like collecting stamps. The tail begins to wag the dog. Last year I flew to Lisbon, crossed from Algeciras to Tangiers, drove across Morocco and then, on impulse, turned around and followed Spring.

Moments of joy are distractions from the tough stuff, the "Grin and Bear it," "Buck up," or "Don't think I like this anymore than you" stuffs. I would lie if I didn't admit to drenching myself in beauty as a solvent for blotches in my life. Hannah wrote about losing her mind over beautiful things. If I were to lose my mind, I would rather do it over beauty than sorrow. Hannah had plenty of sorrow to blot out. She was a sponge absorbing splendor wherever it appeared.

Kindred spirits collecting beauty. A dear California friend of mine went to Guatemala and took an empty suitcase to bring back fabrics of beauty. She and I are sympatico and felt it when we first met, like Hannah and Alice Fraser. Like me and Aunt Ann.

> Dear Stephie,
>
> I have given some thought to your wedding gift! Thought at first a check with which your mother said you would buy china. After much thought decided china breaks, and I would like you to have a treasure of mine that won't break so . . .

A pair of silver candlesticks (plated), dated 1810 – 1820 is yours. They are rare, 'telescopic'. The copper shows through a bit, but adds charm and muted color . . . If you really like antiques you should have it as is. The top part pulls up . . . and on one candlestick this is broken....such a pair is very rare. I think you have a feel for old things . . . Those not interested in antiques would think it "used goods.'

I used to collect these treasures when I saw them way back, and now, have reached the point of no return. Want to get rid of 'things', and no one better to my liking than you. It is fun to collect, and also fun to give away . . .

Do use them . . . You are quite special to me . . . we seem to have a bond, whether illustrated children's books or what.

Treasures passed from one generation to another require care. That is what I told myself after I didn't renew my rental lease and was packing to move full-time to Maine. I faced square-on the oddity that I didn't trust the movers to truck my treasures all together across the country. I didn't have that trouble when moving to California. A seismic shift had taken place with my divorce and parents' deaths. Family treasures mattered more than ever. I packed my treasures into so many flat-rate boxes that the California Post Office clerk memorized my Maine address. I asked myself, why I had not trusted the movers? What if the whole lot was lost? It wasn't rational. There is a problem with living alone. You and yourself have conversations. No one calls you out on odd behavior. I used Hannah's stuff to wrap up other stuff of hers. Handwoven cloth belts I never wear and a turquoise South American skirt that no longer fits were used to wrap the telescoping candlesticks. Most people would have given those clothes away. Not me. That skirt held too many memories. Hannah bought it, my mother wore it, I wore it.

Treasures from Hannah, Ann, and my mother arrived safely in Maine. As I packed and unpacked the stuff, images of Hannah swaying back and forth on a bus taking her to villages nestled in mountains floated in my mind. Images of Hannah taking in the faces of people around her, creating stories about their lives, maybe as a distraction to her life, maybe to enrich it, maybe to learn the secret to hearts that were fulfilled. These were people with "sunshine in their hearts," people who created "things of spirit," who were "people of spirit." My images held puffy clouds in a blue sky, craggy buildings, and flowers in window boxes. I immersed, or maybe I submerged myself, in another time, another world, filled with richness and warmth, as an escape from what weighed me down. Worries of leaving behind my kids and my friends loomed like a heavy fog. Packing Hannah's stuff, like transcribing her letters, distracted me.

Those flat-rate boxes were a lifesaver. Each arrived without mishap. Collect and protect beauty—a family motto I am proud to adopt. The heightened sensitivity of the women in our family who came before Hannah may have fostered in my grandmother both dreams and receptiveness to scraps and reams of beauty and may have been linked to the mountains of tragedy they faced. Gathering mountains of beauty sprinkled with humor offset losses:

> Snows are melting on the mountains. Cold water slides from under glaciers and slips downward thru crevices of rock - - - looks like Rapunzel's hair. Streams meet and like some crazy living thing leap into chasms and lie on rocks below in misted pools that overflow as waterfalls, then race on down into the valleys . . .

> And oh, the valleys! Green, pricked with spots of color. Pink to mauve to violet to brilliant cobalt blue, set off by yellow. Veiled in white. Delicate pink Alpine roses - - Forgetmenots - - blue gentian underneath the windblown buttercups. Long stemmed dandelions; Eidelweiss and dozens that I do not know. I'm beginning to sound silly. Excuse it please. I'll get off the subject and report to the lost and found department.

Writing for Hannah was tutelary, gave cover, and uncovered what was within, permitted a sensuality that was repressed. As she theorized in "They Call It Creative Writing," *Progressive Education*, February

1943: "Images and words must be in a sub-conscious before you can get them out." Hannah's sub-conscious was rich and full, writing was her companion, a way to connect with others. Her unpublished essay on teaching, "Whatever Miss T Eats Turns Into Miss T," put it best:

> It was my job to show them how to make this beauty ever into
> dreams. I don't mean those dreams which are not more than static
> sense impressions. I mean those that come alive, as action. "When
> I write stories," Betty said, "I don't feel lonely now." Adults would
> phrase that differently. "Who lives with beauty hath no need of fear."

I answered my question about where my heart felt at home, about Hannah and her collecting, about my mother and her sister, who kept Hannah's collections, and about me, who did the same. Don't discount the heart. What the heart loves is too precious. And when a heart breaks, and sorrow comes, or loneliness grabs one from the bushes, I will repeat Hannah's mantra: "Who lives with beauty hath no need of fear."

Chapter Twenty-One

Traveling through Dreams and Reality

Even as she approached seventy, Hannah was propelled to travel. In 1956, her hometown newspaper reported she was on her way across Canada to Alaska. No traveling companion was mentioned. She was on the move, intrepid, gathering up moments that were beautiful beyond one's dreams of beauty. I imagine she continued repeating the adage, "Who lives with beauty hath no need of fear." Like mother like daughter, twenty-year-old Ann penned a version of that in her journal while traveling to Poland in 1937:

> "He who loves beauty shall never be lonely" . . . I do not know who
> said that, but mother's favorite quote. And even she found it was not
> true.

Ann changed the word fear to lonely, or did Hannah change lonely to fear? Ann's observation about her mother was astute. By the time Hannah included the quote in her writing, she may have learned that, though she loved beauty, she was lonely. Hannah attempted to banish loneliness. A futile effort. If she couldn't banish loneliness, then banishing fear about being lonely was her replacement. Beauty and loneliness, love, loss, and fear. Longing and belonging. Generations of women in my family sought beauty, felt deeply, dealt with fear.

There was no mention of the word lonely in letters from Hannah's 1957 voyage. Hannah was aboard the Norwegian freighter Ferngrove, bound for ports in the Mediterranean, and her travel partner was Adolph Volderauer. After the death of his wife in 1953, Adolph pursued Hannah. Hannah, in turn, made it clear that she had no intention of giving in to his intentions. He wanted romance. Hannah wanted a friend. Adolph stayed the course. On this trip she referred to Adolph as "himself." Was she making clear he was his own self and not her partner? When two people have different intentions, either one gives up and goes away or gives in and stays. Adolph gave in and took what he could get. Hannah had what she wanted. So far with the men I have met, we end up as friends.

Adolph and Hannah set out on a two-month freighter voyage, though if I believe Hannah, he didn't appear to understand what he had gotten himself into. As I read about the start of their trip, I didn't understand the lessons she would provide about my relationship voyages.

> . . . the first impression of the Ferngrove and the Port of Authority was a shock to "himself." I think he expected a tall beauty, shining with brass and white paint. He stood on the dock, a gentleman to the last drop, guarding our heap of bags and looking about him with aversion. The dock was littered with dirty and dead scraps of things, great and small, in a damp posthumous state. Longshoremen with shoulders and arms swelled out like sausages were slinging John Deere tractors and sacks of flour marked "enriched" . . .

> We were pushed out of their way into the freighter, climbing those silly steps that are slanted the wrong way for coming down as well as for going up. The stateroom assigned to "himself" is around the corner from mine. Fahreeya the maid, was bewildered in Italian when I balked and refused to accept the same one, en famille. "Two bed?" she said, disappointed.

"Two bed" it was. During a visit to Maine when my mother was alive, I posed a question: "Who was Uncle Adolph anyway?" Her eighty-year-old body stiffened up and from her upright perched position on the kitchen stool she replied, "How dare you ask that question." The emphasis was on "dare." I said no more. While I had a fantasy that Adolph and my grandmother had some sort of love affair, that was more than my mother could take in. Her defensiveness surprised me. Why not a relaxed answer with the truth? An answer such as, "He was grandmother's dear friend who looked out for her welfare. A man who hoped she might marry him, yet grandmother didn't want to remarry." With that answer, my next question, which I never asked, would have been: "Why didn't she want to remarry?" I've considered several theories. One: she never let go of her deep love for Arthur, a man who was beyond handsome, a man of stature. Two: Adolph's looks—his sharp features didn't draw Hannah in. The chemistry wasn't there. Three: once she was on her own, she couldn't get enough of her freedom. I have gleaned that my grandfather was a buttoned-up individual, a husband in control; maybe Hannah, a woman who couldn't keep track of her bills, who followed spring on impulse, who wanted to be untethered to chase after beauty, had had enough of that. Four: my mother once told my sister, "Grandmother didn't like the sex part." I didn't pause long to consider that option. In consultation with my sister, we agreed that was projection on our mother's part.

No surprise, on this voyage Hannah's typewriter was ready. From bedding to bathtubs, she never minded sharing intimate details with "Everybody." She knew how to engage her audience, bringing my mother, and later Adolph, into her letter without either of their approvals. My mother wouldn't have approved. Adolph put up with it. Neither had a choice.

> Taking a bath in the Ferngrove is like planned parenthood. If you
> think you know it all, you have no fear. I do not think I know
> it all. When towels slide from my hand I can think of no better
> thing to do than to slide after them. Crouching like a skier brings
> results. The mechanics of the bath are worthy of mention. They

await you on a stick, gooseneck like my floor lamp at home,
at the end of which is a spray like the one on my dish washing
gadget - - without the brush. (. . . the brush idea might pay off. I
shall try to sell the idea.) The spray sits on a horizontal bar, as of
a telephone . . . removed the receiver and pointed the spray at my
stomach, forgetting first to turn on the boiling water . . . Feeling
less confident if possible, I sat down, more or less unexpectedly, on
the toilet - - sidewise. Since the toilet has no lid, I was sucked into
this safety zone, fitting neatly, like the cork in my thermos bottle,
and could drop, first one, then the other leg into the shower. I
sprayed them thoroughly with water . . . snatched a bath towel as
it swung past and bent over to dry my extremities. The plan proved
to be excellent for legs. My topside, however, is shaped differently.
I decided to approach the problem in a different manner. I cradled
the soap in my washcloth, leaned forward toward the basin (you
understand I am still on, or in, as you wish, the toilet) . . . I had
bubbled myself all over with soap suds, I called it a day. It was simply too difficult to rinse me. Anyway . . . Margaret Smith would
not approve of such. She believes in rinsing.

Hannah's sentence about my mother was an understatement. I envision
my mother rolling her eyes in exasperation at her mother's behavior,
accompanied by, "Oh mother, really?" What my mother witnessed in
her mother might have been the source of comments my mother made
to me whenever I crossed her line of propriety. I rolled my eyes with
her comments, "A woman's body is not meant to do that," or "That's no
way for a lady to sit." My mother may have tried to contain her mother,
and she admitted that she tried to do the same with me, adding on the
ending, ". . . with no success." I contained myself for years on behalf of
my mother. Now that she is no longer alive, and now that, years after my
divorce, I am coming alive, containing myself is not what I have in mind.

Unlike what happened next to Hannah, I am not perceived as one
needing rescue. I am the rescuer, a role I consider shedding. Not that
being rescued is my desire. I wouldn't mind now and again being perceived
as someone who would welcome caring arms to take a load off. I have

never forgotten the time the wife of a fellow school board trustee asked me, "Who takes care of you?" I had no answer. I had been self-sufficient for too long. Back to another day with Hannah and Adolph.

> After lunch I left "himself" . . . reading his whodunit. I went in to take a bath . . . I took my dock blanket and spread it on the floor to absorb the shock if and when I fell down. Then I locked the door. The key turned smoothly in the lock. It was a huge key with metal dangles - - the kind that you can drop into the mailbox and they will pay the postage.

> When I stood shivering before the door, one cold bath later, with my arms full of wet towels, shoes and sundries, I found that the latch would not budge when I poked it with the key. Thru the years, when I lose my purse, Margaret has said, "Now don't get panicky, mother." In spite of this early training, I was as mad as a wet hen and jittering, when "himself" rescued me. "I couldn't unlock it," I said. "It wasn't locked," he answered patiently.

With patience, Himself came to her rescue. There must have been many other rescues.

I suspect that Adolph and Hannah knew each other growing up, and that he would have watched her dance through meadows with ferns in her belt, and dangle her feet in the bayou, and would have known she wasn't one to keep track of practicalities, such as keys and locks. She was lucky to have a male watcher-over such as Adolph. Add Adolph to the men in Hannah's orbit: sergeants, captains, diplomats, bankers, military husbands of her friends, and the stray men she met along the way. What she didn't have was a man to vanquish her loneliness, loneliness that could be, as she wrote, "banished by the golden intimacy of a burning ecstasy." Maybe I am projecting that she was lonely without a male love partner and that the burning ecstasy meant sex, the romantic kind. A letter from Ann, which surfaced from a cousin's desk, may disabuse me of the idea that passion for Arthur was the reason Hannah never remarried. Ann wrote that her father felt anything fun was immoral, adding that he had a rigid moral character, was opposed to dancing, and that he had tears in his eyes one day when he came home to find Hannah had rolled up the rug to allow a dancing instructor to teach my mother and her sister the fox trot. He shed tears knowing how much the three of them wanted laughter, song and dance. Widowed, she was out from under. Divorced, I was too.

More Ferngrove adventures were to come, providing more insight on Hannah and Himself.

> "It will be much warmer when we hit the Gulf Stream" the captain said at Breakfast. "I am receptive to the idea," I told him. "I shall spend long, lazy hours on deck, with an unopened book on my lap. The waves will be shot with sparks of intense light, like rain from the sun, and swept with the white wings of gulls . . . porpoises will be at play . . . Above it all, a sky of cobalt blue." I finished my second fried egg and took another hunk of bread.
>
> "Why is the tablecloth wet?" H- - said to the Captain.
>
> "Keeps dishes from sliding."
> H- - is a man who leaves no stone unturned. "I notice that the barometer is falling," he said.
> "Yes," said the Captain.

Himself, now referred to as H, was a man who left no stone unturned. I take that to mean details. I take that to mean Hannah left stones unturned. Numbers had little meaning for her, and she would not have noticed a barometer reading, only the leap of the waves, the glint of the sun, a dapple of joy on someone's face.

> That night a wind from some'ers north of Newfoundland increased in fury. Heavy swells moved in . . . met our little four thousand ton freighter and shivered its timbers . . . At one thirty I waked with a start and switched on my light. The chairs were upside down - - also my table, which was sliding back and forth like a turtle that couldn't

turn over . . . There was a patch of red which I took to be my dressing gown, tangled in the debris. As I tried to lift my head the chest began to slide, throwing up my purse, bedroom slippers and a plate filled with dried orange peelings into my face. Then I was flung against the wall, where I clung.

I thought about "himself" built like Mahatma Gandhi without my per pound resistance and worried. When morning came, hearing nothing from him, I beat upon his door. Because his beds were placed stahbud to port he had spent the night, he said, when he was not crawling on the floor to pick up small objects . . . sliding lengthwise on his bed . . . bumping his head against one end, then smashing his feet against the other. When a swell hit him broadside, the middle of him rose to meet it, he insisted curving upward like the lemon custard we had had for dessert. He told me kindly that he had thought of me, but, knowing that I always had one hand on Plymouth Rock, was afraid to offer help while he wore his pajamas. The thought of dressing was completely distasteful to him. He preferred to let me die.

I hand it to Adolph that he didn't always come to her aid. Hannah, with one hand on Plymouth Rock, sturdy as a pilgrim, a single woman who found it unseemly if her friend appeared in his pajamas, was the woman whose other hand was on a masseuse table, who wrote about toilets, and who marched down a spa hallway in a robe, a woman of contradictions.

But this is digression. I am reluctant to approach my next chapter. It happened after I had gone into the lounge . . . I reached the table with caution, keeping a tight grip on one immovable object while I snatched at another. H - - has a different approach. He chooses an objective, then, in that split second when he and a wave are in accord, makes a run for it, moving with an up and down movement - - tripping thru the tulips, sort of. Sometimes he reached base. He sat down at the table with me and dealt himself cards for a game of Samba. I felt I could not stand that, and anyway, why should I? "I'm going to throw up," I said with finality. H - - glanced at me as he arranged his canasta, "You look fine," he said. That was too much. I pushed back my chair. It suddenly came alive, slid the length of the lounge, taking me with it, hit the wall with a crack, and with added momentum, slid back again, banged my head against a wall . . . and kept on sliding, mad as a March hare. I hit the door with the end of my back and ever since, when I wish to lie on deck, I am accompanied by "himself", who carries the pillows, two longs and two shorts.

Hannah didn't take well to H telling her she looked fine when she was on the verge of throwing up. He made it up by accompanying her on deck with pillows should she fall as the ship lurched. While this may be unfair to both Hannah and Adolph, I picture the queen of hearts followed by her knave. This relationship model never was mine and never will be.

Hannah's Mediterranean trip offered up an unknown nugget on Hannah's personality vis-a-vis napkins, not to mention more on Hannah and her watcher-over companion.

Last night the Mediterranean threw the whole book at us. The Ferngrove cut into the wind in a humping caterpillar crawl, pitching and rolling . . . I lay in bed . . . trying not to think negative thoughts, like kidneys for breakfast, or pale fishballs submerged in white sauce. I tried quotes, like "You can't hold back the dawn." "Consider the stars, my dear." But I kept going back to an Arab I had seen on the docks in Algiers. He stood, as limp as his rags, and slept, with his eyes closed, his feet neatly placed, swaying - - swaying - - his eyes closed, his feet neatly placed, swaying - - - -

"Oh shucks," I thought, "I'm doing that."

"Look where you're going!" Himself cried out sharply from behind me. I snatched at the wooden fence that outlined my parking place at the table and sat down suddenly.

H- - took my napkin from its envelope, unfolded it and laid it on my knee. He had begun by folding it, because, he said, I wadded it into its case. Then, since one thing leads to another, he took naturally to unfolding same. I pushed it back and stood uncertainly, swaying by my chair.

"A merry Christmas to all," I said politely, and got out just in time.

"Himself," who, in spite of Plymouth Rock, was sitting in one corner of the room, on guard, grinned and ruffled thru pages of his whodunit. I suspect he is one of those people, who, living a life of routine, welcomes change, even for the worse, as better than no change at all.

I turned my face to the wall.

Himself called out sharply to Hannah, who no doubt was not as focused as he thought she should be, pointing out she was a "napkin wadder."

Thumbing through my memories of lunch with Hannah at the Women's City Club surrounded by sweet little old ladies, I pulled up no images of her as a napkin wadder. What arose, despite images of her commanding presence, were her eyes radiating a stern warmth of support letting me know I was the one to behave. Whether it was the white gloves my mother insisted I wear when going downtown or the white table cloths, I behaved. Hannah sat upright, her bosom prominent, a chunky silver necklace in the V of her suit jacket. As we waited for our meal, she smiled at me and then immediately looked at my napkin, still on the table. I was giving no thoughts to napkins, distracted as I was by a queasy stomach from the bus exhaust fumes as we swayed down Jefferson Boulevard to the Park Avenue district. The smell of chlorine from the club's pool wafting to our table through the dining room door wasn't helping as my mind floated to the pool's teardrop Pewabic teal and aqua tiles, drippy drops on the walls. I pushed back pool thoughts and told myself there was a reason my grandmother was looking with a smile at my napkin. I was in training, learning to decode looks and obtuse messages. I picked up my napkin and put it in my lap. I was rewarded with another warm smile. If Hannah could have showed me the woman her writing revealed, she might have said, "You done good." I never knew the woman with a sense of humor, and a passion for the extraordinary, who submerged herself in down comforters, who wadded napkins.

~

Back to Adolph and Hannah. He put the napkin on her knee, a kind caring gesture, and she pushed it back, left the table, stomach churning, and dished out a polite yet off-the-wall comment that could only come from the likes of Hannah in the month of May, "A merry Christmas to all." Hannah, seeker of adventure, was humbled by her stomach and the waves. Adolph, who ordered things, kept guard, took it all in, dealt out cards for a game. Quite a pair. I wonder if she ever had a smidge of guilt for pushing back his desires to be her husband while also accepting his kindness and company. I couldn't do it. Maybe it worked for both of them. Her May 3rd letter from Beirut Harbor exposed more:

> Adolph is sending you a carbon of a letter. It is nice having him
> along. There has been not one minute of difficulties. He allows
> me to live my own and I do the same in return. He waits on me
> hand and foot - - I'm completely spoiled. But he always beats me at
> Samba. That burns me up.

Hannah and Adolph, or at least Hannah, had settled into an understanding about their relationship. He was to be nice to her, not give her difficulties, allow her to live her own way, and she would do the same for him, but he was to wait on her hand and foot. That was quite an arrangement. The least she could do is cool off when he beat her at Samba.

Relationships in the last quadrant of life are haunted by history and fraught with "this is really important to me" needs. Settled in

Maine in the house that had a hold on my heart, I would resist any expectation of giving up my house. A friend who is also sorting out the same, sent an article from the *Wall Street Journal*, "More Older Couples Stay Together Because They Live Apart." I'm not sure I want to fully live apart any more than fully give up the house. I could envision house sharing, a back and forth, reciprocity. How likely is it to find someone who captures my heart and with needs which mesh enough for both of us to be content? Comfort not confinement. Compromise figures in there somewhere. Hannah figured out what suited her. I squirm with what Adolph put up with, and want to apologize for her.

Hannah revealed more about her relationship after they came ashore.

Arab drivers are the best in the world and this includes the French. They are fearless, strong and articulate, especially in snarls of traffic. If they were not, they, and we, would be dead. In Beirut, the driver brushed off casualties which he incurred, as one would brush off flies in a bazaar. I closed my eyes at every intersection, so that I might not be called upon to witness.

"What was that you said to him, Tony?" I demanded after one bloody skirmish.

Tony shrugged. "Ah say, 'Awkay, he not have goat legs.'" His smile was as sweet as the honey of Lebanon - - tender as first love, and meant exactly nothing.

In the mountains Abdul took all hairpin curves from the left lane. Fog meant nothing to him. With one hand on the horn, the other arm was freed to sweep the countryside, pointing out the silver beauty of an ancient olive tree . . . In the back seat I became a "wee, timorous, cowerin' beastie" clinging to "himself", who, in these, his most protective moments, did not have the heart to ask me to look where I was going.

This pleasured me, since H- - who no longer dealt with me in the manner to which I had become accustomed. He snatched at me in cities such as Algiers - - especially Beirut. Sometimes, when nothing more deadly than a bunch of goats bearing down upon me, "Damn it!" he shouted. "Look where you're going!" He is irritated when I walk in one direction while looking into another.

I try to be patient with him. "How can I see what I'm looking at if I don't look at it?" I ask. I must be a great trial for him, for at the end of one day, when we were safely off dry land, bobbling back to the ship in a rowboat, he leaned toward me, speaking gently, and said, "If I told you what was the matter with you, would you be hurt?"

"Not at all," I answered coldly.

He signed. "You just don't look where you are going," he said, still speaking gently.

Hannah had someone who told her what she may not want to hear. After ten years, Mr. Apple Orchard, whom I met during my back-and-forths to Maine, did that to me when he popped up from his rabbit hole. On that rare occasion, we talked openly and honestly; that was progress. He grew up with same "the code" to decipher as had I. He helped pull me out of that language. All good except for the red flag which I ignored with my ex and now took heed. His relationship was with his work. Connecting was on his own terms. Reciprocity absent. No can do, I told myself.

Chapter Twenty-Two

Facing Ourselves

The portrait I am painting of my grandmother has many layers and shades. She acknowledged she must be "a trial" to Adolph. Thank you, Hannah. Be nice to Adolph, please, I want to tell her. Hannah was aware that she walked in one direction while looking in another. She was impulsively drawn to whatever caught her eye while on a mission to search out magnificence. She was an intrepid, indomitable woman who also managed to be a "wee, timorous cowerin beastie," who could cling to a man but also push him away. Her mind overflowed with images and wonderings, was filled with playful fiddlings, bursting at the seams to share with "Everybody." A woman who grappled with loneliness, bristled under certain conditions, and was intrigued with others, "And always faces - - faces - - faces." If Hannah's spirit haunts me, there is a reason.

> In bed, I lay happily and thought of many things . . . an Arab child
> with long red hair, who carried water buckets balanced on a hoop;
> puffs of cloud that topple over peaks; that thread of silver mist
> that separates sky from water thru long twilights; Muslim girls in
> sliding slippers, peeking out with one dark eye from yashmaks;

pale light before the dawn; half buried rocks on treeless mountains; blue morning glories climbing on a yellow stucco wall; soldiers armed with Tommy guns; gardens, set with the reflected sunshine of marigolds; others dripping Oriental perfume - - the star jasmine, gardenias, calla lilies, heliotrope; street sounds, dock sounds, cadences like modern music, lifted from antiquity And always faces - - faces - - faces.

I was almost asleep. "Fifty years is little room," I thought hazily . . . "Time to stand and stare" - - Just as I was dropping off again, I remembered clearly something out of something. "But at my back I always hear, Time's winged chariot hurrying near."

That did it! I waked suddenly - - good, land!

I am leaving out most of her last letter, including a three-hundred-and sixty-one-word paragraph, typed single-space. Too much, too long, though the ending is worthy:

This all sounds silly, I know to you. Unless I can talk too much, I say too little. But I have never had such a chance to learn, in all my life. I sure agree with Phyllis McGinley, - - she wrote an actual adventure and discovery in middle age, without having had it packaged.

My collection of sentences that speak of her self-awareness has a new entry: "Unless I can talk too much, I say too little." That made me take stock of someone else who may do that. Sitting at my mother's drop-leaf table, laptop a-ready, the photo of Hannah in her Persian Lamb jacket to my right and my Maine garden outside the window, possibility rose up that I may talk too much and carry the conversation load with men too often. I made note of Hannah's reference to Pulitzer Prize author Phyllis McGinley whose views on women included their need to have the regard of men to feel alive. Then the contradiction. McGinley's book, *The Plain Princess*, includes elements of a feminist fairy tale with the main character portrayed as an independent woman.

Men were not relied upon to solve the complications that arose. Many women besides Hannah, were navigating marriage, independence and intimacy. As Hannah approached seventy she continued to deal with "the one we don't know too well — " the unknowable parts of ourselves. As I approach seventy, I intend to do the same.

The last travel document for Hannah is dated September 3, 1958. "Passenger Boarded at Zurich Switzerland on SR 844. Admitted New York, New York." An identical record existed for Adolph and Carrie. Hannah and Adolph's Ferngrove trip must have been pleasing enough that they were off less than a year later. A photo of Hannah in front of zig-zaggy chalet shutters admiring a rose brings Switzerland to mind. No surprise, she was surrounded by flowers. No surprise, her sweater was draped over her shoulders. Zooming in, there is some junk jewelry pinned to her bodice. Adolph endured. Hannah, age seventy, had a companion.

Travel with a desired male companion lured Hannah, and sensual experiences were captured in word and shared. I would be remiss to not point out the similarities with Ann during her college travels abroad. Travel which she described in a letter to me decades later, her words almost a replica of Hannah's, capital letters for emphasis: "I went to Europe ALONE . . ." If Ann shocked her mother with boys and being ALONE in Europe, Hannah may have shocked her daughters as a middle-aged woman traveling ALONE, talking to strange men. Or maybe shocked her daughters traveling at age seventy with Adolph. Either way, Ann's writing in her 1937 journal is eerily similar to her mother's.

> The energetic, mostly men, walk a mile around the deck . . . Greet each other in passing. Ladies curl up with a cup of bouillon or go to sleep over an unread book. What is wrong with wives? Men are more friendly. A few college students make love in lifeboats swinging above. There is not enough time for the Viennese waltz and too much for smorgasbord. After midnight, we found our way through the hold of the ship to its prow and sat on a prickly pile of coiled rope. Had to hang on tight when the ship rode the waves. Sprayed with salt and showered with rainbow bubbles. "What do you see?"

he said . . . "I see a Christmas tree hung with jewels." "Not really . . .
just iridescence and phosphorescence of plankton." . . . "I want to
hang my tree with emeralds and sapphires . . . turquoise and amethyst . . . not diatoms and plankton. Look! Your arm is on fire with
black opals." "No love. Just the link in the chain of life . . ."

Hannah's voice and views were in Ann's diary. Ann embraced romance
and iridescence, a moment on fire with black opals. I twirled the black opal
on my finger and heard Ann's admonishment that the ring was too valuable
to wear every day. "It should be in a safe," she insisted. "Why keep beauty
locked up in a safe?" was my reply. Some romantics may never know better,
though Ann proclaimed later in life she learned to know better. I haven't.

One entry in Ann's college travel journal included a poem about
moons, "Silver" by Walter de la Mare. Hannah would have read it to Ann
as my mother read it to me. Hannah made poetry part of childhood, a
way to capture dreams.

"Milk Can be Homogenized But Not Children," *New York Times
Magazine*, 1948
   The time I steal, we fill with poems and stories and with intangi-
bles compounded of beauty.

"They Call it Creative Writing" *Progressive Education*, February 1943
   I happen to belong to the outmoded school of thought which still
believes that with or without the urge it is still a wholesome thing to
memorize poetry for rainy days ahead. Although at nine years you do
not know what you will need in the dark of middle-aged nights when
you must combat thoughts that press in upon you . . .

"Intangibles compounded with beauty," a phrase I will repeat and share
with others. I regret not having memorized more poems for my rainy
days, though poetry is close at hand. Hannah's influence once again, a
poem well taught and moons for romantic dreams.

As my mother aged and anticipated her death, she put together a
collection of poems for her memorial. "No service," she insisted. "Just

send the poems." She shared several with me as a child, that I committed to memory. During the period when divorce emails took over, to mute out the gnawing feeling that arose when I saw either the name of my ex-husband-to-be or my divorce lawyer, I signed up for "A Poem-a-Day" emails. Each morning, a poem to read or ignore arrives as I sit in my PJs drinking my coffee. Two years after my mother died, 6:32 am on December 30, dark and minus four degrees outside, my grey pill-covered cashmere bathrobe wrapped round me, there it was, subject line: "Barter" by Sarah Teasdale, one of my mother's favorite poems, one she shared with me many times, one she included in her memorial collection.

> Life has loveliness to sell,
> All beautiful and splendid things,
> Blue waves whitened on a cliff,
> Soaring fire that sways and sings,
> And children's faces looking up
> Holding wonder like a cup.
> Life has loveliness to sell,
> Music like a curve of gold,
> Scent of pine trees in the rain,
> Eyes that love you, arms that hold,
> And for your spirit's still delight,
> Holy thoughts that star the night.
> Spend all you have for loveliness,
> Buy it and never count the cost;
> For one white singing hour of peace
> Count many a year of strife well lost,
> And for a breath of ecstasy
> Give all you have been, or could be.*

I read each line slowly, caught in its power, or was it the power of the poem coupled with the grief that still arose around my mother's death. Then a jolt. I read the last two lines over and over. I uttered one

---

* "Barter," *Love Songs*, Sara Teasdale, 1917

word to myself, or maybe I blurted it out into that cold kitchen, only the refrigerator humming. "What?" My mind took off. Had I glossed over those last two lines all these years? I couldn't have. Did those two lines mean nothing to me before? I doubt it. Now they jumped off the page. I pulled out the scrapbook with her memorial pamphlet and read the "Barter" poem she had included. I was right. I had missed nothing over the years. My mother had left out the last two lines, had always left them out:

> And for a breath of ecstasy
> Give all you have been, or could be.

I slouched down, put my head in my hands covering my eyes. Why had she eliminated ecstasy? Was she embarrassed to even think of a breath of it? Had she never known such delight as Hannah and Ann had, never been overpowered with emotion leaving reality behind, basking in bliss? Or, had she once known that and bartered it away? Hannah would not have eliminated ecstasy. Sarah Teasdale made it clear in her first love poem not to barter away loveliness. Teasdale turned her back on her lover to marry a man who offered financial security. That marriage withered. She turned back to her lover, but he had married another. I think of my mother and John York, the man of the opal ring on my finger, the man she said she wished she had married. I think of the man I married who offered financial security. What marriage isn't without thoughts of, "I wonder what my life would be like if I had married someone else?"

Those lines in "Barter" repeat over and over in my head. I think of twenty-year-old Ann sitting on the Statendam's rope coil with her young man. I think of Hannah writing that loneliness can only be banished by the golden intimacy of a burning ecstasy. I think of myself and the times I have given all I could for a breath of ecstasy. When I first met Mr. Apple Orchard, I fell in the deep end with him, or should I say, I jumped with a smile of apology to my mother. I needed, and still do need, ecstasy of the physical passion variety, moments letting myself go. Something I rarely do. I cried with its richness, his arms holding me close. We reminded ourselves of the comfort our similar backgrounds provided. Proper exteriors and something else within. He understood. He appreciated fine things of beauty. When I was first at his house, I did a double take seeing his antique three-paneled room screen with its hand-painted pastoral scene and muted colors, a partner to the one in my house growing up, an item of beauty Hannah passed along to my mother. He did a double take when I served him lunch on a muted green Nils Royal Copenhagen plate, an abstract image of a flower within. My mother's plates. His mother's plates. He owned an apple orchard sloping down a lush hill to a river. He had a twinkle in his eye. He wasn't boring. He challenged me. I savored every moment, every early memory with Mr. Apple Orchard.

The feeling that I shouldn't let myself go would creep up for a moment, that a woman such as I, raised as I was, shouldn't feel ecstasy. I would hear my mother's warning when I was a teenager, flush with desire for whatever boyfriend I had: "One thing leads to another," and "The woman's always left holding the bag." Were those warnings given because she knew that I took after her sister, that I carried a version of Hannah within? Mr. Apple Orchard pulled me in: sensuous and successful, consumed by his work, self-absorbed, and independent, too much so, no room for a relationship.

Hannah must have known ecstasy. At least that is what I need to believe. She wrote about it, and I doubt she could have done that without having it, feeling it, believing in it. I catch myself with a reminder that maybe Hannah's ecstasy was immersing herself in a flower garden or losing herself with delight over things made from the heart. Ecstasy rises up when I ice skate on the lake, pause for snow falling gently on pines, or when a square of rich dark chocolate melts in my mouth, or when I close my eyes at an organ concert, music all around me. "Barter" is a reminder of the seduction of the sensuous.

Hannah's sentence about ecstasy came as loneliness lingered long after her husband's death. Dreams of ecstasy, golden as it is, burning as it is, intimate as it is, banished her loneliness for a spell. She held on to her memories and created new ones as she traveled and collected whatever pulled on her heart. I imagine she read those last few lines over and over again as I do: "And for a breath of ecstasy give all you have been, or could be." I was in my twenties when Ann wrote in response to one of my pour-out-my-heart letters:

> . . . loved your note about your amours . . . Your grandmother was
> an incurable romantic, as I am, but have learned the hard way, the
> only approach is that of the pragmatic realist.

Hannah was an incurable romantic. Ann was a romantic and was cured. Margaret blocked thoughts of ecstasy. Some marriages do that to women. Maybe it is easier to hold on to dreams when single.

My mother had dreams that may have been the result of her mother's endless pages extolling her travels in vivid details. A matter-of-fact statement that my mother shared more than once: "I would have liked to travel, but your father doesn't like to." In a prominent place on her bookshelf was *Toot and Puddle*, a children's story of two pigs, one whose happiness was staying home to enjoy the riches at hand, and the other who was fulfilled by exploring the greater world. The story mirrored my father and mother, though only one of them lived as they had hoped. My mother never traveled on her own, never gathered up women friends as Hannah did and said, "Let's go." Excerpts of a letter from my mother:

> I've adjusted as best I could – tho, of course Dad says I would be the
> way I am anyway - - independent. Actually my mother brought us
> up to be independent since in her 40s she was thrown on her own
> - - - tho <u>she</u> might have been the way she was anyway - - Truly -- I'd
> just as soon not have to be quite as independent as I've had to be.
>
> Since I have reached an age in which I am no longer so agreeable,
> sometimes it is hard for him, tho he has always said I can do what I

please that he's not holding me back. It's just (like traveling) that he won't do it - - - I should feel free to go on my own, which of course, I'm not quite independent enough as my mother was, to do . . . anyway, happy 40th birthday. Love, Mother

Please throw this letter away when you have read it.

Throw the letter away? I couldn't do it. I tucked it away in the back of my desk drawer. Now here it is, for everybody to read. Apologies once again to my mother.

Hannah and my mother were taken in by the allure of freighters. For my mother, they stayed far out on the horizon of the Great Lakes, a symbol of adventure. She collected prints and books about freighters. Hannah grabbed ahold of their allure, faced any fear of adventure and jumped aboard. Lake freighters were part of my everyday world growing up. Their haunting horn, long, low and penetrating, wafted up to our house on foggy days and nights, the wistful sound calling out its existence, like a meditative exhalation breath, OMMM. Its warning call lingered. The massive ship's imposing structure, long flat deck with its bridge at the far end, appeared like an elongated snail, crawling along the horizon. Danger lurks for freighters on the Great Lakes, and the sight of one on the horizon conjured imaginings for me as it did for my mother.

Adventure and independence. Fear held my mother back. With warnings from my mother not to get too close to the freighter channel, in winter my father and I skated on Lake St. Clair. The ice cracked and moaned. Large blocks of ice which freighters had pushed up upon each other provided a barrier which kept us from skating out too far, making my mother's fear unwarranted, though remnants from her past fear lurked deep within her, pushed upon me. I pushed back. I hear her phrases, "something might happen," "perish the thought," and "I dread the thought." The twelve-year-old girl inside her knew life could be fine one minute and fall apart the next. The trauma of her father's sudden death was never erased, and fear and worry reared up when something seemed out of her control. In a letter, she made clear, in a rare expression of the impact of her father's death, that "going to pieces" was not an option.

> Being 1929 the year of the crash and ensuing depression, to save his
> business his entire life insurance was used as a collateral loan for
> the business and it went. We <u>had</u> to grow up <u>or</u> go to pieces. So, we
> grew up- Grandmother went back to school and started teaching
> and we were expected to pull our share.

Genetically like her father, my mother pulled her share and kept it together through tough times. She found beauty in her garden, gave to noble causes, read voraciously, took great care with the collections her mother passed along, gathered up poems and longed for adventure. Ann, wired like Hannah with her creative impulsive side, traveled, sought out native crafts, was an award-winning photographer, and didn't give much thought to keeping order, whether clothes or house. When life's trials piled up, she struggled with a strained voice, and words were hard to get out as though stuck inside. My father said it was a medical condition. My mother thought it was from the strain of her marriage. Ann's words:

> Perhaps there are those marriages as in the ads, with a Perrier at one's
> fingertip, pearls around the neck, soft lights, piano, with a kiss on
> the neck . . . that is pure fantasy. Sal told me way back after college
> she did not need a man for financial security and she is right. You
> should need them for more than that, but often one does not get
> that something else, and makes do.

I am glad to be out from under "making do." Well before I was married, my parents and I were sitting around the lunch table at Ann's summer place when her husband shot horrific words at her about the burned brownies she'd made and served. I fled the table, pushed back tears and headed out alone down their dirt road. My mother followed, trying to explain the challenges of their marriage. I vowed never to have a marriage with nasty words. That wasn't how it turned out. Hannah,

Margaret, Ann, my sister, and I had different versions of disappointment in love. Sally never married, had many romances and no doubt her own disappointments. I married, made do, and won't make do again. Don't settle, a dear friend told me.

Dear Everybody

Chapter Twenty-Three

Who Lives with Beauty

Ann called her mother "... a hopeless romantic and should have known better." Those words could apply to Ann and to "the one I don't know too well," which would be me. I ask how could I be anything else? Dreamy romantic images surrounded me as a child. I didn't have one fairytale book, I had several, with illustrations by the likes of Arthur Rackham and Jessie Wilcox Smith. These were coupled with fairytale hand-painted wood cutouts that hung on my wall. I had poetry books: the cover of one was of a girl catching silver pennies from heaven. I had Wulfing postcards of young maidens gazing at knights in armor. I had chocolate mice and popcorn strings at Christmas. I had smocked dresses, organdy and polka dot. I had hand-crafted dolls with flower-laden hats. I had a photograph of my grandmother in a wedding dress which any young woman would dream to wear. I had a grandmother who sent postcards scrawled with the words lovingly, darling, and dearest in large flowy handwriting. I had, I had, I had. My childhood overflowed. Becoming a romantic was hard to avoid, resisting rich sensory experiences a challenge. I think of Hannah's words, "I promised me I wouldn't." Her head failed to override her heart. My heart and head vacillate as to who leads whom. I am working on ridding myself of my mother's "should have known betters," pushing back her tendency to be the practical realist. Where is the fun in that? Her words re-surface:

> . . . there were years when I really had FUN - - plain unadulterated
> fun . . . So, try not to lose the side of you that likes a good laugh and
> cuddle.

During a Maine outing, I learned of the quote, "Maine is where subtlety matters and the spectacular distracts," (*A Year in the Maine Woods,* Bernd Heinrich). There was much that was indeed spectacular. There was splendor that I wanted close by: my lush flower garden with beloved peonies and lilacs. No complicated California irrigation needed. There was the ever-changing sky with Maxfield Parish clouds, the deep green and blue summer vistas, the fall leaves on fire, the silent drifts of snow, filigree frost on my windows, the crisp air putting color in my cheeks. All combined, being in Maine brought a life-enriching "Ah." I had no regrets becoming a resident at age sixty-four.

I was captivated by more than what was outside my window. I fell under the spell of another someone. Hannah, a hopeless romantic, would have fallen too, though being able to "hold her own with any man," as Ann shared, Hannah would have wised up sooner than I. The bewitcher did me in with recitations of sonnets while we skated, snowy nights in a hot tub, lilting music, movie nights, and morsels of culinary deliciousness. I was vulnerable to being swallowed up by sensuality and the sway of possible romance. We wallowed in moments "made beautiful by the senses." Mr. Sonnets and Sonatas and I had birthdays a few days apart. Not believing in astrology, I smiled when reading that two Libras "share a blissful, romantic relationship full of beauty, sensuality and utter pleasure." Margaret would have said to watch out, "One thing leads to another." My new Maine friends said watch out. I eventually saw what wasn't there between us, held my own and pulled away, though I was grateful for a gift he gave about my relationship with Hannah.

When first walking into Mr. Sonnet's bedroom, my eye was drawn to the only item on the table near the door, a sizable black and white photograph of a woman in a stunning wedding dress, a forlorn expression on her face, no trace of a smile. Even with the dim light from the late afternoon November sky, the photo stood out in the sparsely furnished oversized room. Beautiful Oriental rugs filled the floor, reminding me of a spread-out stamp collection. A massive Victorian woman's dresser took up one wall with a king bed and two opposing Victorian side tables. Despite the visual feast, I couldn't take myself away from the photograph. Mr. Sonnets and Sonatas was behind me when his question floated over my shoulder, "Is there someone you carry within you?" I absorbed his words without answering. I had never been asked this. Whether out of respect for the woman in the photo or how deeply the question burrowed in, the moment called for silence. I leaned in closer to take in the details of the forlorn-faced woman. "Who is she?" I asked. His reply startled me. "It's my grandmother. I carry her within me." I turned around and faced the man who collected items from the past and recited sonnets. With the wedding dress photo of my grandmother filling my mind, his answer echoed my answer: "I carry my grandmother within me."

On that grey November afternoon, with Mr. Sonnets and Sonatas by my side, Hannah floated around me and within me, whispering and watching, a knowing loving smile on her face. Shortly after Hannah's death, a letter sending "lots of love" arrived from Ann, stating what I realized that day:

> It is true, and sad that she did not know it, that Grandmother left
> more of an impact upon her surviving children dead. She did have a
> great influence . . . and she only visited.

Sad if, when alive, my grandmother never understood the extent of her influence. Sad, if she died unappreciated. I hope she knows otherwise now.

At age sixty-four, Hannah had traveled across oceans, scouting out beauty wherever she went. The woman who lived all her life in Indiana went far. By the same age, I had racked up some trips abroad: a high school AFS summer in Austria, two during my college years, several on business with my husband, and one with Mr. Wildlife Biologist. Never a trip abroad on my own. I gathered up beauty and the delights that were nearby. Mr. Sonnets and Sonata provided just that, as did Mr. Apple Orchard, who put words around it with his comment, "You have been in a sensual desert far too long." My senses were awakening with Hannah on my shoulder.

~

Music is a balm for me, and once I settled into my first Maine winter, I attended monthly chamber music concerts at the local museum. As a solo, I took a seat at the end of a row and while waiting for the performance, both the swirling snow outside the window and my soft pink polka dot scarf soothed what needed soothing. I had a small bag on my lap and was lost in thoughts of a necklace I had bought moments before at the museum gift shop. What pulled me back to reality was a chunky orthopedic black shoe on a wheelchair footrest coming into view on the parquet floor. Hannah's Archlocks came to mind. "Do you have enough room?" a voice asked. As I turned around to answer, the bag on my lap started to slip off. "Yes, plenty of room," I replied, catching the bag.

The face greeting mine was about eighty, warm and serene, a smile that makes anyone feel at home. Her white hair with gentle waves mirrored Hannah's. Her skin said she had been careful with the sun. If there were wrinkles, I didn't notice. I have seen this face before on elderly women. My hope, as I age, is to have such a face—peaceful and serene. Maybe because of her smile, I offered up a personal comment which was unusual for me and explained that I succumbed to a necklace. Was I channeling Hannah?

With more than polite interest she said, "Do let me see it." Her face was an invitation to connect. "A real splurge," I said as I took the box out of the bag and lifted off the lid. "Ah, smoky topaz." she noted. The topaz was the size of a walnut with a small deep yellow gem above, each in an understated silver setting. "My favorite gem," she continued, adding, "When I got engaged, I wanted a smoky topaz ring. The man who was to be my husband looked all over New York City for one." She paused. Lucky her I thought. An unusual engagement ring request. "Did he find what you wanted?" I asked. After another pause, she continued, "He couldn't find one. Maybe that was why we got divorced later."

I sighed, felt a sense of resignation. I nodded with empathy and fingered Hannah's citrine necklace I was wearing. Let beauty touch you whenever it appears, I reminded myself. The concert was starting.

With the new necklace in my lap and Hannah's citrine one around my neck, my mind wandered as it does in concerts. I had thoughts of Hannah at the Badgastein Spa telling "Everyone" she "changed her necklace each night to conform." If I trade out the citrine one for another, that is rare. Since that concert, the smoky topaz necklace has been on my neck one or two times. When I open its box giving thought to wearing it, I put the lid back on. Despite its beauty, I fear it's too much of a statement. It has joined my Hannah necklaces that stay in their boxes, hidden away, only brought out now and again to admire.

Later that winter, I took off the citrine necklace and contemplated wearing another that I had never worn, a heart-shaped beveled rose quartz, the stone that "restores trust and love in relationships." The fig-sized gem set in sturdy gold wires has four prongs peeking around from the back, with a gentle hold on the heart. It borders on being too large for my taste, too sappy and showy, yet many of the necklaces I wear from Hannah are unique enough to draw attention, an inconsistency to acknowledge. Soon after my divorce, I had a jeweler make a gold chain for the heart. Since then, the necklace has stayed as my mother wrapped it years ago, in tissue paper sprinkled with little gold stars nestled in a thumb-size box. I never remember seeing my mother wear the necklace. I wonder if Hannah ever wore it. That morning when I tried on the heart, I had been digging through places where I tuck away the many little boxes that house my jewelry. I was searching for a necklace to wear to a luncheon, a rare occasion in Maine for a dress, and a rare opportunity to wear a different necklace. I overcame thirty years of thinking that the heart was too sappy, thirty years of closing up the box. A friend told me more than once that I box things up, things being emotions. I have lots of boxes. She is right.

I felt the time had come to pull that heart out of its box and wear it. I congratulated myself that I didn't say, "I thought it was time . . ."

I have been accused of saying, "I think I feel." The battle of head and heart, the battle of the parts within that are Margaret and Hannah. That winter, I was full of feelings for a man I met in November. At Christmas, he gave me ice grippers. If I were to spend any time with him, he said I would need them. He was right. It can be slippery hiking up a Maine mountain under icy conditions, and slippery navigating middle-age romance. I thought of middle-aged Hannah and men, how she pushed back Adolph's advances, how she slid about on the freighter with him as the ship lurched through waves, how she commented, almost a boast, on one of her trips traveling alone, that she was on the loose without a sergeant. I don't boast when on the loose without a man.

The man who gave me grippers was the reason I put on the necklace. Two months after meeting, he announced he had something to get off his chest. That is not a comforting opening line. Good thing I was a master at guarding my heart. His former girlfriend asked to meet him for coffee, and he wanted me to know ahead of time. All good, until he called afterward to report he had feelings that he hadn't expected. Feelings of the positive kind. Every nerve in me activated.

"How are you feeling about that?" he asked.

I would have preferred a hard question on a chemistry exam. As much as I hated his question, I admired his ability to bring up feelings. Phone in hand, I leaned back in my pea-green Martha Washington chair, wearing the layers needed for a Maine winter, late-afternoon grey day gloom seeping in the two windows sized for colonial days. Small windows keep out bad weather. Layers fend off the cold.

"What am I feeling?" was my answer, a question to his question. I scanned my inner landscape searching for a word. Where was Hannah's word collection when I needed it? The best I came up with was, "Mixed." I was still sorting out matters of the heart and realized that it may be a journey with no destination, especially challenging when the head is in the lead. I tried again. "There aren't words for some things," I told him. Things was a code word for feelings. It wasn't easy for him to put his feelings out there, and I was trying to do the same.

After that conversation, Mr. Ice Grippers and I zig-zagged our way through emotions, each of us trying to sort ourselves out. All those years Hannah was sorting herself out, musing about who was and wasn't "integrated," she had to have been wondering that about herself. So much to integrate: head and heart, being lonesome with being independent, needing men in her orbit while pushing back the one she called Himself.

If I had grown up in a family who spoke about things of the heart instead of in code or intellectual terms, my head and heart might integrate with more ease. Would I say, "I felt loved," instead of saying, "I knew I was loved?" Love was present, just not talked about. If there were problems in our family, they were kept quiet. There would be a hush. As a child with my ear to my bedroom floor, searching for any sound of emotion in conversations below, I was on my own to sort things out, things being feelings.

Mr. Ice Grippers did more than make me talk about feelings. He got me on downhill skis after a twenty-year hiatus. He might also be called Mr. Supportive, cheering me on to take a ski lesson. The instructor repeatedly told me, "Stop over analyzing. Just FEEL the edge, lead with your big toe as you turn." After my lesson, she told Mr. Supportive, "She over-analyzes." Mr. Supportive looked at me across the beaten-up wooden table in the ski lodge, a face full of smile, our protective helmets next to our shared cup of coffee. She looked at me, then at him, then both looked at me. I had no choice but to look within and tell myself, it is time to get to work on letting go. The part of me that took after my mother needed adjusting. It was time to loosen up, let in the repairman for inside jobs as he was at my front door. Time to wear that heart, not just collect them as Hannah did, or box them up as I did.

The winter plowed on. While it wasn't a freighter trip, my journey was navigating a Maine winter and this relationship. The upcoming forecast was grey and warmer than frigid, with no snowflakes. It was the kind of Maine weather that depressed my mother. Even with my delight of having moved to Maine, a forecast like that got to me. Nothing outside my window called, "Come out and play." I chilled just looking at the January "dead-of-winter-green" grass, a green if in the Crayola 64 box would never be used, the crayon tip unmarred. My dead-of-winter thoughts digressed to cemeteries. I decided if Hannah's mind could wander to "tootlejohnnys" and hat trees that kept her company, I could digress to thoughts of the cemetery up the street and the gravestones of my great, great and many more greats paternal grandparents. In Evansville, Hannah's headstone is next to Arthur's. I pushed back thoughts of my headstone and who, if anyone, might be next to me.

Back to the scene outside my window with ice rinks sized for chipmunks, a result of spring-like temperatures of days now gone. A wool shrug around my shoulder like a tea cozy helped warm me and gave rise to thoughts of firing up the cold wood stove, a dust of ash on the floor from a fire long before. The yo-yo of this winter's jet stream was wreaking havoc on dreams of winter adventures. It was a winter of one day at a time.

I called a California friend, one of those friends who don't come along often, one who came into my life by chance. We met two weeks after I moved to California. She was standing under the redwood arch at the Town Commons, waiting for her son to come out from summer day camp, and I walked up looking for my son, looking like an alien in an outfit my daughter dubbed "SO back east." I was looking for that boy of mine whose smile would beam me to him. I was a back-east mother in California, a woman with no girlfriends at hand, and I was seersuckered with whirlings of worry about this California life. I had been wrenched from an historic sleepy town outside Pittsburgh on the Ohio River, and to be a good wife had followed my husband to sunscreen California. I gag at palm trees. I moan with too much sun. I couldn't fathom being one of the women I had seen who wore sprayed-on exercise capris and built-in bra tops from dawn to dusk, faces with a yoga residue gaze. The woman next to me wore a baggy mid-calf jumper that looked like it came from L.L. Bean. She sensed my ill-at-ease stance. Her smile beamed a warm hello which saved me from myself. Years later, she was there for me during my divorce when the California culture had solidified the Grand Canyon gap between my husband and me. Then it was my turn; I was there for her divorce. We rescued each other. We had been in lifeboats together. We traveled into the land of online dating together. On that frozen winter day with cemetery thoughts, I needed one of her smiles to beam across the country. Then the phone rang. It was Mr. Ice Grippers. I sent a news alert to her voicemail. He called asking if I would lend a hand. It was about beds. One a queen and the other a California King.

In my house, a queen is the biggest that fits up the narrow twisty stairs. After the house became mine, I got rid of my parents' single beds. Seems I advanced up in royalty with the limit that there couldn't be a king on my second floor. Mr. Ice Gripper's queen needed to be taken down into his cellar to make room for the king platform bed recently given him by his ex. This was not a humpty dumpty project. Two people were needed, and one of them was invited to stay over for the night. It could be a day trip, but it was a seventy-minute journey north, plus it was about beds. Unexpected sun for this grey-sky weekend. "Woo hoo" voicemail back from my friend. She is a woman who woo hoos. "Woo hoo," I echoed back.

I traveled up Route One to his house with ease, no icy roads, no threatening snow. I was almost the girl on the flying trapeze, singing away with the Wailin' Jennys, hitting that replay arrow several times as "Some Good Thing" played . . . "lookin ahead just a little . . . keep your eyes on the road . . . can you be sure this will be some good thing . . . lucky stars appear again . . . can you believe all that has brought you here . . . come on baby let's go and live." I channeled Hannah. While she had many delights, I wager she wasn't a car-singing woman.

Up his driveway, an open garage door welcomed. The motorcycle caught my eye as it did each visit, a nice partner to the red pickup, both of which Margaret wouldn't approve. The flatbed trailer was loaded with a mattress and bed parts. I stepped onto the breezeway carpet, which I carbon dated by traffic to the 1950s, his skis leaning up against the wall. I crossed the threshold into the kitchen, feeling the radiating warmth of his living room woodstove, my black underlayers ready to do the job of offsetting the chill in the rest of his house. I dropped my overnight bag near the door and melted with his smile and wrap-around hug. Smiles do it, so do eye twinkles, I become "a jellied mass of non-resistance."

While he and I were never short on conversation, we cut it short to head off to the bed project, down the narrow hall with no carpet, to the room with no pictures, no excess of pillows. A sparse room, a cold room. The job was explained: Queen mattress, box spring and frame down the hall and down to the cellar. Next, a trip to a store with discount rugs. He wanted a rug to match the dimension of the platform to avoid scratches in the wood floor he had installed. I have a soft spot for men who love wood. We measured the platform.

"Not your standard rug dimensions," I advised. "A bigger rug will be expensive. Maybe a rug pad cut to size so it wouldn't show." No response. I repeated the sentence, maybe even three times, words with no response. He claimed I repeat things. Correct, I do. Getting a rug was on his mind. Following that, we were to haul in the bed parts and haul ourselves carefully as we put it together. We were at the age where one hauls things with care, even our hearts that have been banged around. "Got it?" words asked with that charming smile. "Yes, got it," I repeated. "Yup, got it." Said twice for good measure.

Mr. Ice Grippers was good at checking on how I'm doing. He wanted to be sure I had a grip, on the mattress that is. The mattress handles were useless, aligned for horizontal transport and a team of four. This was a vertical job and a team of two. I am the queen of getting a grip, even though I had been working to discard that crown, working to let go, let it flow. I am also the Queen of Sorry. "Sorry, I can't reach the handles." "Sorry, give me a minute to pick up the end."

I told myself to get a grip and stop saying sorry so often. This job had the potential for many apologies that were not needed, tapping my inheritance of saying "sorry" for things I haven't done. Time to shed some of what I inherited and keep the best. I am also the Queen of the Midwest "okey dokey." Mr. Icegrippers, the king of smiles, smiles at my okey dokeys. "Okey dokey, I have the end now."

What came next was a verbal relay: watch the ceiling fan, watch the door trim, watch the wall thermostat, watch your step. My father's words were in the air. As a child when I helped him, he shouted all the watch-outs. Dinging woodwork my father had painted was not what he had in mind. There can be comfort hearing words from the past, even if it is "watch out." We watched out as we navigated the queen. We were careful types, navigators of mattresses, relationships, and hikes. There was a reason he gave me ice grippers. He smiled when I wouldn't trust their grip and slid down iced granite ledges on my derriere, grabbing branches and limbs. He scampered down mountains, quick as a flash, light on his feet. I think of Hannah and Adolph's approaches to managing the freighter as it lunged from side to side, she the napkin wadder and he the who-done-it.

With the queen delivered without mishap to the cellar, we headed to a store with discounted rugs. Don't discount what you haven't tried, I told myself. Nothing in this store looked like it was made by craftspeople with sunshine in their hearts. Before we split up to divide and conquer rugs, he smiled and squeezed my hand, realizing I was out of my element. We reunited to report back. I reminded myself to keep my thoughts to myself, but was overruled by impulse. The Hannah in me couldn't resist. "The rug you need isn't in your price." No reply despite being elbow to elbow. I told the me within not to repeat myself. I repeated that reminder, "Keep your mouth shut about a rug pad cut to size." I succeeded. The Queen of Repetition and Sorry was pushed down to my cellar.

"May I help you?" queried a Maine-sized man for a Maine-sized store of stuff. Mr. Ice Grippers served up the situation. The Maine-sized man returned the serve, "What about cutting a rug pad to fit your dimension?" I smiled, looked up and repeated myself with a smile. A smile came back my way. He knew and reached for my hand and gave a squeeze. "Ten dollars" said the man. A deal it was.

We completed the job of the bed from his former wife. "You don't mind?" my friend asked later. Meaning, did I mind a former marriage bed. My mind didn't seem to mind, which she hinted was a bit unusual. Being a little unusual is OK, I heard Hannah whisper in my ear.

Now that I am paying attention, I notice when Hannah is within. I have her tendency to dance somewhat on the edge of what is typical. Her mind leapt like a rabbit in the spring. Mine can leap, stop, sniff, take it all in, leap another direction, stop, sniff. Something good to find, something troublesome to avoid. I am sniffing out too many similarities. We both were lucky in one regard. Adolph was patient with Hannah. Mr. Ice Grippers was patient with me. With a glint of a smile, he declared, "This bed is really for you," words said by the man who slept in a recliner as his shoulder, wounded from the past, hadn't found a way to smile in a bed. I would be the queen alone in a king bed as we navigated our two worlds. My handcraft world was miles from that store of discounted stuff. I loved literature. He didn't read. I needed physical passion. He had given that up. Grand Canyon gaps. Terms of endearment continued from him long after their expiration date. My visits waned. We parted friends. My collection of very dear men friends had begun. Hannah explored foreign countries as a single woman. I explored relationships, many of them foreign lands.

Chapter Twenty-Four

Inheritance

The Hannah project led me to embrace the similarities and heed warnings on traits that may lead me astray. "Don't be like Sally, you'll scare off the boys," and "Watch out, you are going too fast, just like Ann." I look down at my hands, smile when I see them at rest, in a pose identical to my mother, Fanny Rose and Sarah Ann, and I say "Ugh" when I see the knobs and ridges. Fanny Rose's body type seems closest to mine. Other relatives are too tall, too short, too stocky, too large boned. Margaret, Ann, Sally, and I inherited Fanny Rose's mouth. Piecing together family parts, Ann did the same when I was in my early twenties. Her words to my father:

> She does look astonishingly like Sally, which I never saw. Her mouth
> is like Sally's and the way she smiles, and her nose.

And in one of Ann's letters when I sent her a photo of me:

> Like you, I was a bit confused at first . . . was it me or Sally? Your
> father told me once that you were like Sally, and I hope so . . .

The shared traits anchored me to those with whom I belonged, as do the Hubbs and Basnett forks and spoons. I open the kitchen drawer each day, there they are: Sarah Ann Basnett and Fanny Rose Hubbs. Generations connecting, reminders that the past moves into the present and part of it lingers, fossils of the past.

When I step into my garden, I thank each generation who tended the flowers. When others comment on my hair, I give credit to Hannah. When compliments surface on my citrine necklace, once again I bow to Hannah. When I repeat myself or realize I am about to give an opinion that wasn't needed, I check myself, don't want to offend others as Ann and Hannah could do. I remember the words of my cousin George: "Any man who can't stand a Trimble mouth doesn't deserve one." He knew. He wanted to reassure me I was deserving.

In a prime location on my refrigerator door is the photo of my great-grandmother Fanny Rose seated with Thomas on a backyard glider, her head tilted toward him, relaxed hands crisscrossed one over the other on his knee, her knuckles unmistakably mine. Well into their seventies, they look at peace with one another, content, sharing affection. Given all the tragedy that Fanny Rose had been through, I take heart in knowing she had someone to lean on. I could embrace having that. I was finding my way. Sorting out what I valued. Determined to be integrated and age with grace.

Discouraged by the men I had met with Grand Canyon value gaps, a kindred spirit appeared with a passion for beauty, the sensory, the woods and water, a man with a tender smile, an embrace that felt like home. Those were his words to me, "You feel like home." He said I was like his mother. I said he was like my father. No one has given me advice on whether that means watch out. Sympatico feelings. We sang songs from our youth, laughed at jokes, paused for beauty, valued words well written, let chocolate dissolve slowly, melted and swooned together. Then he said, "It's hard having a relationship when two people are so independent." There "it" was again, being so independent. I sensed a path existed balancing independence and connectedness. A path I was determined to find. He shared there had been relationship issues in his past. That declaration fit my past.

My mother's words floated through my head, "One thing leads to another." My Marin friend who, decades before, crawled through my dog door when I was out of town when she discovered her husband had been unfaithful, shared, "Wait and see. It will reveal itself." I wanted to picture my kindred spirit and me, like Thomas and Fanny Rose on the glider. Whatever "another" is, I will wait for it to reveal itself.

What was leading one thing to another were the years. One summer night when reaching over to my bedside table, I caught sight of my arm. Maybe the summer tan made it more noticeable, or the angle of the light, or the fact that I had lost weight during the move from California, there was no denying the loose skin with wrinkle lines running parallel to each other, looking like a twisted shirt that needed ironing. I had a flashback to Hannah's arms. First hands, now arms. During our card games when she held out an arm, loose flappy skin hung down from under, like the waddle on a rooster. There is no beauty in waddle. I remember being brave, tapping on Hannah's arm, making it wobble. It was time to check mine. I swim laps and from time to time, lift weights, so my upper arms were in the early wobble state. The wrinkles disturbed me. My arms were not matching the age I felt inside. My hands didn't match either. I didn't want to reconcile the age I saw on the outside with how I felt on the inside. Best not to. I vowed not to write the words which Hannah wrote at sixty-four, an age younger than I was that summer night. Her words, "Now that I am getting old . . . " Sixty-four is not old, it is old-er. I use age-related words with care. The older I become, the more my mother and grandmother appear in me. Maybe I am looking more clearly at myself, lingering longer over the changes, realizing I can't avoid what I see. A birthday card pointed out the inevitable: "The evidence shows, women who exercise, age." Ugh. One word says it all.

Hannah aged and her "guerrilla warfare" approach to old age bore no resemblance to the "dreamy" approach to getting old which she wrote about when age fifty in "Intangibles":

When Sally and I return from walks, because I am her grandmother,
I am hung with dreams she wishes me to share. In every button-

hole - - - there is a little faded flower. My pockets bulge with acorns
and on Sally's head and mine there are crowns of leaves, which have
been pinned together with the long, strong, red stems of the wild
grapevine.

There is another less tangible beauty which children sense and out
of which they sometimes make little singing dreams. Only happy
children sing them. Sometimes they are soft, like bird sounds, with
no words. Sometimes they have wonderful words with no meaning.
Sally is full of such dreams. She sings them when she sets the table,
or when she buttons the dresses of her dolls.

If, because you have been a dreamy child, you find yourself a too
dreamy adult, don't worry. All of us are lucky enough at one time or
another, to be disciplined by Life. Then we give up this fascinating
pastime in a hurry. At least I did.

If, in spite of everything, such dreams persist, look out! When you
feel one coming on, take a cold bath, drop a light bulb, pinch the
baby. Try anything. I know of only one cure. This is brought about
when you are forced to realize that you love someone more than you
love yourself. Then you will be too busy for bad dreams.

It occurs to me that I am being very free with advice. That is, of
course, because I, myself, am no longer vulnerable. I am a smug and
contented grandmother. I talk back even though I do not know the
answers, and laugh out of turn in domestic crises. It does not give
me pain to recall the mistakes I have made.

I think, in my older age, I shall do little last minute dreaming on my
own again. I also want to get an iron kettle and stir apple butter in
my backyard.

Hannah wasn't stirring apple butter. In her old age, she had no backyard.
She had an apartment. She stopped coming to visit as travel was hard.

For a time, Hannah's dreams about how her life could unfold might have comforted and helped as she marched forward. When those dreams didn't become reality and the dark well of loneliness was harder to offset with fountains of beauty, the reality of old age may have made smiles rare.

~

Among the many photographs which hit me deeply, one is dated 1960: four women, three generations, only one with a smile. The photo was taken in front of our mantel filled with Christmas boughs and pinecones. On the wall behind hung Hannah's Swedish wall sconce with a heart. There is a little girl sitting with red ribbons in her braids, one hand on her bare feet sticking out from her blue jeans, her other hand on the floor as she looked at the photographer, beaming. All are wearing red for the holiday. Three in skirts. Of these three, one is mournful and glancing off to the side, one is lost in thought glancing downward, and one glowers at the photographer telling him how unhappy she is about posing for this photo. One is about ten, one about sixteen, one about forty-two, and one named Hannah about seventy-four. My mother, my sister and I were having a Christmas photo taken with Hannah. Throughout each life there has been looking and loneliness, longing and love. A search for a something that fulfilled to the depths of each heart, a sense of belonging, a sense of oneself. Nothing faint about it, nothing shrinking or small. Somewhere along the years, three lost their smiles. I was the one with the smile, too young to know better. I was smiling at my father, the photographer.

At eighty-five years of age, Hannah fell and broke her hip. Humor didn't entertain her as she had hoped it would in her *New York Times* article on aging: "I have developed 'mental resources' and in rarer instances, a sense of humor, which should succor my old age and entertain me even if I fall down and break a hip." She pulled out her IVs and fought the nurses. She fought so hard she successfully ended her life. She refused to be any more aged than she was. Hannah died on November 2, 1972. I was in college. My mother said not to disrupt my studies, not to come to her funeral. I never challenged that decision, but I wish I had.

Friends thought it odd. For other families, going to a grandparent's funeral would have been a must. All I have is the memorial program. The minister's words:

> Her apartment spoke of her love of family, her appreciation of painting, carving and the value of the printed word. In Mrs. Trimble's possession was a yellowed clipping from a subsequent issue (NYT with her article An Old Lady Refuses . . .), containing a letter to the newspaper from a doctor in Washington DC . . . I quote it today: "Anyone who faces life as resolutely as Hannah Trimble . . . is destined to stay young. She has truly lived to have extracted so much fragrance, flavor and fun from the other side of sixty. It's refreshing to see oldsters grasp the 'twilight-teens' with the adventurous spirit and adamant audacity of a high school freshman . . . Yes, there's more than a thimbleful of fun in Trimble. And the inspiration she has given the rocking-chair crowd to follow her lead should help us to stand up, keep alive, and look with faith to the fun-filled future.

I hold on to the words that exemplify the best of my grandmother, "more than a thimbleful of fun in Trimble," a woman who "extracted so much fragrance . . ."

Before that day in July when my father stood in front of me, I had examined the least of what formed me the most. He, at the end of his life, gave me a gift never imagined. In piecing together what shaped my grandmother, I pieced back myself and my sense of belonging, which my mother thought I had decades ago:

> At least you know who you are and who your family is, and what we stand for, and the fact that you are part of all of us . . . Really, the only security any of us can have, in the end, is security within ourselves.

As the years go by, if there isn't a beloved at my side, I am determined to not lose heart. I will seek out beauty, link arms with girlfriends, and hold on to my smile.

I know I've told you stuffs you will not want to read about – and have forgotten to say the things you'd like to have me say - - But I thank you awful much for everything.

Goodnight and love from me,
Hannah

The Family of Hannah Hubbs Stevenson Trimble

<u>Maternal Family</u>
Benjamin Hubbs Sr. marries Sarah Ann Basnett (child of Hannah
& Charles Basnett)
Children: Charles, William, George, Hannah, Benjamin Jr., Sarah
Ann (Sadie), Samuel, John, **Fanny Rose.**

<u>Paternal Family</u>
Thomas Burke Stevenson Esquire marries Sarah Elizabeth Combs
Children: Elizabeth, Mary Cassandra, Sarah (Sally), Lousiana (died
as a child), Martha (Mattie), Julia, Susan, **Thomas Burke Stevenson Jr.**, John Burke, Louisa, Anna (died as an infant), Horace.

> **Fanny Rose Hubbs** marries **Thomas Burke Stevenson** –
> children: Twins Sarah Ann and Fanny Rose (both die as
> infants), Louise (Lulie), Thomas Basnett, Frank, **Hannah**.

<u>Married in Family</u>
George Trimble marries Ellen Haley
Children: James, John, **Arthur,** Tom, Joseph, George, William,
Eliza, Maria, Margaret

Arthur Trimble marries Alice Hilliard
Children: Mary Ellen, Edith Otillia, Alta Marcella, Annie Elizabeth
(died age 2), Margaret, **George Arthur**

> **Hannah Hubbs Stevenson** marries **George Arthur
> Trimble** – children: Ann marries Kenneth - children: twins
> Thomas and George Arthur (George Arthur dies as an
> infant), George, Sally. Margaret marries Richmond Smith –
> children: Cecily and Stephanie

Fanny Rose Hubbs Stevenson

Born, January 24, 1858, Madison, Indiana

Age **Life Event**

1	Charles, brother, commits suicide, 1859
3-4	Hidden from a Native American who wants to buy her
7	Father commits suicide, 1865
11	Brother Benjamin disappears, presumed drowned, 1869
16	Grandmother Hannah Basnett, dies, 1874
22	Marries Thomas Burke Stevenson Jr., 1880
22	Twins Fanny Rose and Sarah Ann, born 1880
22	Twins Fanny Rose and Sarah Ann, die of cholera 1881
24	Daughter Lulie (Louise) born, 1882
26	Son Thomas Basnett, born, 1884
27	Mother Sarah Ann Basnett Hubbs dies, 1885
30	Daughter Hannah born, 1888
34	Benjamin, brother, dies in San Francisco, 1892
40	Son Frank Barbour born, 1898
43	Samuel, brother, dies of alcoholism, 1901
44	William brother, dies of chronic mania, 1902
57	Carrie, sister, dies 1915
59	Granddaughter Ann, born, 1917
60	Granddaughter Margaret, born 1918
60	Niece Fanny Rose dies at age 36, 1919
63	Hannah, sister, dies, 1922
66	Sadie, sister, dies, 1924
71	John, brother, dies, 1929
71	Son-in-law George Arthur, dies 1929
81	Husband dies, 1939
81	Daughter Lulie dies, 1939
84	Great grandson George Arthur dies, 1942
88	Fanny Rose dies, 1946

Hannah Hubbs Stevenson Trimble

Born Evansville, Indiana, March 6, 1888

Age	Life Event
28	Married George Arthur Trimble, January 24, 1916
29	Ann born, February 1917
30	Margaret born, February 1918
41	George Arthur dies, November 25, 1929
51	Thomas B. Stevenson, father, dies, 1939
54	Ann's infant twin, George Arthur, born & dies June 1942
57	Fanny Rose, Hannah's mother, dies, April 19, 1946
61	RMS Queen Elizabeth, New York to Southhampton, June 15, 1949, "transit to France" UK incoming passenger list
64	Pan American to Lisbon, Portugal, March 27, 1952, with widow friends Edna Page and Alice Fraser of Minneapolis
65	SS Uruguay Rio freighter to NYC, Summer 1953
67	SS American Planter freighter to Le Havre, May 6, 1955 TWA flight from Paris to Boston, August 8
68	Canada to Alaska, June 1956
69	Ferngrove freighter to Beirut, Istanbul, Trinidad, May, 1957 left Genova June 8 (with Adolph)
70	Zurich, Switzerland to NY, Vessel SR 844, Sept 3, 1958 (with Adolph)
77	Adolph die, February 10, 1964
82	Friend Josephine Foster Leich dies, March 1969
85	Hannah dies, November 2, 1972, Evansville, Indiana

Hannah Hubbs Stevenson Trimble

Known Publications

"We Learn to Read," *Childhood Education*, September 1938

"We Tap Our Subconscious," *Childhood Education*, February 1941

"We Write Poetry," *Childhood Education*, April 1941

"They Call It Creative Writing," *Progressive Education*, February 1943

"To Milly, On Her Birthday," *Southern Literary Messenger*,
    July-August, 1943

"And Gladly Teach," *Southern Literary Messenger*, 1943

"Round Trip," *Southern Literary Messenger*, Sept-October, 1943

"Thoughts of the Very Young," *Parents Magazine*, April 1944

"Out of the Mouths of the Third Grade," *New York Times*, June 22, 1947

"Meteorologists, Age 8," *New York Times*, March 7, 1948

"Milk Can Be Homogenized But Not Children,"
    New York Times Magazine, May 2, 1948

"An Old Lady Refuses to be Aged," *New York Times Magazine*,
    November 12, 1950

"Tommy Was Busy," *Baby Talk*, 1950

Lippincott Managing Editor request to turn "The Old Lady" into a
    book, November 13, 1950

New York Times permission to write a book based on her "The Old
    Lady" article, 1951

"Cherchez Le Spring," *New York Times*, March 7, 1954

"In All Innocence," *Literary Cavalcade*, December 1961

Acknowledgments:

Many thanks to family members Sally, Tom, George and Cecily who provided their memories and opinions on our grandmother, Hannah, and the deepest appreciation to Richmond Smith Jr MD, Hannah Stevenson Trimble, Margaret Trimble Smith, Ann Trimble Warren, and Thomas Burke Stevenson Sr. who each wrote and saved letters. Without the practice of letter writing this manuscript would not be possible. To my friends who read segments of Hannah's letters and pages of my writing about Hannah, your encouragement was my motivation. Finally, the patient coaching provided by Kathrin Seitz pulled the story within me out, urging me to let go of my reticence to put myself "out there." To all, I am ever so grateful.

Dear Everybody